WAS PRESIDENT NIXON OUT OF HIS MIND?

Dr. David Abrahamsen, a distinguished psychiatrist, comes closer to the mind of Richard Nixon than any other observer. By studying Nixon's childhood and adolescence, by interviewing friends, family, and close White House associates, by reading his speeches and listening to the White House tapes, Dr. Abrahamsen provides fascinating new glimpses into the unconscious dynamics that caused the man who had achieved the very pinnacle of power and esteem to literally bring the house down on himself. This is Richard Nixon's life story as it has never been told before. . . .

NIXON VS. NIXON

"A CONSIDERABLE ACHIEVEMENT . . . it will make even an inveterate Nixon-hater feel a measure of sympathy."

—NEW YORK TIMES BOOK REVIEW

Dr. David Abrahamsen, M.D., a practicing psychoanalyst, is a Fellow of the American Psychiatric Association, of the New York Academy of Medicine, and of the American College of Psychoanalysts. He has taught at Yale, the New School for Social Research, and the College of Physicians and Surgeons at Columbia University. He is the author of many books, among them *The Murdering Mind, The Psychology of Crime, Our Violent Society, The Emotional Care of Your Child,* and *The Road to Emotional Maturity. Nixon vs. Nixon* is his second psychobiography, his first being *The Mind and Death of a Genius,* a study of Otto Weininger, psychologist, philosopher, and author of the book *Sex and Character.*

MENTOR and SIGNET Books You'll Want to Read

NIXON
VS.
NIXON

AN EMOTIONAL TRAGEDY

by

David Abrahamsen, M.D.

A SIGNET BOOK

NEW AMERICAN LIBRARY

TIMES MIRROR

TO LOVA
WITH LOVE AND AFFECTION

This is an authorized reprint of a hardcover edition published by Farrar,
Straus & Giroux, Inc. Published simultaneously in Canada by McGraw-
Hill Ryerson Ltd., Toronto.

Library of Congress Catalog Card Number: 76-49827

The author is indebted to the following: *The* (Whittier) *Daily News,
East Whittier Review,* and *The Fullerton Daily News Tribune,* for permission to quote from articles in those newspapers. Doubleday & Company, Inc., for permission to quote from *Six Crises,* copyright © 1962
by Richard M. Nixon. Reprinted by permission of Doubleday & Company, Inc. Doubleday & Company, Inc., for permission to quote from
Before the Fall: An Inside View of the Pre-Watergate White House,
copyright © 1975 by William Safire. Reprinted by permission of Doubleday & Company, Inc. Doubleday & Company, Inc., for permission to
quote from *Nixon and Rockefeller: A Double Portrait,* copyright ©
1960 by Stewart Alsop. Reprinted by permission of Doubleday & Company, Inc. Harcourt Brace Jovanovich, Inc., for permission to quote
from *Hide and Seek: A Continuing Journey* by Jessamyn West. Harper
& Row, Publishers, Inc., for permission to quote from *Richard Nixon:
A Political and Personal Portrait* by Earl Mazo. Peter H. Irons, for the
use of his letter to Alger Hiss. Donald Jackson, for permission to quote
from his unpublished manuscript "Coming of Age in America: The
Youth of Richard Nixon," and from his article "The Young Nixon,"
published in *Life* magazine, November 6, 1970. *The Los Angeles Times,*
for permission to quote from "Whittier '34 Most Likely to Succeed" by
Lael Morgan, copyright 1970, Los Angeles *Times.* Reprinted by permission. *The New York Times Magazine,* for permission to quote from
"The Bismarck Connection: Why Kissinger Must Choose Between Nixon
and the Country" by Thomas L. Hughes, © 1973 by The New York
Times Company. Reprinted by permission. Random House, Inc., for
permission to quote from *Nixon in the White House: The Frustration
of Power,* copyright © 1971 by Rowland Evans, Jr., and Robert D.
Novak. *Writer's Digest* and John Brady, for permission to quote from
John Brady's interview with Gloria Steinem in the February 1974 issue
of *Writer's Digest.* Victor Zorza, for permission to quote the anecdote
told by Sigmund Freud published in *The Washington Post.*

Preface

The human personality is immensely complex. Experts in many fields—historians, political scientists, and psychoanalysts, among others, with all the resources at their command, may devote themselves to the interpretation of a single person.

I have tried to apply my experience and training in psychoanalysis to present the emotional development of Richard Nixon, one of the most interesting subjects for psychoanalytic inquiry of this generation. In writing about a public person, psychoanalytic theory must weigh historical evidence. My book, therefore, is based on an exhaustive study of Nixon's own writings, including *Six Crises;* his public statements; and long hours of interviewing many of his closest associates, members of the family, and people with whom he worked. I have also read seemingly innumerable newspaper and magazine articles and books about him. I have studied in detail the transcripts of the White House tapes, the Judiciary Committee's Impeachment Report, the entire transcript of the Watergate Hearings, and the report of Nixon's tax returns from 1969 through 1972.

But to be long on history and short on psychology is as inadequate as the reverse. However exhaustive my researches, I realize that I can offer only my professional insight into the character of Richard Nixon. At the same time, I am aware that the divisive emotions he aroused in us are still within us.

There are important questions to be answered. Was Nixon a dreamer, idealist, astute politician, ambitious self-promoter, realist, bungler, actor, puppet? Was he intelligent and sane? Did he honor his family background, his Quaker code of ethics? Or did he act only on what he believed was best for his advancement? How did he react when things were *not* going his way, and how did he get along with himself? Only after we answer these questions can we ask why he failed at the height of his career.

My primary concern is not to place Nixon, or anyone else, in one particular diagnostic category. Rather, it is more important psychoanalytically to understand the hereditary and environmental elements, the developmental factors, and the psychodynamics that determined his personality makeup.

Psychoanalysts are more concerned with exploring the *why* than the *what* of human character and behavior. As doctors, we are also interested in human development. We too appreciate the wisdom of Wordsworth, who believed "the Child is father of the Man," and of Alexander Pope, who wrote, "Just as the twig is bent, the tree's inclined." Psychoanalytic insight can provide understanding, and understanding can lead to greater charity in our judgment of others. We are all, in a very important sense, the victims of victims.

I have tried to explain the complicated relationship between Richard Nixon's personal life and his political life. The books written about him do not provide a descriptive and comprehensive psychodynamic view of his emotional development. I am primarily concerned with the emotional side of his life: with his personal projection of himself, the impact he made on others and they on him. In determining Nixon's pattern of behavior—his actions and reactions, constructive or destructive—I shall deal with the constellation of his emotions from early childhood until the present. Most important are the critical periods in which the aggressions of childhood and adolescence formed the personality structure of a man who became a conflicted, ambivalent, secretive President.

Psychoanalysis is, at best, a difficult and often lengthy process. Not everyone is able to endure this kind of scrutiny, particularly if he fears the truth about himself. The former President has refused to make himself available or talk with me, and it is therefore hardly likely that he will submit to a psychiatric interview by me, or anyone else. However, even when the subject is not available for examination by the psychoanalyst, analysis of the inner man is possible. In fact, secondhand material can sometimes reveal more than patients themselves can. Such psychological studies have been fruitful indeed—Freud's study of Leonardo da Vinci, his controversial study with William C. Bullitt of President

Woodrow Wilson, and my own of the gifted Otto Weininger come to mind. Alexander L. and Juliette George, who did not know Wilson, were nonetheless able to make a penetrating study of him. Of note also is Erik Erikson's study of Martin Luther. An excellent example of behavior analysis is Walter Langer's *The Mind of Adolf Hitler,* which he wrote for the United States government during World War II. Besides predicting accurately that Hitler would commit suicide, the author stated that each military defeat would shake his confidence and that he probably would try to compensate for his vulnerability by acting out his sadism and brutality—a prediction which proved to be true.

Other psychiatric evaluations of people made without examining them include two studies of Daniel Ellsberg by physicians of the Central Intelligence Agency.* Another valuable study, *The Presidential Character* by James David Barber, comes to mind. Although I do not agree with Barber's fundamental conclusions about Nixon's personality makeup, his book has broken new ground. Here also should be mentioned the psychohistorical study by Bruce Mazlish, *In Search of Nixon.*

The historian and the psychoanalyst are both faced with a special problem in trying to grasp the mind and actions of a public figure. In addition to character traits which may elucidate the intimate connection between the man and his actions, traits rooted in the unconscious often determine his public behavior. While the uniqueness of a person most often rests in the unconscious, we can examine his behavior and discover the clues it reveals about his character. And even if we do not know the exact details of the person's childhood and dreams, we can, through a study of his daydreams or fantasies (which express his unconscious wishes and fears), learn much about his inner core.

In Richard Nixon's case we are fortunate in having information from his own hand. It is axiomatic that a man un-

---

* The second one was requested in 1971 by the White House "plumbers" and was later released by the House Judiciary Committee.[1] These studies resulted in two profiles. The first suggested that Ellsberg's motivation for leaking the Pentagon Papers derived from patriotism and a need for recognition; the second attributed it to aggression against his psychoanalyst, his own father, and the President. From the start, the "CIA doctors had reservations about the project, fearing that it could be misinterpreted and mistakenly considered to have been derived from the doctor-patient relationship."[2]

consciously reveals himself through his writings, and, with Nixon, we also have his lengthy and revealing conversations recorded on the White House tapes.

This book endeavors to illuminate the war Nixon fought within himself, the long years of inner struggle which led him and his presidency to disaster. In seeing Nixon through the eyes of a psychoanalyst, we may better understand his complexity. I shall attempt to show how Richard Nixon, the defender of "law and order," came to believe he was innocent and above the law. From psychoanalysis and, in particular, criminal psychopathology, we have learned that even if a person does not admit to having committed criminal (or noncriminal) acts, by using our insight into his instinctual and emotional makeup we can determine whether it was within his realm of probability. Was Nixon's personality, his character, constructed in such a way as to instigate or mobilize criminal tendencies that manifested themselves in unlawful acts?

In examining Nixon's emotional development I shall first try to describe the personality characteristics he showed as a child and adolescent. The second step will be to determine whether these personality traits are substantially the same as or different from the characteristics he demonstrated during his political career as congressman, senator, Vice-President, and President.

While some may believe that facts speak for themselves, we must be careful to look for the facts beneath the surface which sometimes do not appear even to the well-trained eye of a reporter or journalist. Let me share an anecdote with you:

> Freud once told the story of how an East European Jew . . . observed in the train which was taking him home to his village a young man who seemed to be going there too. As the two sat alone in the compartment, the Jew, puzzled about the stranger, began to work things out: "Only peasants and Jews live there. He is not dressed like either, but still, he is reading a book, so he must be Jewish. But why to our village? Only fifty families live there, and most are poor. Oh, but wait, Mr. Shmuel, the merchant, has two daughters: one of them is married, but for the other he has been seeking a husband. Mr. Shmuel is rich, and lately

has acquired airs, so he would not want anyone from the village for his daughter. He must have asked the marriage broker to find a son-in-law from the outside. But Mr. Shmuel is old and cannot travel to meet a new family, so he would probably want a son-in-law from a family he knows. This means it would have to be one that had lived in the village but moved away. Who? The Cohen family had a son. Twenty years ago they moved to Budapest. What can a Jewish boy do there? Become a doctor. Mr. Shmuel would like a doctor in the family. A doctor needs a large dowry. The boy opposite is neat, but not well dressed. Dr. Cohen. But in Budapest, Cohen wouldn't do. Probably changed his name. In Budapest? To Kovacs—a name which comes as naturally to Hungarians as Cohen to Jews."

As the train drew into the village station, the old Jew said to the young man: "Excuse me, Dr. Kovacs, if Mr. Shmuel is not waiting for you at the station, I'll take you to his home and introduce you to your betrothed." Replied the astonished young man: "How do you know who I am and where I am going? Not a word has passed between us."

"How do I know?" said the old man with a smile. "It stands to reason." [3]

In my profession such deductive reasoning cannot always be used. My fundamental concepts are based upon my years of training and experience and rest upon a vast body of scientific knowledge.

While my emphasis is on the development of Nixon's character—his ego, superego, and instinctual forces, as well as the conscious and unconscious aggressive, defensive, and passive feelings that determine a person's behavior pattern—this study concentrates on the substance of Nixon himself and the kind of political climate and administration he created. My concern is not *what* he wanted, but rather *why* he wanted it. My concern is not primarily with the political acts themselves, but rather with the motivation that prompted them. *Nixon vs. Nixon* offers a picture of the inner man. It does not attempt to give a political evaluation of Richard Nixon's presidency.

The resiliency of Richard Nixon is certainly as fascinating as the reasons for his many reverses. I have tried not to let the fact that he was our President influence my analysis. I sympathize with the magnitude of his personal problems. I saw with amazement the exuberance of his startling comebacks. I admire his tenacity. I deplore his duplicity. I shared the pain of his ultimate downfall—the dissolution of his presidency. The title *Nixon vs. Nixon* is not intended to suggest a court case. Rather, I hope it suggests the conflicting emotions which created a pattern of behavior that became more and more destructive.

To write about Richard Nixon is difficult, since he is a complex person. To offer a summary judgment of his personality would be impossible. To the public, and even to most psychoanalysts, he has been a challenge to understand. Easy as it is to condemn him, it is just as difficult to understand him.

This is not a biography in the ordinary sense; rather, it is a study of the emotional development of a man who became the President of the most powerful country in the world, and left that office as a result of actions that caused both a personal and a national tragedy.

Acknowledgments

In my study of Nixon, I have drawn on the insight of many professionals outside the field of psychiatry. I am grateful to William J. Foltz, Associate Professor of Political Science at Yale University, for his painstaking work on the manuscript, and Osborn Elliott, Deputy Mayor of New York City. I also have conferred with C. Richard Arena, formerly Professor of History, Whittier College; Elie Abel, Dean of the Graduate School of Journalism, Columbia University; A. M. Rosenthal, Managing Editor of *The New York Times;* and George E. Jones, Associate Executive Editor of *U.S. News & World Report.*

Daniel Reed, Assistant Archivist of the Presidential Libraries, directed me to material about Mr. Nixon and his family. Dr. Raymond M. Bell, Washington and Jefferson College, Washington, Pennsylvania, furnished me with a genealogy of the Nixon and Milhous families.

Much of Richard Nixon's early life was particularly illuminated by my communications with Jessamyn West, and also with her brother Merle (Rusty) West, both second cousins of the former President, who, besides being most generous in sharing with me a genealogy of the Milhous family from 1854 to 1904, also told me much about Nixon's family, his childhood, and early adulthood.

I would also like to thank many of the residents of Whittier, California, including some of Nixon's classmates and members of the Nixon family; Clinton Harris for his information about Nixon's early school years; and Ola-Florence Jobe, née Welch, who told me about her long relationship with Nixon, and Lois Elliott Williams, who disclosed to me pertinent material. In particular, I would like to mention Nixon's aunt, Rose Olive Marshburn, sister of his mother, Hannah, and her husband, Oscar Marshburn, who were most responsive to my questions and who gave me family photographs and provided the kind of sensitive material on Nixon, his brothers, and his parents that made this kind of study possible. I am especially indebted to Donald Jackson, formerly of *Life* magazine, who provided valuable material about Nixon's early life and photographs of the family. My thanks also go to Edwin P. Hoyt, to Harriet Van Horne for her help in directing me to sources about Nixon's past, to Roy M. Cohn and Alger Hiss for their information about Nixon's career, and to Allene Talmey, former White House correspondent, for information about Mrs. Nixon.

I am grateful to Bradley Morrah, who provided me with background material about Duke University Law School, North Carolina, and about Nixon's conduct there, and, also, William Perdue and Frederick Albrink, who graciously informed me about Nixon's life and behavior at Duke Law School, particularly about the break-in at the office of the dean in which he was involved.

I express my warm thanks to Irving Wallace and to a prominent lawyer who prefers to remain anonymous, both of whom provided me with information about Nixon's career as a young lawyer in Whittier, California, from 1937 to 1941, particularly about his first court case; to Philip Mayher, at that time lieutenant, who graciously extended to me information about the service of Lieutenant (j.g.) Nixon in 1943; to another person preferring to remain anonymous who gave me a detailed account of Nixon's service in the South Pacific, and to the Navy Office of Information.

I would like to extend my thanks to Howard Gotlieb, director of the Mugar Memorial Library, Boston University, Boston, Massachusetts, who graciously made available to me material, such as the "pink sheet" which Nixon used in 1949 in the senatorial election against Helen Gahagan Douglas, unpublished photographs of the Nixon family, as well as a transcript of *Richard M. Nixon: A Self Portrait*. I am most grateful to Ted Slate, Chief Librarian of *Newsweek*, who was most helpful in locating this transcript at the Mugar Memorial Library, Boston University, and also for finding other valuable material. Through the help of a federal agency I was able to track down the film of *Richard M. Nixon: A Self Portrait*, and in a private screening was able to observe Nixon's reactions and his behavior. Through a member of Nixon's campaign staff in 1968 who does not want his identity known, I was able to obtain transcripts and a film of Nixon's speeches in the 1968 primary of the presidential campaign in New Hampshire and in the Oregon primary in 1968.

My research brought me several times to Washington, D.C., where I attended the Watergate trials, discussed material with Richard Ben-Veniste, the Assistant Prosecutor, with newspaper editors and with persons connected with an agency of the federal government who wish to remain anonymous. Robert Finch, in Los Angeles, Nixon's one-time Secretary of Health, Education and Welfare, shed light on the former President's feelings about the Watergate scandals.

I also would like to thank Charles K. McWhorter, assistant to Nixon during his second vice-presidency; Anthony M. Lowell, M.D., Statistics and Analysis Section, Tuberculosis Control Division, Atlanta, Georgia, for information about the prevalence of tuberculosis in the United States; the East Hampton Free Library and the New York Academy of Medicine for their cooperation in tracing books for my study.

As much as I would like to acknowledge my appreciation to all those who contributed to this book, many former colleagues who worked with Nixon in the White House and in agencies close to him have asked to remain anonymous because of their past professional involvement in politics.

In a book such as this, it is particularly important to record faithfully the information provided from individuals as well as from published sources. It is equally important to state that the interpretation of the information is solely my own and does not necessarily reflect the opinion of my sources.

In closing, I want to give warm thanks to my secretary, Louise Kragelund, for her numerous retypings of the manuscript, to Gay Stebbins for her many excellent suggestions, and to Arthur W. Wang, my editor, who with enduring stimulating help painstakingly devoted much time and effort to the manuscript.

My greatest debt is to my wife, Lova, who through the long hours of research and writing in this large undertaking diligently assisted me in the step-by-step development of this book.

Contents

"In the case of the criminal it is a secret which he knows and hides from you, but in the case of the hysteric it is a secret hidden from him, a secret he himself does not know . . .

"[Pointing] out the chief difference. With the neurotic, the secret is hidden from his own consciousness; with the criminal it is hidden only from you. In the first we have a genuine ignorance (though not altogether complete), whilst in the latter this ignorance is merely simulated. Connected with this is another difference more important in practice. In psycho-analysis the patient consciously helps to overcome his resistance because he expects to gain something from the investigation—cure. The criminal, on the contrary, does not co-operate with you; he would be working against his whole ego."

—SIGMUND FREUD,
"Psychoanalysis and the
Ascertaining of Truth
in Courts of Law"

PART I

Beginnings

1

In the study of human conduct it has been found that behavior patterns are often carried down through several generations. In Richard Nixon's family, though the records are sparse, patterns can be discerned. James Nixon came from Ireland to Delaware in 1731. His son George fought in the American Revolution. And this George's son (also George Nixon) fought at Gettysburg. We have more information, although that too is sparse, about the Nixon family since the Civil War. What happened to Nixon's grandfather and father, however, has had an important and clearer bearing on the life of the future President.

Samuel Brady Nixon, Richard Nixon's grandfather, was not sixteen when his father, George, died in the Civil War in 1863. Samuel's mother died not quite two years later, in 1865, leaving her eight children orphans. The trauma of the violent and seemingly inexplicable death of Samuel's father was an important element that undermined the emotional security of Samuel and the other children. Samuel's tragic youth was made even more difficult when parts of his father's Ohio farm had to be sold at a sheriff's sale. Family finances were in an almost hopeless state.

On April 10, 1873, Samuel Brady Nixon, aged twenty-six, married a twenty-year-old schoolteacher, Sarah Ann Wadsworth. Their marriage produced five children, three boys and two girls. The second-oldest, Francis (Frank) Anthony Nixon, who was born December 3, 1878, in Vinton County, Ohio, was to become Richard Nixon's father.

Samuel first tried to make a go of what was left of his father's farm, but he did not succeed. Unable to support his family, he gave up farming and became a teacher. Since the pay was poor, he also worked as a mail carrier. Trying times set in when Sarah Ann contracted tuberculosis, a disease which in the nineteenth century was particularly dreaded because it killed more people than any other. It was also believed to be hereditary, not contagious as we now know. Samuel, after selling his Ohio farm and most of the family belongings, took Sally Ann, as he called her, to the Carolinas and Georgia, where he took on odd jobs. He hoped Sally Ann might recover in the warmer climate, but she grew weaker, her condition became acute, and in despair the family returned to Ohio, where, in January 1886, she died in her father's home.

President Nixon described his father's youth:

"My father was orphaned when he was a very young boy, nine years of age.* There were four brothers in addition to himself and a sister. And once this orphaned family in Ohio broke up, they had to face up to the problem of self-support." [1] As a matter of fact, the children were scattered around and taken care of by different members of the family.

The gloom and despair brought about by Sarah Ann's illness and death were later to afflict Frank Nixon's own family when two of his children (Richard Nixon's brothers) died of tuberculosis.

Frank was sent to live with his uncle Elihu (Lyle) Nixon, who was twenty-six years old and had two young daughters. The girls were soon followed in close succession by five other children. Frank, who we know was highly sensitive even as a child, found this new life difficult.

The fact that Samuel Nixon's financial troubles began well before his wife's death, and despite his hard work, suggests that he was inadequate as a provider. The same would be true of his son Frank.

Samuel, even without the financial burden of his children, had a hard time getting back on his feet. In Vinton County, he struggled to earn a meager income, once again teaching school and carrying mail. He also worked occasionally in a pottery factory whose products were peddled on the side of the road. Four years after Sally Ann's death, he was somewhat better off.

Frank's adult personality was strongly influenced by his childhood. The loss of his mother and his home when he was seven and the long separation from his father, which must have seemed an eternity, no doubt had an effect upon his development. Living with an uncle was a difficult dislocation

---

* Nixon was in error; his father was seven at the time.

4

for him, and so as a child he found no stability in his family life. Those who knew him later found Frank's personality to be turbulent, argumentative, and offensive. His rebelliousness was surely an expression of anger—at his helplessness and the rejection he must have felt at being cast adrift as a child. His parents had been powerless to protect him.

The impact of a parent's death on a child's emotional development can be significant indeed. When a parent dies—or is absent for long periods of time—the child's identification with him becomes confused or delayed, often leading to complete rejection of both authority and parents.

The parallel is striking between Frank's childhood loss of his mother and the long separation from his father and that of his own father, Samuel, who, when he was not sixteen, had lost his father in the Civil War and his mother a short time later. In successive generations family life had been seriously dislocated by the loss of one or more parents.

At the age of fourteen, seven years after his mother's death, Frank was, because of his interrupted schooling, only in the fourth grade. There is some doubt about the actual length of his formal schooling. Nixon says, in his book *Six Crises:* "Because of illness in his family he had had to leave school after only six years of formal education." [2]

Nixon has never written that his father's mother died of tuberculosis—perhaps because the nature of her illness and death is too painful to think about. One cannot, however, attribute Frank Nixon's lack of schooling solely to his mother's illness, even if he had attended school while the family lived in the South. His younger brother Ernest, five years his junior, worked his way through college, earned a Ph.D., and became a distinguished agricultural expert. Frank, on the other hand, impatient and rebellious and therefore with a high opinion of himself, resisted discipline in and out of the classroom, and preferred to be free of authority, to do as he pleased. His rebelliousness was reinforced when, four years after his mother's death, when he was eleven, his forty-three-year-old father married Lutheria Wyman, who was twenty-seven. She proved to be a harsh stepmother. Where could the boy turn for affection? He found himself deserted at an even earlier age than his father. Moreover, his father's financial condition no doubt provided partial self-justification for his decision to leave school in order to help support the family.

There was, though, another important reason for his leaving home. Lutheria was a strict disciplinarian. She dominated the household, partly because her husband was weak and often absent, seeking work wherever he could find it. Frank felt threatened and powerless against her. He reacted to her strictness with anger and defiance, which in turn made him think of himself as an outsider.

When Samuel died in Ohio in 1914, Frank's stepmother, Lutheria, moved to California, where she married Dr. M. W. Marshburn, who had a son, Oscar, by a previous marriage. Oscar, in 1918, married Rose Olive Milhous, whose sister Hannah was Richard Nixon's mother. Having lived with his stepmother, Lutheria, Oscar Marshburn came to know her well. During the course of a long interview, he told me in a voice in which I could sense his anger, "When she was married to Samuel, she was hard and beat Frank." These beatings would provide a further stimulus to Frank's rebelliousness. He no doubt was deeply angry at his stepmother, and her beatings may have been the reason for leaving home—not his stated purpose of wanting to work to help support the family, although that probably was his hope.

Family brutality and abuse, which is far more widespread than most people realize, is often passed down from one generation to another. It is ironic that those who have suffered physical abuse from their parents frequently use brutality as a way of dealing with their own children and others in the family. This became a pattern in the case of Frank Nixon.

Frank left school in 1894, when he was sixteen. During his first summer of work, Frank did not spend money on his family, as he had declared he would, but instead spent all his money on clothes. As his brother Ernest said, "He was a fancy dresser." [3]

Jessamyn West has said that young Frank was very active, interested in everything that went on around him. His lack of schooling did not prevent him from speaking his mind. He was often belligerent and combative when others disagreed with him. And like his father, Samuel, but without as much formal education, Frank took on any work that came his way—as a farm hand, a painter, a potter, a carpenter. When he moved westward from Ohio to Colorado, he worked as a sheep herder.

In 1896, at eighteen, he returned to Ohio, having saved enough to buy himself a horse. As Frank explained it, "My father, Samuel Nixon, was an Ohio Democrat. But one day I rode a horse in a William McKinley parade. McKinley himself admired my horse and told me so. That did it. I voted Republican for McKinley then and ever since." * [4]

Another version of the story is related by Edwin Hoyt, who states that McKinley asked him how he was going to vote, and Frank, too young to vote, nevertheless answered, "Republican, of course," [5] a reply which expressed both the defiance and the tremendous self-assurance which were central to his personality. It also reflected Frank's natural—but no doubt very intense—gratitude for praise and attention.

Frank voted Republican not only because of the chance meeting with McKinley but also because he opposed the "hard money" policy of the Democratic President, Grover Cleveland. Then, too, Frank's father was a Democrat. Becoming a Republican was a rebuke to his father, a way of avenging his father's inability to care for him, which he may have experienced as desertion—a pattern of behavior Frank was to repeat.

In 1896, according to Hoyt, he again worked on the farm, then got a job in a brick works; bored with that, he began to raise potatoes. But tiring of that, too, he moved to Colorado, where he worked as a day laborer. In 1901 he traveled to Columbus, Ohio, to better his fortunes. It is reasonable to surmise that he had become well known for his stubborn and rebellious behavior. One avenue open to him was to start again where people wouldn't know of his difficulty in keeping a job and would not be aware of how antagonistic he could be toward people in authority.

In Columbus, he first worked as a day laborer and, later in 1901, was employed by the new electric-streetcar company as a conductor. While he liked his job and was especially proud of his bright uniform, he complained of the bitter winter weather. Standing day after day, hour after hour, on the front platform of the streetcar, he developed a painful case of frostbitten toes. Moreover, the low pay infuriated him, and he set about organizing a movement to better the working conditions for himself and for his fellow employees, but without success. Frank realized that he could not better his lot in Columbus and he also concluded that he would be hap-

* In 1936, Frank voted Democratic.

pier in a milder climate; and so, in 1907, he packed his bags and boarded a train for California. Once again Frank was on the move, this time seeking new adventures in the Far West. He was restless, lively, and, besides, he had little to lose.

In Los Angeles, Frank worked as a motorman on the Los Angeles Street Railway connecting Los Angeles and Whittier. As he tells it, he was a motorman until he hit an automobile as it crossed the tracks. This led to his dismissal, which suggests that he was responsible for the accident—or that he had incurred the dislike of his superiors. He next worked as a farm laborer.

Early in 1908, at a St. Valentine's Day party given by the streetcar conductors, Frank met Hannah Milhous.

The Milhous family had migrated in the late seventeenth century from Germany to Ireland, where, probably on their arrival, they anglicized their name from Mulhausen or Milhausen. It was in Ireland, too, that they joined the Society of Friends. Little is known about the family; records are scant. There is an old Quaker cemetery in Timahoe, county Kildare, but there were no family markers until President Nixon arranged for one. The inscription on it reads: "In memory of the Irish Quakers of Timahoe, dedicated October 5, 1970 by Richard Milhous Nixon, President of the United States of America, whose maternal ancestors are resting here." [6] Nixon was proud of his Quaker heritage and proud, too, of the fact that the first Milhous, Thomas, arrived in America from Ireland in 1729. The Milhouses moved from Chester County, Pennsylvania, to Ohio in 1805, and then to Indiana in 1854, and, finally, to California in 1897. Nixon's paternal ancestors, as we have seen, had an equally long heritage in America. The Nixons, like the Milhous family, had slowly moved west: from Delaware to Pennsylvania, to Ohio and Illinois. It was Frank Nixon, as we have seen, who had uprooted himself and gone to California in 1907, and it was Hannah Milhous's father, Franklin, who, ten years before, moved from Indiana with his family to Whittier, California.

As we look at the history of the Milhous family in America, we are struck by the recurring pattern of tuberculosis. We know that Joshua Milhous, born in 1820, married Elizabeth Price Griffith and was the father of eight children. Two of his sons, William and Amos, died in 1866 within one day of each other.[7] That both children died within such a short period of time would suggest a highly infectious disease such as tubercular meningitis, which was rampant at that time.

Franklin Milhous, Joshua's youngest son, must have grown up with a fear of this dreaded disease. Franklin is important to us because he was the father of Hannah Milhous, Richard Nixon's mother.

Franklin Milhous married twice. His first wife, to whom he had been married five years, died in childbirth in 1877, leaving Franklin with two small children. His second marriage, two years later, was to thirty-year-old Almira Park Burdg, a schoolteacher who was thought of as a "frontier" woman and who "rode to school on horseback." [8]

Franklin and Almira had six girls and one boy, Ezra. Their third child, Hannah, born March 7, 1885, in Butlerville, Indiana, was to become Richard Nixon's mother.

Franklin was an orchardist and nurseryman. Believing that he had inherited the Milhous "weak chest" and a predisposition to tuberculosis, he and his wife decided to move to California, where the climate might improve his health. So, in 1897, when Hannah was twelve, Franklin piled his furniture, nursery stock, oak doors, sills, and beams for a new house into a freight car and, with his wife and nine children, headed west. They settled in the little town of Whittier, some twenty miles from Los Angeles. Named after the Quaker poet John Greenleaf Whittier, the town had been founded ten years before as a Quaker retreat.

There is little to tell about Hannah's infancy, childhood, or adolescence, with the exception of one incident that occurred during her Indiana years, which she recalled when she was interviewed in 1959. This incident was brought to light at the time of her death in September 1967.

"I was one of a large family and father never paddled us," she said. "Mother switched my ankles once with an apple twig. I was about 5 and had told my 2-year-old brother [Ezra] it was all right for him to go wading, even though my mother would not approve. The switching didn't amount to anything but I felt terrible about it." [9]

Though Hannah minimized the punishment—"the switch-

9

ing didn't amount to anything"—she nevertheless remembered it, and remembered it well. Evidently this event had stayed in her mind for seventy years because of her strong feeling about it—and her guilt.

There must have been more to the story. Probably, as is not unusual, she was jealous of her little brother, feeling that had he not been born, their mother would have paid more attention to her. We don't know how deep the creek was, but a two-year-old child could easily stumble and fall in, with disastrous results.

Hannah was brought up in a devout Quaker home dedicated to hard work and prayer. Her family, from the very beginning, had belonged to the conservative branch of Quakers. Raised to be concerned about the immortality of her soul, she lived in a strict and disciplined environment. Strict discipline puts conscience to work. We have the impression that while growing up she may have been secretly troubled and concerned about her conscience.

A quality of self-absorption emanates from the early photographs of Hannah. Although one cannot judge a person's mood and character from one photograph, a series of photographs taken at different ages can be suggestive. One Milhous family picture, taken when Hannah was no more than five or six, includes fifteen adults and eleven children. It is a somber group; not even the youngsters are smiling. In another family photograph, Hannah, about eight, looks solemn, determined, and fearful; perhaps just a little arrogant. Of the eleven people in the picture, she is the only one who is not looking straight into the camera.

In a photograph taken when Hannah was about ten, we again see a grave and determined young girl. Although she is quite attractive, one senses sadness in her face. These traits of determination and seriousness reappear in a striking way in a photograph of her as a young woman in which her face is controlled and tight, with no suggestion of radiance or joy. She looks at the world as if preoccupied with serious matters and hiding something she resents. This same expression is found in a much later picture in which Hannah appears with Frank and their children, Harold, Donald, and Richard. Once again, she is somber, intent, and sad.

In all these pictures, a repressed anger is revealed in the

lines of her face. She was brought up not to show anger. She was taught control. But anger will inevitably surface in all of us, and Hannah was no exception. As the *Los Angeles Times* reported in 1967:

> [She] could—despite her Quaker religion—get angry. She did during the 1952 presidential election when her son was seeking the Vice Presidency under the ticket headed by Gen. Eisenhower.
>
> It came in the aftermath of disclosures of a "secret Nixon fund"—money contributed by businessmen.
>
> "I was completely shaken," she said. "What they were saying or intimating was very bad. There was no foundation. As a Quaker I can't say I got angry, but I was terribly put out."[10]

Living in an orthodox Quaker world, Hannah was isolated from the mainstream of American life. Preoccupied with herself, brought up in a self-contained subculture, she may have felt that only she could defend her interests, for if anything traumatic happened to her, no help could be expected from the outside.

This attitude she had learned from her mother and her grandmother, Elizabeth. Elizabeth Milhous was an interesting and domineering woman. After her husband had died in 1893, she continued her calling as a Quaker minister.

Elizabeth's staunch and conservative faith would pervade the home, and the lives, of her children (Franklin, her oldest son), her grandchildren (Hannah, Franklin's daughter), and her great-grandchildren (including, of course, Richard Nixon). At the time of her death at ninety-three on May 3, 1923, in Whittier, California, Richard Nixon was ten years old and had lived within the sphere of her strong religious influence. It was in this environment that Hannah developed a deep and underlying need to keep things to herself. Her need and desire for secrecy reinforced her belief in total self-reliance in an unfriendly world. Furthermore, she shared the family streak of stubbornness. The desire not to seek help from others could also derive from lack of trust in people. What is apparent is that this combination of stubbornness and lack of trust in others became a predominating pattern. As we shall see, because of the strong affinity

11

Richard had with his mother, he developed these same qualities.

Even in adolescence Hannah remained quiet and withdrawn. But then something happened to change her life. When she was twenty-three, she met Frank Nixon.

2

Frank Nixon and Hannah Milhous were married on June 25, 1908 in Whittier, California. His courtship was not only short but overpowering. He admitted as much: "I immediately stopped going with the five other girls I was dating, and I saw Hannah every night." [1]

Dating many girls concurrently suggests an aggressive attitude toward women. While Frank's boasting may imply bravado, sources confirm that he was sexually and emotionally aggressive. As Jessamyn West says, "I doubt that Frank Nixon could do anything halfheartedly, and this trait is appealing to young people." [2] This may explain why only four months elapsed from the time Frank met Hannah until he married her. Frank was dramatic in his courtship, a characteristic we will see in Richard Nixon's behavior.

One stumbling block in their courtship was the difference in their religious upbringing. Whereas Hannah was a Quaker, Frank had been raised in a strict Methodist home. We do not have detailed information on how they were able to reconcile their religious differences, but we do know that, after meeting Hannah and prior to their marriage, Frank became an active Quaker.[3] Hannah, who on the surface was mild and subdued, was able to persuade her fiancé to renounce his religion for hers. There is also the possibility that the Milhouses may have insisted, either directly to Frank or through Hannah, that Frank would have to become a Quaker. It may also be that Frank was predisposed to be a Quaker, since, according to Merle (Rusty) West (Jessamyn West's brother),* Frank, who roomed with a family of Quakers, had attended services at the Meeting House. Knowing that Frank was erratic, that he always had

_____
* Merle and Jessamyn West's maternal grandfather, Jesse Milhous, was Franklin Milhous's brother.

a definite opinion on everything, we may ask whether his conversion was soley out of love for Hannah. We do know that once Frank had decided on a course of action he would not rest until his goal had been achieved. Being persistent, he may have concluded that becoming a Quaker was something he would do to win Hannah's hand. She was worth it. While from his viewpoint conversion may not have seemed to be a major concession, the fact that she or she and her strong family were able to have their way reflects her strong and commanding determination to make religion an important part of their married life. And yet, as Jessamyn West says, Frank "was very unlike my birthright relatives, who were quiet, subdued, inclined to see both sides of every question. Frank saw one side: his; and he was not bashful about letting you know what was wrong with your side." [4]

Since he felt his side was "right," it is strange that he gave in to his fiancée on the issue. But part of the explanation may lie in Frank's youthful rebelliousness against his father. Samuel, as we have seen, was a Democrat; Frank had chosen to become a Republican.

Although not temperamentally inclined toward becoming a true Friend, Frank's willingness to change did fit his defiant personality and his need to repudiate his father. It is doubtful to me that his conversion was sincere: that, as Jessamyn West claims, he "had become a Quaker by conviction." In any event, he had to show that he was a true believer, that he was a better Quaker than anyone else—better, even, than Hannah and her family. "Frank was certainly ardent in his Sunday-school teaching," Jessamyn West has said. "His cheeks flamed, and his voice trembled."

Miss West also described Frank some years after his marriage:

> I was a member of a Sunday-school class of young people between the ages of fourteen and twenty, taught by Frank Nixon, Richard Nixon's father. Frank was an ardent and energetic teacher, and his class had outgrown one room after another until finally we were occupying the entire platform reserved, once church began, for choir, preacher, and visiting dignitaries. . . . He was the first person to make me understand that there was a great lack of practicing Christianity in civic affairs.[5]

We might infer that Frank's decision was made in an effort to ingratiate himself with Hannah's family. Ordinarily, the true believer feels no need to flaunt his convictions. Faith is an intrinsic quality securely anchored within oneself which nobody can touch.

The renunciation of his childhood faith must have been unsettling to Frank. He, the strident, argumentative man, gave in to his wife's (or her family's) demands. In any case, he had given up something closely identified with his father's family, and as a result he may have felt guilty. His conversion shows that despite his bravado and intensity he was capable of yielding to pressure as long as he did not feel it posed a fundamental threat. Intimidating as Frank could be, it is likely he himself could be intimidated.

Frank's passive accommodation to his fiancée's religion could, in addition, undermine his identity and independence in their marriage. Hannah used her indirect, controlling passivity to dominate him on the issue of religion and to dominate him later as they sought solutions to other problems—problems caused not only by their different personalities, but also by their different backgrounds. He was a day laborer, she a former college student. The point is that she didn't seek him out; he pursued her. These differences to a great extent influenced their relationship.

Hannah's shyness had probably prevented her from finding a young man who was more or less her equal—a college classmate, for example. According to some sources, Hannah met Franklin when she was a sophomore at Whittier College.* It is reasonable to conclude that she decided to marry Frank because he pursued her so ardently and there was no one else in her life. Her reserved nature and her sheltered life no doubt made it difficult for her to meet new people and feel comfortable in their company. "He was a fast worker," her sister, Rose Olive Marshburn, told me. "Hannah sometimes went out with a group but she never had a single date before meeting Frank."

What did Hannah admire in Frank? His bravado? His enthusiasm? (He certainly turned out to be a forceful and popular Sunday-school teacher.) His looks? Clearly this was no intellectual match. Frank tried to compensate for his

* Rose Olive Marshburn told me that Hannah had done some teaching and had stayed out of college a year. She did not finish college.

limited education by being more talk than substance. We also suspect that Frank's sexual needs were intense and that he looked upon Hannah as a sexual object, as an object of conquest. The forcefulness of his pursuit apparently appealed to Hannah, whose repressed nature responded positively to his attention. He posed as a man of the world who had traveled, who knew life and could deal with "the real world."

Frank married Hannah because she was young and attractive, and he himself was alone and without family.

At the outset of their married life, Frank worked as a farm laborer outside Whittier. Jessamyn West and others have said that he was also a carpenter. It was not long before Hannah became pregnant, and in 1909 her parents, Franklin and Almira, requested that she return home for the birth of her first child. Rose Olive Marshburn told me that "they stayed on the ranch owned by my father, on which Frank worked." Frank and his wife were absorbed into the crowded Milhous home, where six of Hannah's brothers and sisters lived, as well as Franklin's strong-willed mother, Elizabeth Milhous. On June 1, 1909, Harold Samuel Nixon was born.

By contemporary standards, the Milhouses, who lived in a large house, were well off. They were also a well-structured family. In contrast, Frank was in many ways footloose, and he had worked and lived wherever he could. Although we have no information regarding Hannah's feelings about her husband's difficulties in making a living, we may surmise that she resented it. We may also suspect that the Milhous family felt that Hannah had married down, which may have brought additional anguish to her already troubled mind.

Observers who have studied the Nixon family background generally agree that Hannah had married beneath her station. "Hannah was," as Stewart Alsop wrote, "rather widely regarded in Whittier as having made an unfortunate marriage . . ." [6] To Frank, marriage to a woman of higher social status may have been a way of affirming his own worth. The need to measure up to the Milhouses, to compensate for his lack of status, made him even more competitive, more combative.

Living in the Milhous household was neither easy nor relaxing, for there were sharp restrictions on how life was to be conducted. For example, every morning before breakfast a chapter from the Bible was read either by Hannah's parents or by her grandmother, Elizabeth; this was followed by a prayer by each person present. Only then did breakfast begin.

Frank, who developed bleeding ulcers in later life, was clearly a tense man. At first he endured this regimented life quite well, but we must suspect that he soon began to resent it. Then, too, there was the ever-present problem of how to make a living. Frank had neither money nor much vocational training. His father-in-law gave him a few acres at Lindsay, where he could plant an orange grove. This venture failed. Within two years he was back in Whittier working as a foreman on a citrus ranch, a job which lasted only a few months.[7] Then, in 1911, again with the help of his father-in-law, he bought property in Yorba Linda, a few miles from Whittier, and tried his hand at growing lemons. One biographer says that he had chosen his land badly; the topsoil wasn't deep enough.[8] Another source says that the price of lemons fell and Frank Nixon sold out at a loss.[9] In any event, the venture failed. Frank, who had now failed several times, was not able to support his family. His household may not have been at the level of abject poverty, but money was not readily available. It was a constant struggle to meet expenses.

Frank spent a good deal of his time in Quaker religious and educational programs. And the family continued to grow. Frank built a small frame house in Yorba Linda, where their second boy, Richard Milhous, was born on January 9, 1913. Three boys followed: Francis Donald, born a year after Richard; Arthur Burdg, born four years later; and Edward Calvert, born seventeen years later.

In contrast to Harold, his quiet older brother, Richard "was known in the family as a screamer." [10] The first characteristic that impressed Hannah was his "decided voice." [11]

It certainly is not unusual for children to cry in their early years. But persistent screaming surely indicates a problem. We might say that a newborn baby's responses are conditioned. For an infant, harsh sounds or strong lights are acute biological and emotional shocks, and crying is the child's way of protecting himself against them, of communicating his discomfort.

To his great-grandmother, Elizabeth, the boy's loud voice meant that he would be either a preacher or a lawyer; a psychiatrist or pediatrician would reason that he was either uncomfortable and needed attention, or felt lonely and wanted

17

company. He was in the first year of his life, in the oral period, which lasts for about one year. During this year all the child's feelings center on food and nursing.* He sucks the breast or the bottle, and his thumb. He puts everything into his mouth, or he babbles away. When he is fed or cuddled, he is satisfied. Unable to postpone satisfaction, he wants to be fed at once. Until he is taken care of, he cries and whines, and this is his only way of making his wants known.

To an infant, love is felt mainly through receiving food. The infant starts his contact with the world through his skin or his mouth, which are fundamental sources of pleasure. He unconsciously associates the oral sensations of taking in food with love and security. When children are fed, and at the same time fondled, they learn to enjoy these pleasurable feelings, and their sense of being secure and loved grows. The quicker their needs are gratified, the happier they are. But if they are not taken care of at once, they experience rejection or pain. Once the child has become used to oral gratification, he likes to prolong it because this satisfaction gives him pleasure. He craves indulgence. But if he is denied emotional gratification through the mouth, he feels rejected and unloved; and this may lead to oral aggression.

This is an important point. If a child is denied normal satisfaction through the mouth—for instance, being weaned too abruptly—or the mother or father has not had the time to take care of him, he feels this as a loss of love. He wants it back—and he may go on wanting it back for the rest of his life.

As we follow Nixon's life we will find that behind all his actions as a child, and later as an adult, was a person who had been cheated out of love. He wanted it back at all costs.

The oral stage is followed by the anal stage, which usually occurs between the ages of one and two and a half. For the first time the child has to learn self-control, and he has to learn to keep back, not to let go. A person with anal characteristics may to the outside world be compliant, but this withholding is like keeping a secret. Secrecy was one of the most predominant of Nixon's traits.

People exhibit traits stemming from both the oral and anal stages. The oral influence makes us generous, easygoing, kind,

---

* According to Rose Olive Marshburn, all Hannah's children were breast-fed.

flexible, lackadaisical or carefree, and unconcerned about material things. But it also makes us dependent and childish, excessively ambitious and attention-seeking. It causes us to become impulsive, self-righteous, and calculating; we develop contempt for others, show undue passivity. The oral influence can make us feel rejected and cause us to be suspicious and always want our own way.

The second group of traits, rooted in the anal stage, when we are concerned with defecation—either elimination or retention—tends to make us miserly, impatient, manipulative, rigid, tense, controlling, and cruel. There is a need to be perfect; it becomes important to be right and there is a concomitant fear of admitting mistakes. On the other hand, the anal stage can make the individual careful and cautious, thrifty, foresighted, and orderly.

To some degree, some of each of these traits are necessary for healthy development. In extreme form, they create a self-destructive personality. In those whose emotional development has become stunted because of neglect or a threatening parental environment, these traits can become exaggerated, strongly entrenched, or fixated.

The oral and anal stages are pregenital. These pregenital stages and the genital phase of emotional development overlap. The child's genital drive, as we understand it, is an outgrowth of his pleasure-seeking urge. Little by little, the boy's sexual urge is directed toward his mother (the girl's toward her father). The boy and girl first experience a phallic-Oedipal stage which creates a self-centered preoccupation with their whole body. As their genitals become the predominant erotogenic zone, the boy and the girl enter the Oedipal stage. The Oedipal stage—the classic mother-son, father-daughter attraction—usually occurs when the child is between two and a half and about five years of age. The boy's unconscious sexual urge is not limited to the mother; it is partially directed toward the father, because the child does not want to lose either parent. But whether or not he would like to lose his mother or father, normally he has to identify with the parent of the same sex.

In the case of Nixon, we have noticed his early screaming; later on, his oratorical activities, indicating his oral orientation, show that he was orally fixated. We also will see that he was anally fixated. Both his oral and anal traits were deeply anchored in him. With both oral and anal fixations there could be very little genital orientation; that is, genuine sexual expression. We might anticipate that he felt more comfortable when he could express himself orally and anally instead of genitally. By and large, Nixon did not develop beyond his oral and anal stages. Both these stages stayed with him; they were to become ingrained, fixated. As a result, his emotional development was stunted.

As an infant, Richard reacted to his home environment by screaming because he found it disturbing and unsettling. Resistance to his surroundings upsets the child's emotional balance, so that he becomes disoriented, unable to organize positive and normal feelings about his home environment. Cold, noise, and unrest in the environment, however, do not invariably trouble a child. His own personal reaction to outside stimuli is also a determinant.

From Earl Mazo, who had talked to Hannah, we learn more about the house in which the family lived:

> The small frame house, perched on a knoll above a deep irrigation ditch . . . , was difficult to heat. . . . nights were often cold, particularly in January and February. When the town was cold, the Nixon house was very, very cold. The family dressed in the kitchen, huddled around the cooking stove . . . But on the night of January 9, 1913, the whole house was warm and comfortable, especially the tiny alcove that served as master bedroom.[12]

Whether it was warm in the house that night or not we can't be sure, but Yorba Linda on the night Richard Milhous Nixon was born was experiencing the worst freeze in its history.[13] Inexplicably, none of Hannah's family was with her.

> . . . Mrs. Ella McClure Eidson Furnas remembers the day, probably because it was the only time in her life that she played the role of midwife.
> That was on January 9, 1913, and the infant she took from the doctor becomes the 37th President of the United States on Monday.
> . . . [She] resided then in Yorba Linda across the irrigation ditch from the home of Francis and Hannah Nixon.
> She recalls that Nixon's father came to her house a

few hours before the birth of Richard. He was worried. . . .

Francis Nixon asked if Mrs. Furnas would look out for his wife until the doctor arrived. Her role of midwife was cut short by the arrival of Dr. Horace P. Wilson, but she remained at bedside to become the first to hold the infant Richard after he was handed to her by the doctor.

"I wrapped him in a blanket to keep him warm and put him in a laundry basket," she said in a recent interview.[14]

The poor protection the house provided against the cold, damp winter days may have contributed to the high incidence of illness in the family. Nixon seems to have been very susceptible to childhood diseases. When he was four years old he had pneumonia, which nearly killed him; he suffered from hay fever; in his last year of high school (1929–30) he contracted a fever, with temperatures up to 104. It was thought that he had undulant fever. The exact duration of his illness, however, is not certain. His aunt Rose Olive Marshburn told me that he was out of school only a few weeks, certainly not most of the year, as some have suggested, and she, like others, thought the cause was undulant fever. Knowing that this illness is rare and that it can very well be mistaken for mononucleosis or a neurotic condition, we cannot say for sure whether Richard really had undulant fever or whether he was suffering from another illness. It is possible that he had a mild attack of tuberculosis. The comments of one of his college classmates about his health are illuminating.

> Dick lived somewhat abnormally. He studied a great deal and worked in the store. It wasn't uncommon for him to work himself ill. On one occasion Dick was home ill. His mother called me at the college and asked to have his books brought home. When I arrived Dick was really ill with the flu.[15]

Frank's financial problems must have contributed to a disharmonious home life, filled with heated outbursts and repressed anger. Frank must have more than once yelled at Richard when he screamed. We are told that by the time his brother Donald was born, when Richard was a year old, he

21

had "quieted down." [16] Young Richard may well have quieted down to some degree because he was intimidated by his father's threats, which would have awakened resentment and fear, fear of a man who was loud and demonstrative, a man who moved his hands quickly, almost violently, as if striking at some invisible target.

The fear Richard felt must have increased the stress and strain between Frank and his son. Naturally, Richard's antagonistic feelings were not conscious. He must have felt conflicted. At times he would be aware of a woman talking quietly, in measured tones, seldom raising her voice. But there were times when she spoke up loudly and insistently, and this too must have frightened and bewildered Richard.

A strange house it was. Two contrasting emotional antagonists, one parent usually quiet and unyielding, the other often unruly and violent. Richard was caught in the middle. To survive in this atmosphere was like walking a tightrope—a feeling he never forgot. That his attitude toward his parents became ambivalent is not surprising. Based upon the data we have of Richard as a child and upon what we know about the psychodynamics of an infant growing up in a conflicted home, we can safely assume that through his crying and screaming he sought solace, and received it, more from his mother than from his father.

Further, since in early infancy a boy's attraction toward the mother is greater than toward the father, we may conclude that the closer Richard felt to her, the more he felt estranged from his dominating father—whom he disliked, resented, and feared. The unhealthy relationships produced in Richard an unusually early and strong bond to his mother. At the same time an early and unconscious hostility was mobilized toward his father which Nixon later projected onto adults, particularly authority figures.

Hostility toward a parent is, of course, very common; many of us go through this phase. Some people, however, never succeed in outgrowing it. Richard's closeness to his mother, reinforced by the vicissitudes she suffered, resulted in a syndrome centered on absolute loyalty, which became extremely important to him in his adult relationships. Hostility toward his father made identification with any man not devoted to him difficult, a trait which was to determine much of his later choice of his close associates and of his relationships with them.

Although we cannot predict what the adult's behavior will be in any particular situation, we can single out patterns of behavior that are evident in childhood; since we know that the responses learned in childhood will persist, we can project patterns, although we cannot predict precise actions.

Many people, however, refuse to accept, or would like to minimize or disregard, the importance of childhood feelings or the existence of the unconscious, which dictates our actions. Further, some people believe that past emotions have little or nothing to do with adult behavior. To admit that emotional difficulties are rooted in childhood experiences would mean we would have to acknowledge that we have not grown up emotionally.

But we know that when children are satisfied and affectionate, or hostile and sullen, they will in all probability grow up retaining these predominant characteristics. Or when they waver between friendliness and anger, trust and hostility, we are not surprised that their childhood insecurity reflects inconsistent, vacillating, and ambivalent feelings and behavior which become apparent later in life.

In this respect Richard Nixon is no exception. By crying or screaming loudly, young Richard learned how to get attention, and this pattern continued as he grew older. By crying or seeking attention in other ways, he unconsciously found a way to control his mother and, to a lesser degree, his father. We can easily believe that his childhood screaming represented a pattern that would cause him in later life to continue to use his mouth, to proclaim his wishes loud and clear, particularly in an emergency or crisis. We see this pattern in his political career; for example, in the Watergate period he said he would "fight the impeachment like Hell," which caused Illinois congressman John Anderson to remark, "Nixon is not going to fade away like one of MacArthur's old soldiers. He always was going to be dragged kicking and screaming into oblivion." [17]

Drawing attention to himself became a predominant trait in young Nixon, one reason why he loved to talk, argue, and debate. What he had to say was to become more important than what others would have to tell him. Using his voice, therefore, became more important than being loved or giving love. His verbal facility, however, is not so much a matter of using well-turned phrases; he learned to talk about and around the aspects of any issue. His success as a politician

23

was based on his skill as a debater. Orally oriented and orally fixated, speech was his way of releasing his aggression.

Much of this behavior was conditioned by Nixon's loveless home environment. In all his writings and speeches, I have not discovered any mention of the word "love." Its absence is noteworthy. If children do not receive love, they cannot learn to give it. Frank Nixon was a tyrant who intimidated his children. He spanked them on the slightest pretext.

Frank was unpredictable. His children feared him; although he could be jovial, he punished them often. One example, related to me by Jessamyn West, underscores this point. When the Nixon children were small they went swimming and wading in the Anaheim ditch close to their house. Playing in the ditch was dangerous and forbidden. Frank happened to discover them. He ran to the ditch and ordered them to come out. After the children crawled out, Frank shouted, "Do you like water? Have some more of it." Whereupon he began to throw the crying children back into the water. A person who observed this terrible scene called out, "Frank, stop! You will kill them." He finally stopped.

We may imagine how petrified the children must have been when, after crawling out of the water in a state of fright, they were in the next moment thrown back into it by an angry father. The thought must have gone through their minds: "Is he trying to kill us?" It certainly must have been an experience that left a lasting mark.

Frank was a powerful figure who tried to control everyone around him, young and old alike, either by force or by flattery. However, as Jessamyn West explains, he also had difficulty controlling his sexual aggressions.

> To offset his truculence, he had a boisterous geniality, which none of my Milhous relatives ever evidenced. He never saw my mother, a plain woman, without exclaiming, "Grace, I swear you get prettier every time I see you. How do you do it? I want your recipe. Come here and let me give you a hug."
>
> Mama always protested afterward. "What does Frank want to embarrass me that way for?"
>
> She may have been embarrassed, but she was also secretly pleased. No woman takes permanent offense

from a man's praise, even though she recognizes its foundation in truth is shaky.

Quakers—and Frank, after his marriage to Hannah Milhous, had become a Quaker by conviction—did not believe in dancing. Frank had, apart from doctrinal precepts, his own reasons for not dancing. He did not use Dr. Johnson's language, who told his friend the actor David Garrick that he could not visit him back-stage because the sight of half-clad actresses "aroused his amorous propensities"; but it was for this reason Frank told Papa that he would not dance. When his arms went around a woman, his amorous propensities were instantly aroused. Today when this kind of re-sponsiveness is valued and whole books are written on the most effective means for males and females to in-duce such an arousal, Frank's scruples may seem ridic-ulous. But our need of such books today may bespeak our lack of understanding the strength of such propen-sities in an ardent man fifty years ago.[18]

Interestingly enough, when one of Jessamyn West's cous-ins asked her about Frank's sexual aggressiveness and if he had ever pinched her, Jessamyn West replied, "He never pinched *me!*" Even though there were attractive young girls in the family old enough to be kissed, Frank was careful for the most part to keep his distance, because he wanted to control himself.

In view of this abnormally strong sexual drive, we can better understand Frank's frustrations and angry and irri-table, even brutal and uncontrollable outbursts. Sex and violence are closely related. Sex gives violence its strong character. And being sexually aggressive, he also must have been violent. When his sexual desires did surface, they also served to conceal his violent temperament.

Thus, we see Frank as a strongly orally oriented person who drew attention to himself through his loud, impulsive, and often violent temper, and by talking about how he felt about women. He was therefore highly visible to people out-side the family and feared by his children and wife.

In many ways, Hannah was the opposite of Frank. Be-neath her calm exterior there was a tension, a toughness, combined with resolution and strength; she was hard as flint. These characteristics seem to have been overlooked by previous observers. In contrast to Frank, she usually managed to control her anger. When Nixon was under heavy attack in 1952 because of his secret slush fund, Hannah controlled her anger to a great degree.

They were similar in that each wanted to have his own way, Frank directly and Hannah indirectly. Hannah was a strongly suppressed and repressed woman, and at the same time a controlling wife who manipulated and subdued her husband. She became the model for Richard, who developed at an early age an ability to manipulate others in order to get what he wanted.

From what we have seen, we can begin to picture how Nixon's personality and behavior were shaped by family influences. Nixon's forebears were wandering people, perpetually seeking new lands which held greater promise. But despite their hard work, they were never successful. They were never "well-to-do," and they survived on the margin of poverty. Nixon's grandfather Samuel Brady Nixon and his father, Frank, were both failures. Their often strenuous efforts to compete in the business world failed; their personality structure was too weak to withstand enduring stress. That economic failure was manifested in two generations may be considered a strong indication of a deeper failure. Furthermore, both men, who were weak, married very strong women. These patterns were strongly pronounced in Frank, and later became readily apparent in Nixon. Even though Richard Nixon *did* succeed, he ultimately failed.

Not only were the Nixon children deprived economically and socially; more important was their emotional deprivation. Samuel Brady Nixon and his son Frank each lost parents when they were children, and so their homes were lacking in stability, love, and affection. Illness left an indelible and traumatic impression, often producing overpowering despair. While there was tuberculosis in the Milhous family, it was more devastating in Frank Nixon's household. Two of his five children died from tuberculosis, and a great fear of this affliction plagued Nixon.

Frank Nixon and Franklin Milhous both came to California for their health. This concern was transmitted to Hannah and later to Nixon. It came from both sides of the family. Like the Nixons, the Milhouses were wandering people, but they were able to reach a state of family stability. This sense of balance was partly achieved through their

26

strong religious faith. Hardworking as they were, they also were stubborn and tenacious.

From Nixon's father's side there was a great deal of erratic and aggressive behavior. In Hannah we find characteristics—quietness, secretiveness, control, stubbornness, self-reliance, and an instinct for self-preservation—which in many ways tended to cause Nixon to repress much of his hostility and aggressiveness. These strongly conflicting influences created elements of insecurity, indecisiveness, and hesitation in him. Under acute pressures, he compensated for his passivity by becoming aggressive and hostile, often overreacting by "punishing" those who crossed or opposed him. While it would seem that his mother's usual control over her own feelings would have been a healthy influence on the development of her child, particularly in curbing his aggressions, the influence of her outward, seemingly controlled passivity complicated Richard's psychological makeup. Therein lies much of the core of President Nixon's behavior.

As we observe Richard's home life as a boy and as an adolescent, we will find that his appearance of control was only a façade that hid a deep and smoldering anger which was to erupt and play a major role in his career.

PART II

Childhood and Formative Years

3

When Richard Nixon was forty-five years old, enjoying status and recognition as Vice-President of the United States, he said about his boyhood, "It wasn't easy." [1]

There were indeed many respects in which his childhood wasn't easy. There was, first, the conflict between his parents, which created tensions within him and the desperate need to attract attention. He was also accident-prone and perhaps suffered more illness than most children—and later, as we know, two of his brothers died of tuberculosis. There was the hard work and poverty which in his adolescence and later years he would grow to resent. In addition to the parental conflict, there was the dominating influence of the many strong women in the Milhous family. Above all, there was fear, fear of his parents and fear that death would strike him as it did his brothers. Nixon's statement suggests that he knew his early life wasn't easy, but, as we will see, he tended in almost all cases to distort the truth; he could deny it and he could exaggerate it, not only to the public, but also to himself. He changed the truth—or covered it up—even as a grown man.

Judging from what we know about his early home life, even Nixon's admission glosses over the emotional deprivation. This kind of distortion is not surprising. Many of us, when describing our youth, like to remember the pleasurable and carefree times and overlook or repress the painful experiences. This need to protect ourselves explains why we often remember childhood as pleasurable and wonderful. Time is a great healer because it seals off conscious memories of early hurt and pain—which, nevertheless, remain to plague us as adults.

Nixon's home was joyless, as joyless as he himself was when he created his own home in the White House. His home life was dominated both by the strict orthodox Quaker

31

code of his mother and by the tyrannical rule of his egocentric father. The atmosphere was depressing and frightening. There was little beauty or love. The fact that Richard was a sickly child, and accident-prone, made those years even more grim.

An account of an incident which could have ended in tragedy is revealing:

> President-Elect Richard Nixon came close to serious injury or death in his third year of life in Yorba Linda. He was saved by Ralph Shook, Sr., still a resident there.
>
> It happened some 53 years ago, Shook said, while he and Francis (Frank) Nixon were working on a drainage project.
>
> "The little boy crawled behind our team of horses and when Frank backed up I grabbed him just in time before the animals passed over him," Shook said.
>
> The project, a tough job, required that a drainage pipe be placed under the Anaheim Union Water Company ditch. When the ditch was originally placed, workers did not take into account rainwater runoff.
>
> ". . . The little boy was just like any other little tow-headed boy in Yorba Linda. He was a fine little boy, but he had to be watched around the team," he said.
>
> He doesn't remember just why Mr. Nixon had his little boy along that day at the location near the Shook residence. Perhaps, he said, it was because his mother, Hannah, was at a church or Woman's Club meeting or "maybe it was just because the little boy wanted to be with his daddy that day."
>
> "He came close that time. The team was rearing and straining to pull the auger and I noticed the boy just in time. They backed up and their hoofs trampled the spot where the little boy had been crawling only seconds before," he said.[2]

We must ask whether this near-tragedy was not caused by Frank Nixon's negligence. Richard, two years old, like any small child would have needed careful watching around a team of horses.

About a year later, three-year-old Richard Nixon nearly

lost his life in a wagon accident between Placentia and Yorba Linda:

> Young Richard was riding in the wagon with his mother when he fell and a heavy wheel grazed the side of his head, cutting it open.[8]

> "I held Donald, the baby, in my lap [Hannah remembers] and drove the buggy. I couldn't handle both boys because Richard, then three, was too lively. So a little neighbor girl * came along to hold him."
> As the buggy rounded a steep curve along the bank of the irrigation ditch, Richard outsquirmed his young guardian and fell into the road.[5]

We have no information about whether or not he lost consciousness. However, he had to be rushed twenty-five miles by car to a doctor, who sewed up his long scalp wound, which left a scar.

That Richard fell or escaped from the girl's lap may perhaps, but only perhaps, indicate that his being "too lively" was not the full explanation; his restlessness may also have been caused by the desire to sit on his mother's lap.

As we have suggested, the cause of his first near-accident was his father's carelessness. Whether or not Richard had innocently blundered into the path of the horses or whether he did it to get attention we do not know; Richard at that time in 1915 was two years old. What we do know is that (certainly later) a great deal of attention-seeking was ingrained in him.

We know that when a child comes from a family where there is a great deal of domestic strife and brutality, such a child may become accident-prone. Richard as a child must have been very agile, moving fast without thinking very much of where he was going. As a result, he got into situations or circumstances in which he was exposed to serious danger. After the buggy accident he must have suffered emotional shock. Later he developed motion sickness, pneumonia, hay fever. In 1952 he had a foot injury; in 1960 two knee injuries; in 1964 phlebitis in the leg, and also in 1974.

In short, Richard was a sickly child who craved maternal

* Bela Kornitzer describes her as an aunt.[4]

attention. This craving may, in part, explain his illnesses. Hannah, in turn, must have felt guilty about Richard's accidents; and his illnesses bound mother and son even more closely to each other.

While Hannah had a natural maternal concern for her children, the main bond between them was a mutual fear of Frank. Richard himself said in *A Self Portrait:*

> My father was strict, and he didn't believe in that—let me put it this way: he didn't believe in any of the modern methods of raising children. He said, "You spare the rod, you spoil the child."

Although Hannah was loved by her children, they also feared her. Nixon continues:

> . . . my mother was very firm, but in her whole life, until she died when she was eighty-three, I've never heard her raise her voice. But like my [maternal] grandmother [Almira], she could be immensely effective with that voice. I remember once, one of my younger brothers had engaged in some prank. And what it was actually was that . . . in those days before cigarettes became common . . . of course, in my Quaker family, they didn't drink, they didn't smoke, all of that sort of thing, in addition to using the un-Quakerish language was out. But I remember my . . . my, in those days, before tobacco became common, what the young kids would do sometimes would be to go out and smoke cornsilk. You know, you take dried cornsilk and wrap it up. And so my, my younger brother, the one who later died, my brother Arthur, had smoked some cornsilk and one of the neighbor ladies had informed on him. I've never liked her since incidentally, and my mother had known about it and so I went and talked to Arthur about it to ask him whether he had and I remember he said to me . . . he said . . . "don't" . . . he said, "if mother knows," he said, and he knew of course that she had to know, and he said, "tell her to give me a spanking," he said, "don't let her talk to me." He said, "I just can't stand it, to have her talk to me." And so we always, in that family, in our family, we would always prefer . . .

my mother used to say later on that she never gave any one of us a spanking. I'm not so sure. She might have, but I do know that we dreaded far more than my father's hand, her tongue. Not that it was very sharp, but she would just sit down and she would talk very, very quietly and when you got through, you had been through an emotional experience.[6]

"We dreaded far more than my father's hand, her tongue." Even Hannah, whom Nixon called "a saint" in his farewell talk to his White House staff on August 9, 1974, created a deep sense of fear in the children. We know that she was a serious, somber woman who rarely smiled. She was reserved and withdrawn, and thus it was difficult for her to project warmth and affection. It may well be that in her frustration she cared for her child as much out of duty as out of real love. As a result, he was a child in whom feelings of insecurity and uncertainty were heightened because he was closed off from normal parental affection. He was left to figure things out for himself. Worst of all, he was left with fantasies and impressions of being abandoned, rejected, and unloved.

We might also question how much attention Hannah could give to her children when she had a husband who was aggressive, hostile, uncooperative, and impulsive. Their marriage did not abound in love or affection; quite the reverse. The bond that held them together during their perpetual financial crises and the prolonged illnesses which caused the death of their two boys was apparently the need to sustain the other sons. Frank and Hannah had a difficult and complex life together.

A modicum of peace was maintained in the home by conceding at times to Frank's will, by a combination of capitulation and manipulation. Hannah's way was usually to remain quiet. On the surface she appeared in control of herself, but deep down were emotions which smoldered and at times burst into heated verbal reactions—regardless of Nixon's recollection. We will later see the same behavior in Richard Nixon, particularly during his presidential years. It may be that it was from her that Nixon learned how to subtly manipulate and control others.

In *A Self Portrait* he tells how he learned to handle his father to avoid being spanked, but when he was spanked, he took it without a whimper. He also gives us an interesting insight into his family life:

> . . . this was not a family that just grew up completely outside the pattern that you normally expect. We had our arguments within the family and there were times when I suppose we were tempted to run away and all that sort of thing.

But then he goes on to say:

> None of us ever did [run away], but on the other hand, it was a happy home.[7]

Nixon's mention of his home as "happy" exhibits his pattern of glossing over the true state of affairs. When children contemplate running away from home, they usually are angry and upset because they feel they have been mistreated. We can be quite sure that he and his brothers wanted at times to escape the emotional discomfort of the home. His statement, however, tries to minimize the severity of the home situation, which was probably more strained and explosive than even he as a child could realize, or remember as an adult.

The Nixon children were taught the importance of hard work, and this principle had been ingrained for three generations. Great-grandmother Elizabeth Griffith Milhous, who set the standards for the entire family, was reported by Nixon to have said, "Honesty, hard work, do your best at all times . . ."[8]

While hard work is indeed a good thing, Nixon's parents were compulsive about it, and such obsessiveness can be emotionally unhealthy. Work was considered the solution to all problems of life. If you worked long hours everything would be all right and your soul would be saved. There was, of course, the need to earn enough money to survive. Nixon describes his early days in *A Self Portrait*:

> Up until the time I was ten years of age, we lived in Yorba Linda on a lemon ranch and there were always chores there too. I remember I used to get out on the ranch, in those days we called it a ranch, and hoe weeds. That was before they developed the modern

scheme whereby you left the weeds around the trees for purposes of fertilization and the rest. Then you had to dig them out. I've done irrigating on the ranch. I've worked in a packing house, but then after we came to Whittier and this is at about ten years when I was in the fifth grade, we had the store and service station; and one of these family enterprises where everybody had to work. So you'd come home from school and go to work and work 'til the end of the day . . . six o'clock when the store closed and then for an hour or so afterwards and then after that, studied. We combined that too with work early in the morning. It was mostly study and work. Not much play and Sundays we were all taken with church activities; four times a day,* Sunday school and church in the morning and Christian endeavor and church in the evening.[9]

Not only was there compulsory work; there were also compulsory religious observances. Frank, as Jessamyn West has commented, was as compulsive as his wife about religious devotion, even though their motivations differed sharply. But Frank, who was popular as a teacher, was far different at home.

In a home where work and religious activities were frenetic, it comes as no surprise that there was "not much play," as Richard Nixon admitted. Being sensitive, perhaps hypersensitive, and already introverted, Richard grew up with a solemn attitude toward life similar to his mother's. Jessamyn West confirmed this view for me in her comment:

I am older than Richard, but I have a brother [Rusty] just his age who went to school with him and found him to be at an early age serious, introspective, interested in history and politics, and no happy-go-lucky playfellow.

Richard Nixon's early seriousness about life was an expression of his introverted personality which led to his self-consciousness.

The Nixon family's poor economic circumstances intensified these feelings of insecurity and self-consciousness. In

* Another source says three times a day.

explaining the family's poverty, Nixon admits it but denies it at the same time:

> Looking back on it though, I think my reaction is somewhat like the . . . I think that wonderful statement that General Eisenhower made at Abilene. You may recall, his first speech after he became a candidate for President, and he was talking about his early days in Abilene and he said, "I suppose that we were poor, but the glory of it was that we never knew it." And that was what we were then.[10]

The details Nixon remembered as a man confirm a sense of hardship:

> We were poor. We worked hard. We had very little. We all used hand-me-down clothes. I wore my brother's shoes and my brother below me wore mine and other clothes of that sort . . .[11]

He goes on to say, "but we remember the little things." Here, too, he is admitting and making capital of his poverty at the same time. He recalls one particular Fourth of July:

> We were the only ones in the neighborhood that didn't have any . . . we didn't have the money frankly for firecrackers. In those days you could get them. But my mother wanted to do something, so what happened was she in some way got some bunting and I remember she fixed the table with red, white and blue bunting and my father went out and got some ice cream and what a feast we had! Well, I remember that Fourth of July more than all the ones that I've been through in my whole life when I made speeches before huge audiences, because it was such a rather wonderful thing for them to do.[12]

In this last statement we detect a defensive attitude which skirts the topic of poverty to focus on the Fourth of July when his parents created a festive occasion despite the lack of money.

During the closing days of the 1968 presidential campaign, when some polls indicated that Nixon was falling behind, he went on the *Face the Nation* television program because he thought he might lose the election to Hubert Humphrey. He needed to win votes and he talked again about the Fourth of July experience. By admitting that his parents were so poor that they couldn't afford firecrackers, Nixon made political use of being the underdog. He exaggerated his parents' poverty because he realized it would gain the sympathy of underprivileged people and make him appear heroic. Nixon understood how he could use his past to win votes. In an interview with Stewart Alsop he had said earlier:

> It's been said our family was poor, and maybe it was, but we never thought of ourselves as poor. We always had enough to eat, and we never had to depend on anyone else. Sure, we had to be careful. I was dressed in hand-me-downs mostly in grammar school. Once in a while we'd go to a movie, but that was a luxury. We never had vacations—well, once in a long while we'd have a week at the beach, maybe. But I never went hunting or fishing or anything like that—there wasn't time. We never ate out—never. We certainly had to learn the value of money. But we had a pretty good time, with it all.[18]

The last sentence—"But we had a pretty good time, with it all"—expresses Nixon's defensiveness. He makes political use, but only defensively, of the fact that his family was poor or that his childhood was not like that of other boys. His life was, indeed, different because he had to work to help support the family. But he exaggerates.

Although he was unaware of it, the real poverty of his life was not economic; it was emotional. He covered up the lack of love and affection, particularly from his father—a lack which was reflected in Nixon's later personal and political life. This attitude toward his childhood is an important part of his character structure. As an adult he wanted to give the impression that his home life was simple, even poor, difficult at times, but good, because the emotional environment was too painful for him to deal with. To protect himself from these memories, he needed to construct an image of an orderly and harmonious home. When a person says his home is good when in fact it is not, he is distorting the truth to give a false impression. It is this need to push painful situations out of his mind which became a vaunted Nixon quality. It was his way of rearranging reality so that he did not have to face up to and cope with his repressed anger and the emotional stress of his early years.

Poverty is not necessarily a matter of possessions. A family can have very few material goods yet feel an enormous sense of well-being through love and warmth. It is easy to see sharp differences between Miss West's attitude toward her home environment and Richard Nixon's. She made a good point when she explained to me:

> It is of course impossible to speak for another's state of mind. Perhaps Richard thought of himself as poor. I am sure that no one else in Yorba Linda did so at that time. Perhaps it is politically expedient to put on your log cabin clothes when you run for office. I don't know about that. Perhaps Richard felt when his early political success brought him in contact with Kennedys and Rockefellers that he had an "underprivileged" youth. I don't know.
>
> I only know that I, living in the same neighborhood, in the same kind of house, with more or less the same money or lack of it, wearing hand-me-downs, working every summer, did not then feel poor—and now feel that those years were a Midas-time in my life.

My impression is that Richard Nixon resented his poverty, exaggerated it, and made greater political use of it than others. But most important, though, was the emotional deprivation. Children usually learn to accept hard times. Richard didn't accept it. He was humiliated. Although the wearing of hand-me-downs is not uncommon, as Nixon says, not only clothing was involved here, but also shoes. There was a three-and-a-half-year difference between him and his older brother, Harold, and one can well imagine Richard's feelings when he had to wear his older brother's cast-off shoes. To a youngster, a pair of new shoes is very important, since they also represent greater status for him. Children have been known to take their new shoes to bed with them. Nixon, highly self-conscious and shy, must have felt resentful. I also suspect he resented his handsome older brother, who was outgoing and fun-loving, as much as the poverty and the necessity to wear hand-me-downs. And this sense of resentment must have made him determined to accumulate wealth to compensate for what he considered the humiliation of his childhood. Therefore, poverty was not respectable, and he had an inordinate need for the respect of others. This desire to collect wealth, a manifestation of the anal traits in his personality, had a great bearing upon his later lack of generosity, which became increasingly evident as he grew more and more prominent.

Observing his father's inability to provide for his wife and children, and witnessing the many arguments between his parents during which Hannah must have unleashed the full force of her resentment and anger against Frank's incompetence, Nixon saw his father as a failure. This impression also was augmented by resentment at his Oedipal situation —caused by his unresolved longing for his mother's love and approval.

Richard feared his father, and also began at an early age to compete with him. At the same time, he was afraid of Hannah, a domineering (castrating) woman. Rejection by her was a direct threat to his good image of himself. This fear also was heightened because he grew up in a family where strong women dominated life at home: in addition to his mother, there were his great-grandmother, Elizabeth Griffith Milhous, who died in 1923, when Richard was ten years old; his grandmother Almira, who lived until 1943; and Frank's stepmother, Lutheria, who died in 1948.

He was surrounded by strong and long-lived women whose husbands and sons had died young. Combined with his proneness to accidents and illness, observing the women around him may have unconsciously strengthened fears for his own life. Naturally, he was influenced by them, and unconsciously he adopted their attitudes, particularly those of his mother.

To young Richard his mother seemed to be the opposite of his father, who was strong, aggressive, active, a man who could "explode" violently. She, on the other hand, was controlled, restrained, usually disciplined. Richard was her child too, and accordingly was taught to control himself, to repress strong emotions. But self-control was difficult to learn. Richard was too self-preoccupied, too egocentric. He wanted to "show off" his abilities, both in school and at work. And he was a "good" boy because he wanted to be in his mother's good graces and because he wanted to excel. He had to work hard, especially because his mother did; his primary identification was with her.

My impression is that Richard Nixon exhibited practically the same mental makeup and behavior pattern just after the early childhood stages as he did when he was a man thirty or sixty years later. Since his emotional pattern remained the same, it is evident that he had been strongly fixated at his early childhood stages. Although Freud has said that we all remain children in our imagination, he did not say that all of us are fixated.

It is interesting to note that his mother said of him, ". . . even as a boy I never knew a person to change so little. From the time he was first able to understand the world around him until now, he has always reacted the same way to the same situations. . . . He was very mature even when he was 5 or 6."[14] Apparently there seems to be a misperception on the part of his mother when she says that he was "very mature" even when he was five or six years old. Certainly this is not maturity in the sense that we know it. Being stubborn and reacting in a fixed pattern is not mature. Even though it is unusual for a mother to regard a five-year-old son as being "very mature," the fact that "he has always reacted the same way to the same situations" means that he continued to react and behave according to the emotional pattern he had developed as a child. He apparently was unable (or refused) to deepen his responses and become more open and sensitive in dealing with his emotional conflict. Instead, he became defensive and continued to block out situations which might force him to deal with his real and painful feelings.

In this connection, his mother says:

> As far as Richard's being emotional is concerned, I can say that in his later years he developed a wonderful talent for keeping his emotions under control. Some people like to blow off steam and then some burn down inside.[15]

Her second statement contradicts her earlier quoted statement. To suggest that when younger he was unable to control his temper implies that his level of behavior was unstable. In Nixon's later years we find examples when he publicly lost his temper, revealing his inability to contain the rage he earlier had repressed.

Richard was stubborn in defending his opinions. This trait

42

came to him from both his mother and his father. Coupled with this intolerance of the opinion of others were feelings of hostility and impatience with the obstacles he felt were unjustly put in his way. Nixon's idealistic strivings adopted from his mother's ideals of peace and tolerance—and his father's hostile, aggressive outbursts and relentless criticism of what he thought was wrong with society and the government—created an emotional conflict. There was, in sum, an abyss between his higher, noble intentions and his aggressive, lower inclinations. This gulf resulted in generally unstable levels of activity and behavior which in his career took on an erratic form.

The early conflict between constructive and hostile tendencies led to an ambivalent attitude; he wavered between passivity, the repression of anger, on the one hand, and aggressiveness on the other. Lacking a strong stable male to identify with, his masculine identification was impaired, thereby giving further rein to the feminine inclinations of being receptive and passive. In his struggle against passivity, this tendency to remain passive and his inability to resist external forces intensified his emotional instability. He thus became self-protective and withdrawn. He responded by covering up or denying obstacles which he came to feel only he faced and which he alone had to overcome. Difficult situations had to be covered up or denied. He therefore conjured up the idea that he had to work around obstacles which to his mind other people didn't have, and this state of mind gave rise to bitterness, self-pity, manipulation, and suspiciousness, all creating an unresolvable conflict.

4

When Frank Nixon moved his family from Yorba Linda in 1922 after his lemon ranch failed, he settled in East Whittier with Hannah and their children. Times were hard. To make a living Frank started a gasoline station at Whittier Boulevard and Santa Gertrudes Avenue, and, in addition, Hannah began a small grocery store in the same place.* 1 To start the family business he had to choose between two pieces of property, and settled for the smaller one. Ironically, oil was discovered soon afterward on the other property in Santa Fe Springs. Suspecting that there might be oil on Frank Nixon's property too, a speculator offered a considerable price for it; but Frank, who also thought that his land might contain oil, refused to sell. Characteristically, he never found oil. He followed the pattern of failure that had predominated in his family.

The whole family had to work hard to survive, particularly Hannah, who "repaired and pressed the clothes for the whole family, worked in the store during the day, and at night thriftily emptied the shelves of fruit that might spoil in another day and baked it into pies, which she put on sale in the morning." 2 Nixon family life was spartan, but not uncommonly so.

> They [the children] were reared to frugality and hard work. There was little time for play. They walked a half mile to school every day. When the children were not busy with school work, there always were jobs to be done about the store and filling station.
> "I sold gas and delivered groceries and met a lot of people," Mr. Nixon recalls. "I think this was invaluable as a start on a public career."

* Other versions have it that at first Frank sold bread and milk from his refrigerator as well as gasoline. As the demand for other foods rose, he added to his supplies, and thus began the grocery store.

Old neighbors remember the boy who was to be President as bookish and withdrawn. He found science and mathematics difficult, so he worked especially hard at these subjects. He practiced the piano dutifully, if unenthusiastically, and later learned the violin too. . . .

Religious training was emphasized. . . . Card playing and dancing were forbidden. Church attendance three times on Sunday and once at midweek were compulsory. Richard once taught a Sunday-school class.[3]

In a household where money was scarce and every member had to make a contribution, Richard was his mother's "best helper." His brothers noted that his most outstanding distinction was as a potato masher. "He never left any lumps," Hannah said. "He used the whipping motion to make them smooth instead of going up and down the way the other boys did." [4]

While this activity is perhaps trivial, it does reveal a significant trait. Even as a child, Richard loved to excel and be recognized. His mother said, "He was the best potato masher one could wish for. . . . Even in these days, when I am visiting Richard and Pat in Washington, or when they visit me, he will take over the potato mashing. My feeling is that he actually enjoys it." * [5]

Richard helped his mother in the store and in the kitchen; he also washed the dishes. Before he would stoop to perform this latter task, however, which he must have thought was girlish, he would draw the blinds very tight so that no one would see him.†

That a boy wouldn't want anyone to see him washing dishes would not be considered unusual. But that his mother noticed his shame would indicate that his discomfort was uncom-

---

* Nixon's fascination with potato mashing had psychoanalytic implication. Most children his age release aggression through play, athletics, and peer-group activities. What is unusual in Richard is that he chose to release his energy through potato mashing, which was one way to be close to his mother, to win her love, to be her favorite. The extent and intensity of this activity might suggest that this potato mashing was a form of aggression against an inanimate object which was a substitute for people. Potato mashing allowed this apparently tense and moody child to express his unconscious anger.

† This is known from Earl Mazo, who talked with Richard's mother. James David Barber also refers to it.[6] I have also discussed this point with Mrs. Rose Olive Marshburn.

monly severe. To Richard, washing dishes seemed degrading; "only girls did it." It is possible, but unlikely, that he regarded having to wash dishes as a humiliating proof of their poverty. Richard's status as mother's best helper was one cause for his brothers to tease him. They may have resented him because they felt he was Hannah's favorite. Nixon in turn resented them. As his younger brother Donald said with a great deal of vehemence:

> Dick used his tongue more than his fists. One time he lit into me and gave me a dressing-down I'll never forget. I've forgotten what his beef was, but I had it coming. He didn't just talk about the problem at the moment; he aired all his gripes of the past two or three years.[7]

Nixon used his tongue as a weapon, and he seemed to bear grudges for a long time. He held in his feelings, and he was not to change as he grew older.

Certainly his later relationships with his surviving brothers were distant. Richard's closeness to his mother was deep, and was in all probability heightened by his own daydreams and fantasies. Although some thought him to be her favorite—and he may indeed have been—Nixon's relationship with his mother was at times pathetic. A letter that he wrote to his mother on November 23, 1923, when he was almost eleven, illustrates both their relationship and his fantasy world.

> My Dear Master:
> The two boys that you left with me are very bad to me. Their dog, Jim, is very old and he will never talk or play with me.
> One Saturday the boys went hunting. Jim and myself went with them. While going through the woods one of the boys triped and fell on me. I lost my temper and bit him. He kiked me in the side and we started on. While we were walking I saw a black round thing in a tree. I hit it with my paw. A swarm of black thing came out of it. I felt pain all over. I started to run and as both my eys were swelled shut I fell into a pond. When I got home I was very sore. I wish you would come home right now.
> Your good dog
> RICHARD [8]

Nixon's letter is succinct, but his account and his imagery suggest a high level of confusion and despair. Although we do not know whether the incident actually occurred or whether it is a purely imaginary story, the fact that he assumes the role of a dog, not a human being, is highly significant; it shows a strong sense of fantasy. The action he describes is significant: "I lost my temper and bit him." Not only does biting indicate emotional instability; it also expresses an oral drive—his mouth is a weapon to inflict punishment.

From a psychoanalytic point of view, this letter is highly revealing. Biting at the age of ten or eleven is rare; usually it occurs during the first, the oral, period, which lasts until a child is about one year old (and may in certain abnormal circumstances continue until perhaps the age of four or five).

Biting is one of the most primitive responses we have. It is an animal reaction and belongs to the earliest stages of human development. In young Richard's mind, it was the only recourse for dealing with an adversary. During the latency period of childhood (from seven to twelve years) the practice of biting will normally disappear, though it may appear again in puberty or adolescence as an expression of oral hostility and aggression. That Richard wrote that he bit one of the boys at an age when a child would normally have passed through this stage long before, reinforces our impression that the oral hostile aggression Richard harbored as an infant had been prolonged beyond the norm and had become fixated. The degree to which he regressed into a fantasy is abnormal.

We can surmise therefore that the details were not incidental: they reflect an instinctive response which stayed with him long after he had learned that biting was not socially acceptable. Expressions of this kind of response appear in his adult behavior. In his political life, Nixon was often vindictive and revengeful. He was sarcastic, cutting, and caustic. His mother, too, had a "dreaded tongue," and Richard had learned how to use his mouth to express his biting power.*

Returning to his curious letter, we are struck by the final sentence—"I wish you would come home right now." It is a cry for help—a pitiful and despairing wish that his mother

---

* The bite impressed itself deeply upon Richard. We can say that he took the bite in, incorporated it into himself. To take in (or be taken in) gives a feeling of cheating, capturing by trickery or by surprise—a behavior which Richard later on repeatedly exhibited. This is a psychological defense mechanism which we often encounter in psychoanalysis.

would come to console him and soothe his hurt feelings. He feels alone, rejected, surrounded by a threatening world, with someone described as "very old" who "will never talk or play with me." Clearly, this pathetic letter, filled with self-pity and hurt, pictures a hostile world against which he feels vulnerable.

The "very old" Jim he mentions may be his father, who never talks or plays with him and whose name he is obviously afraid to use. If it is, he felt threatened and wanted another father.

We must also note his description of "a black round thing in a tree" which "I hit . . . with my paw." Then "a swarm of black thing came out of it." They stung, and he was blinded and ran and fell into a pond. We suspect he is referring to wasps or bees, which are not black, although they may seem so to a frightened child. Richard became so surprised and shocked when the insects flew toward him that they appeared to be black. Black connotes a sense of evil or, more fundamentally, danger, death. Not only did he run away, but his emotions—his fears and anxieties—also ran away with him.

The story he relates must be taken seriously because it mirrors his state of mind as a child. His account reveals fantasies of depression and loneliness, which draw us closer to the inner Nixon.

Although we don't know, of course, whether Hannah was actually away at this time, we do know that in 1923 Arthur was five years old and may already have been ill and needed the full-time attention of his mother. Richard felt her absence acutely.

He subserviently addresses the letter to "My Dear Master," indicating that he regarded her as his master and guide, the person who controlled him and to whom he owed his loyalty. Without her, he seems to be lost and vulnerable to attack from a hostile world. The person who was closest to him had "left" him. It was an early feeling of betrayal, a feeling which later grew in him as he became more prominent.

The fact that Richard closes his letter with "Your good dog" shows a sense of fidelity and subservience and a lack of self-esteem. But it also suggests an indictment. Why had he, who had worked hard and had obeyed his mother, been deserted? Richard looked upon himself as a victim in a cruel and heartless world. He had always believed in his mother, had always thought she was right, but how could she desert him when he was being attacked by other boys and by a swarm of bees? When he sat down to write this letter, he was filled with anger and dejection. His letter, which may reflect a real or imaginary fight with his brothers, may also have been a way Richard released his anger against his mother (and father), who had forsaken him.

Young Richard Nixon not only thought of himself as a victim; he was also concerned that he would become seriously ill. Frank surely had told him years before about the death of his mother, Sarah Ann. His illnesses and accidents may have had a psychosomatic root, suggesting an unconscious need to attract his mother's attention.

Certainly the two most tragic events in his adolescence were the death of his brother Arthur when Richard was twelve and the death of his brother Harold when Richard was twenty. Arthur died a horrible death at the beginning of Nixon's adolescence; Harold died at the end of it.

There is disagreement about the duration of Arthur's illness. Not only Nixon's recollection but most accounts of Arthur's illness say that the boy was acutely sick for one or two weeks before he died. What seems possible, or more likely, is that Arthur had been ill prior to the week which culminated in his death. It is my belief that Arthur's illness had two phases, and that the recollections reported deal with the acute and terminal stage. We do know that in the spring of 1925, Nixon, who was twelve years old, was sent to stay with his aunt Jane and uncle Chauntree Beeson and that this stay lasted for half a year. The terminal phase of Arthur's illness was acute and dramatic, as seen in tubercular meningitis. This disease is the result of a tubercular infection elsewhere in the body and occurs most often in children between one and five years of age. In many cases the onset is insidious, the earliest symptoms being listlessness, irritability, and loss of appetite.

Arthur may early on have shown the usual symptoms of tuberculosis: sore throat or upper respiratory infection with fever, irritability, vomiting, and loss of appetite. The duration of the illness may vary considerably. In the case of Arthur, who was seven years old, his symptoms, also associated with influenza, may have deceived the doctors. Arthur's early condition may have varied in intensity, with fluctuating fever, so that the illness was acute at one period, then followed by improvement, again to become more intense.

If Richard was away from home for a long period of time—as I believe he was—we do not know for certain whether he knew why he was sent away. However, late in the summer of 1925 Richard returned and began to work in the family store. Did he feel that being sent away was a form of rejection by his mother? In his sensitive mind, he may have wondered why he was forced to give up school and the everyday pattern of life to live in a strange household. Could it, though, have been that the family, suspecting or fearing the true nature of Arthur's illness, acted to protect Richard by isolating him from his younger brother? Why, then, did he return when he did? Was it because Arthur's condition had improved? Or had it worsened? We do not know.

Richard Nixon's account of this incident emphasizes the short duration of his brother's illness. "My youngest brother Arthur died of tubercular meningitis very suddenly . . . within a week he was dead, and he was kind of the family favorite . . ."[9]

But the important point is that no matter how short or long his illness, the acute stage and death must have had a traumatic effect on the Nixon family. The terminal stage of meningitis leaves an indelible impression. It is a terrible experience. The patient's fever often climbs to 104 or 105, and his body is racked with pain. His head hurts; he becomes so weak he cannot lift an arm or cry out in pain. He becomes drowsy and finally lapses into a stupor. As convulsions begin, intracranial pressure mounts and the patient loses consciousness, sinking deeper and deeper into a coma from which he never wakes.

Arthur's illness and his death on August 10, 1925, not only came as a great shock, but also dealt the Nixon family a severe financial blow. On top of trying to feed and clothe four growing boys there were doctors' bills and other heavy expenses. This illness, as Nixon said, "ate into the income." As we know, the Nixons were proud people who believed they should rely solely upon themselves despite hardships.

Richard had strong and intimate feelings about Arthur; on the conscious level he loved and admired him, and on the unconscious level there were feelings of envy and rivalry. His emotional attachment to his younger brother was strong, and Arthur came to play a larger role in Nixon's life than he himself understood. Unable to perceive the emotional complexity of their relationship, Nixon developed a sense of guilt which later was deeply intensified by Harold's death. Would he, too, die like his brothers?

The death of Arthur, and of Harold in 1933, and the guilt he felt concerning his brothers, has haunted Richard. It intensified his drive to make himself felt to the highest degree, and at the same time furthered his tendencies toward self-inflicted humiliation and self-destruction. The illness and death of these two brothers provided terrifying and traumatic causes of his divided self and further reason for his inability to mature.

After Arthur's funeral, Hannah confided to a neighbor, "It is difficult at times to understand the ways of our Lord, but we know that there is a plan and the best happens for each individual."[10] She was confident that He knew what was best. To members of her family, she was a model who imparted faith and suppressed pain.

In view of his own proneness to illness, we can be sure that Richard in particular was upset and frightened by Arthur's death. He suspected, not without cause, that he too might become a victim of tuberculosis. He may have felt that he had to prove he was in excellent health. His compelling need to project virility was one reason he tried out for the high school football team and later in college became an ardent (though inept) football player. His combative instinct was an overreaction to his fear of being struck down by disease, of being humbled and defenseless. He developed a persistent pattern of behavior that internalized these fears. His home was an intense world filled with struggle. At school he compensated for it. They were different worlds.

Nixon was—even before Arthur's death—busy and hyperactive, trying to move ahead, to excel and be respected. He tried to establish himself, to emulate and at the same time compete with his father. He pushed himself to take on extra jobs. In 1924, when he was eleven, Richard wrote to the *Los Angeles Times* "asking for an office boy job, citing his grade school principal as a reference. He didn't get it."[11]

Why did he feel so compelled to seek more work at such a young age? Was it a compulsion? Was it the strict religious ethic that had been fostered in him by his parents? Or did he want to escape from home? Perhaps it was a combination of all these. We know that Richard Nixon had a fear of becoming emotionally involved with his immediate family, relatives, and friends. Like his father, he did not want to be tied down to anyone.

Incidentally, Nixon's remark that "Dad played no favorites with us"[12] should not be taken literally. Richard, possibly more than his brothers, had a strong need to placate him because he feared his violent temper. In contrast to the other boys, he accommodated his father's wishes and advised them not to argue with him in order to "keep the peace"—a lesson he had learned from his mother. This need to please is related to Richard's shyness and passivity, which he compensated for with his aggressiveness. This personality trait was to become increasingly conspicuous over the years.

Nixon, in his early years, unconsciously felt that his father was not a person to be respected. As a result, it became imperative that he win the respect that his father never had. He battled to gain it throughout his adult life. We shall see how he tried to do that—and to compete.

Many biographers feel that Richard Nixon's entry into politics was accidental. I don't believe this is the case. It is my conclusion that the antagonism between father and son led Richard Nixon into the combat of politics. He was interested in politics as a young man, and there is little doubt that he was influenced by his father's political interests.

Frank's strong feelings, particularly about politicians whom he suspected of being unreliable and self-serving, created an early sense of political awareness in Richard's mind. According to a newspaper account:

> . . . young Richard also heard his father's diatribes against "crooked politicians" and "crooked lawyers" when he became upset over theft of government oil reserves during the Harding administration.[13]

For weeks his father carried on about the men in the Teapot Dome scandal of 1922 who had corrupted and failed the country. This relentless ranting about corruption in the light of later events is ironic. It leads one to think that Frank, who was a failure, unconsciously had his own corruptive tendencies in mind. What is clear is that his father's interest in politics provided a strong role model for Richard, a point confirmed by Jessamyn West:

> Frank was, in his thinking and feeling, a political ani-

mal. He cared about what public officials did. At the age of seven, his son, Richard, on the way to his second-grade class in Yorba Linda grammar school, explained to his classmates the merits of some upcoming candidate [Harding] and the issues he represented. Rusty was one of those instructed. "I didn't understand a word he said," Rusty tells me now.*

"Where did a boy of seven pick up such ideas?"

"Frank, of course."

I do not remember, though he may have preached them, any partisan politics in Frank's Sunday-school classes. I was a socialist, he a Republican, and what Frank had to say about probity in politics pointed, as far as I was concerned, straight to Norman Thomas. The entire class felt somewhat as Nader's Raiders or a group of Vista Volunteers do today. Christianity was not just a matter of the blood of the Lamb, but of seeing that the blood had not been shed in vain.

So when the next revival was held in Yorba Linda, my going up front was not very emotional for me; and perhaps once again not very religious, either. All of us who had been in Frank's class had been convinced that Christians should be political, and that politics, if not Christian, should at least be ethical.[14]

Being strongly rebellious and competitive with his father, young Nixon may have thought that he would show the world that he was an honest politician. As a nine-year-old boy he said to his mother, after he had heard his father talk about the Teapot Dome scandal, "Mother, I would like to become a lawyer—an honest lawyer, who can't be bought by crooks."[15] It is unusual for a boy so young to make an issue of honesty. Any person, young or old, who is sure of his own honesty does not usually make such a conscious, explicit declaration. The fact that this remark comes from a boy reveals a concern about the nature of honesty, which he views not as an unquestioned and fundamental virtue, but only as a public virtue.

Not only did Richard want to follow his father's admonition about fighting against the corrupt politicians; he also

* Merle (Rusty) West recalls that he was somewhat disgusted at Nixon's penchant for such serious discussion, figuring that other things were more important.

wanted to outdo him, a desire which sprang from his unconscious Oedipal desire to replace his father.

Embedded in Richard's oral tendencies was a latent and unusually strong need to draw attention to himself and to show off by being dramatic. A person with hysterical traits has a desire to appear something more than he is. He has a need to exhibit, and thus proclaim himself, in order to attract attention. Even if he tries to hide this need for exhibition, it still comes through. While the hysterical person is not always upset and emotional to the point of being irrational, he has an urgent need to display himself and his ideas to the point where he impresses others and becomes dramatic.

Even as a little boy talking to his classmates, Richard was trying to impress others with his knowledge of politics, although he was too young and inexperienced to speak with authority. Still, he enjoyed observing the dramatic impact of his rhetoric on his young peers. With rhetoric, an insecure (and poor) boy could wield a great deal of power; he was more powerful than his peers because he could confront them and persuade them. That he was able to arouse their interest meant he also was able to mobilize their feelings and win them over. As we have seen, Merle West was impressed with Richard, although he didn't understand a word of what he said.

In the first years of school Nixon's mouth became an important means of winning attention and respect. His career as a speaker began in school, when he distinguished himself as a skillful and argumentative debater, and this ability, of course, played an extremely important role in his political career.

He early acquired an ability to argue both sides of an issue. To be equivocal and remain convincing takes a certain skill. One often has to be a juggler of facts. But more important, one has to be able to find the most vulnerable spots in the opponent's arguments, and Nixon here proved to be a master. It is interesting that he himself says:

> I remember my first debate, in fifth grade at school. The subject was "Resolved, that it is better to own your own home than to rent." I was on the renting side. Father sat down and did a lot of figuring and proved that it is more economical to rent than to own—he very much wanted me to win.[16]

On the other hand:

> [His mother] recalled her son's introduction to oratory.
> It was in 1925, when Richard took part in a debate at
> the East Whittier Elementary School. . . .
> "Richard debated the issue, 'Resolved: It is better to
> rent than to own.'" Richard won.
> His mother said he had been taught at home that it
> was better to own than rent, but he was determined to
> prove the reverse point for his team.[17]

He carried his talents further. Later in his career, many people felt that he couldn't be relied on. In political campaigns
he went for the jugular. He distorted. He degraded his talents.
As we have seen, his father was a good speaker and had
been a successful Sunday-school teacher. Nixon's mother,
however, had thought that her son was going to be a preacher
because of his clear, penetrating voice. She remarked:

> There is a story that I tried to influence Richard to be-
> come a Quaker Minister. This story is inaccurate. We
> Quakers don't believe in exerting influence, or pressure,
> on people. We believe in counseling and discussing the
> issues, but the actual decision must rest with the indi-
> vidual. I remember one time I said to Richard: "Would
> you like to study for the ministry?" I felt that he seemed
> to carry quite a weight for a boy his age. But he didn't
> respond with enthusiasm to my suggestion and so I let
> it drop.[18]

The fact is that Nixon had a strong psychological need to
become a politician. He loved to talk politics, an inclination
which deepened with time. In high school he began to dispute,
to argue, to debate issues. He debated in college, he went to
law school, and in 1946 he entered politics and campaigned
with ruthless energy. In 1966 President Johnson described
him, quite aptly, as a "chronic campaigner."[19] Debating was
his first step in achieving power.
In his ability to verbalize and his persistence in having his
opinions prevail, Nixon emulated his father. This kind of identification we also see in his desire to become an "old-fashioned
lawyer," reflected in his father's concept of returning to the

"good old days" when politicians, like "old-fashioned lawyers," were honest.

It may also be that by debating he wished to fulfill his mother's hope that he would become a preacher. Like a good preacher, Nixon could hold an audience. He therefore could identify with her controlling emotions. As important as it was to carry out her desires, he essentially followed his father's model. Through his mouth, Richard was able to combine both his mother's and his father's ambitions for him. With one stroke he unconsciously had secured his position as their favorite.

In the fall of 1926 Nixon entered Fullerton High School, which he attended for two years before enrolling at Whittier High School. He was a good student, as his classmate Charles Rothaermel recalls, "friendly, but not a guy you'd put on a backpack and go fishing with."[20]

Arguing had by now become second nature; "he entered . . . the Constitutional Oratorical Contest three times; three times he won. He led winning debating teams both in high school and at Whittier College, and when he entered the Southern California Intercollegiate Extemporaneous Speaking Contest, he won that."[21]

In the 1929 school year, Nixon's speech in the Constitutional Oratorical Contest sponsored by the Kiwanis Club was entitled "Our Privileges Under the Constitution." He won the contest on the school and district levels. In the Whittier High School preliminaries, Richard defeated fifty other high school students.[22] The following year, when the contest for the first time was conducted on an extemporaneous basis, he spoke on "America's Progress—Its Dependence Upon the Constitution."

For this he was awarded the ten-dollar prize and also received a prize of twenty dollars from the *Los Angeles Times*. He placed second in the district competition at Monrovia High School.[23]

In "Our Privileges Under the Constitution," he states the following:

> Truly it is a great privilege to hold office, but it is also a great responsibility. . . . It is [the officeholder's] duty to give his services willingly, no matter how insignificant the position; to perform his work to the best of

his ability; and to defend, maintain, and uphold the Constitution. . . .[24]

Nixon was sixteen.

And in his second speech, "America's Progress—Its Dependence Upon the Constitution," he said:

> . . . the Constitution has been the underlying force in America's progress. . . . at the present time [1930], a great wave of indifference to the Constitution's authority, disrespect of its law, and opposition to its basic principles threatens its very foundations. . . . If this nation wishes its progress to continue, this wave of indifference to the laws of the Constitution must cease.[25]

Did Nixon speak these words of fervent admiration and belief in our Constitution without personal conviction? Were they empty words arranged and spoken to make an impression upon his audience?

From the tone of his text, we suspect that he felt threatened. All over America, he thought, there were large numbers of people who were out to destroy the Constitution, and at seventeen he had already begun to do battle against them. He personalized his conflicts, his war against them. In Richard's adolescent mind there already lurked a marked suspiciousness against other people's motivations which would later develop into a system of feeling threatened and persecuted, culminating in Nixon's top-secret Domestic Intelligence Gathering Plan in July 1970, which also included the White House "Enemies List."

We see that Richard's persuasive debating technique clearly reflected his personal feelings far beyond what he had been taught would be good for his public image. To express an opinion would be the same as making a personal commitment, which threatened him. This trait was to become the core of his debating skill—in fact, it became the *character* of his combative way of disputing matters.

Nixon's love of debate revealed the oral orientation of his personality. Of course, we all depend on words to express ourselves; but this is not the only way to communicate. We often show our affection and feelings through gestures—by smiling, by slapping one another on the back, or, more intimately, by hugging or kissing. Conversely, we often show our anger and disgust by throwing up our hands in exasperation or pounding our fist on a desk.

Orally fixated people do not usually rely on other expressions of feelings. The mouth and words are the tools used to control others. By changing their voice from a quietness, almost a whisper, to a loud and hostile tone they command others to listen.

Richard's skill in debate was personally satisfying because it made him the center of attention. His audience was obliged to listen to him, which in turn gave him a sense of approval that his ego needed. Then too, the fact that he could address a crowd and master it showed his strong need to control others. As his mother wryly commented, "People seldom dictate to Richard."[26]

His success in winning debates, being on top, was evident during Richard's high school years. In his senior year he was elected president of the California Scholarship Federation's Whittier High Chapter, but lost when he ran for president of the student body. It was his last defeat until 1960.

While Nixon's debating skill placed him high in his schoolmates' estimation, this ability to control others created in him a sense of suspiciousness and cynicism. It may well be that it was too easy for him to gain power over people, and that when he had the power he felt unworthy of it. He distrusted his own worthiness and held in contempt those who had given him their respect. Success made these feelings stronger. He thus became dissatisfied and frustrated. At the same time he felt, paradoxically, that he had been insufficiently rewarded.

Behind his compulsive hard work was a strange shyness. Lacking personal warmth, he didn't easily attract close friends, even though in high school Nixon was elected by his peers to positions of leadership.

As a child he had maintained a distance from others. "He wasn't a little boy that you wanted to pick up and hug," Jessamyn West said. "It didn't strike me that he wanted to be hugged. He had a fastidiousness about him." A child who is unfriendly usually has a deep sense of frustration, based on a deeper feeling of not having achieved anything which would attract the attention or respect of other people.

Nixon was a tense, frustrated, isolated, angry child who felt abandoned by his mother and father. All these emotions were buried and impossible to articulate. In order to interact positively with his environment and win recognition, he began to debate in school. However, debating was rational, and did not reveal his deep emotional feelings. But this kind of articulation did serve his ego needs. It was a means to exhibit himself, to dominate, and to attract attention. Essentially, Nixon was a closed person who did not want to talk about himself or to communicate his inner feelings. His anger was too profound.

Preoccupied with and angry at himself, he became increasingly trapped in his inner world. Even in these early years we see in Nixon a sense of aloneness, strangeness, and alienation.

5

Nixon's "Dear Master" letter to his mother is certainly a dramatic example of his emotional outlook at the age of ten. There is other evidence bearing directly on his emotional development during his puberty and his high school and college years. A composition Nixon wrote at seventeen throws light on his sexual identity feelings, reflecting his attitude toward himself.

Arthur's death in 1925, when Richard was twelve, had so unsettled Richard that five years later he wrote a sentimental composition about his younger brother. The highlights of this composition are interesting:

My Brother Arthur B. Nixon

We have a picture in our home which money could not buy. . . . let us examine the picture closely. The first thing we notice, perhaps, is that this particular boy has unusually beautiful eyes, black eyes which seem to sparkle with hidden fire and to beckon us to come on some secret journey which will carry us to the land of make-believe. Then we would probably admire his neat appearance; his well-pressed, little dark-blue sailor's suit; his shoe strings, tied in bows which match each other exactly. Even his hands are crossed in front of him to complete a perfectly balanced picture. We find that only his hair is unlike that we would expect in a portrait of a boy. For instead of neatly combed locks, we see a mass of brown curls which seem never to have known the touch of a comb.[1]

Fascinated with Arthur, Richard writes about him very much as though he were a girl. The composition reads like the expression of a fantasy. And this is due to his own repressed desires for some secret journey and indicates his own repressed sexual wishes. His observation that "only his hair is unlike that we would expect in a portrait of a boy" is most revealing, as he perceives Arthur as a girl. He continues:

> One day in May, 1918, when I had reached the age of five years, my father came home from work a little later than usual. After talking with my grandmother, who was taking care of my two brothers and me while Mother was away on a visit, he came over to where we boys were quarreling over some toys and told us that there was a little doll over at the hospital for us, a real live doll! Naturally we then began to quarrel over whose doll it would be, although each of us wished to have it merely to keep one of the others from getting it. My father, however, assured us that our rights would be equal, and then he asked us what name we should give our doll. After learning that it was not a "girl doll," we finally decided that its name should be Arthur.
>
> Several days later, Grandmother scrubbed us all up, especially gouging into the depths of our ears, and helped us to dress, for we were going to see our "doll," which we had learned by this time was a baby. At least, that was what brother Harold, who had reached the all knowing age of nine, had said it was. He had told us secretly that it wasn't a doll but a baby. He warned us, though, not to let on he'd told us so.
>
> Anyway, doll or baby, we were greatly excited over the prospective visit and could hardly control ourselves until the family Ford finally got us to the hospital. All I remember about the visit was the fact that I was rather disappointed in the baby, because, after all, a tiny baby is not as pretty as a doll, at least in outward appearances.

These memories of Arthur reveal Richard's own feelings toward girls and boys and about himself as a male. When the father told the children that they were going to the hospital, where they would find a "doll," clearly it reflected Frank's wish for a girl. What is important, though, is Richard's excitement, apparently stimulated by his still-present Oedipal feelings toward his mother, when his father told them that they were going to the hospital to pick up the "doll." Then, too, Richard must have been fascinated with the prospect of having a sister, a girl, who in his mind would be more amenable to his unconscious wishes than his brothers, with whom he quarreled. It is unfortunate that apparently the children had not even been told that their mother was pregnant.

Richard must have been disappointed when he discovered that the "doll" was not a girl. This may also be the reason why he was preoccupied with Arthur, with whom he instinctively identified. Undoubtedly the baby brother awakened feminine traits in Richard, reinforced in part by his father's sadistic joke that a "doll" was waiting for them at the hospital. Frank was a fooler, and of course enjoyed his sadism; he liked to tease. He had fooled his children with what appeared to him to be a harmless joke, but it undoubtedly left a more profound impression on his young son, who was highly vulnerable.

In the same composition Nixon tells of another incident, which reflects doubts about his masculinity. It occurred when Arthur was told to be a ring bearer at a wedding. Arthur, perhaps not unnaturally, at first refused, because it would mean walking with the flower girl. "I remember how my mother had to work with him for hours to get him to do it." Nixon's attitude is unusual:

> Then I remember the grief he experienced over his hair. My parents had wanted him to be a girl in the first place; consequently they attempted to make him one as much as possible. Each day he begged my mother for a boy's haircut, and when he finally did get it, there was not a happier boy in the state. Again, I shall never forget how he disliked wearing "sticky" wool suits. As soon as he was able to read, he used to search the mail order catalogues for suits which weren't "sticky."

Richard was fascinated with his younger brother's refusal to take part in any girls' undertakings:

> . . . I learned from letters sent from home that he was doing exceptionally well in all things except drawing. He absolutely would not take interest in anything he thought common to girls. . . . As soon as he saw me alone, he solemnly kissed me on the cheek. I learned later that he had dutifully asked my mother if it would be proper for

him to kiss me, since I had been away for such a long time.*

Unintentionally revealing is his interest in Arthur's reaction to girls; it reflects Richard's deep concern about his own sexual feelings, indicating not only an identification with his mother but also his concern with how to be a man.

Every boy wants to grow up. A father serves as a model, as a mother does for a girl. A boy cannot wait for the moment when he becomes an adult like his father. Even if he grows slowly, one secondary sexual characteristic follows another—the pubic and axillary hair, the deeper voice, the beard—and his daydreams or fantasies help him anticipate his manhood.

Although a certain amount of fantasizing is normal, young Nixon indulged in daydreaming to an extreme; much of his libido was spent on making his manhood come through. Richard's childhood fantasies constitute a unique source of his unconscious feelings, his frustrations and fears, his yearnings as he sought to grow up. Everyone experiences some degree of an identity crisis in order to achieve emotional maturity. In Nixon we will find this maturity crisis repeated again and again.

We know that what we cannot achieve in real life we fantasize. The most intense wish of the child in his early years is to be like the parent of his own sex and to be grown-up like his mother and father. Since children feel helpless, through day-dreaming they escape into a world where they feel powerful and successful. Daydreaming creates the illusion that the dreamer is already grown-up and able to live in the adult world—to be a glamorous adult figure such as a pilot, fireman, astronaut, actress, doctor, or President.

By daydreaming the child is trying to change his own situation. Daydreams have two basic components—the erotic and the fulfillment of ambitions. The sexual, however, is most often hidden.

Within certain limits daydreams, which typically are products of the childish imagination, are normal; however, when carried to extremes daydreams are often indicative of emotional instability.

Nixon's aunt Rose Olive Marshburn told me she "had seen

* Nixon was in Lindsay, California, at the home of his aunt Jane Beeson.

Richard lying on the lawn, gazing up at the sky, stargazing and daydreaming." In vain she called him to come in. Unable to get his attention, she went out and shook him.[2]

Typically, the way we daydream depends largely upon the kind of childhood we have had. If a person has had a healthy childhood, his fantasy life tends to be healthy and he can still participate actively and spontaneously in most situations.

The first daydreams a child has are asexual; in them he emulates his parents. But as he goes into his Oedipal phase, his fantasies become sexualized and feelings of revenge, hostility, and retaliation come more to the fore. If the father has been kind to the boy, their later relationship will be friendly. When a father is hostile, the child fantasizes about taking revenge upon him, and may continue to do so for the rest of his life. Despairing and frustrated, he is unable to interact in a meaningful way with others. It is this profile that best defines Richard Nixon.

A daydreaming youngster like Nixon would be preoccupied, overly serious, thinking too much about himself to enjoy life. Would he ever have what he most wanted? When a child is excessively preoccupied, it means he is frustrated, confused. Finding more satisfaction in daydreams than in reality, he doesn't have a grip on what is happening around him. He is unable to perceive the reality of his situation; it isn't the way he thought or wished it might be. Nixon worked hard in school and in the store, yet he was functioning in a perfunctory manner. He was brooding and secretive, preferring his own company to that of others.

Still, being on the debating team, repeatedly winning and speaking out forcefully, he was trying to project himself, his divided self. He did not give up trying to become a real person.

In *A Self Portrait,* Nixon tells us about his first daydreams:

> I think my earliest ambition was to be a railroad engineer and the reason for that, was that in the little town [Yorba Linda] in which we lived in California, one time of day a train used to go by, a steam engine train, and at night I would lie in bed and hear the whistle of that train and think of all the places that it went. So from that early time, I seemed to have in me some wanderlust. I wanted to travel. I wanted to see the world. In fact, geography was my best subject when I was in grammar

school, as we called it in those days. Geography, history
. . . the whole sweep of world history and the world
around me.[8]

His ambition to become a railroad engineer did not derive
from an interest in engines. In *Six Crises* he wrote, "I have
no mechanical aptitude whatever."[4] It was the whistle of the
train that captured his imagination, taking him to all the far-
away places the train would travel. That Nixon remembers
this daydream so well—it is also reported in *Six Crises*—
indicates how important this particular fantasy was to him.
His desire to travel was not accidental. He may have felt
that his horizon was limited, that he was fenced in, and he
could not tolerate barriers. His desire to "see the world," however, would be fulfilled when he became President of the
United States.

His statement that "geography was my best subject when I
was in grammar school" tells us that his wish to expand his
horizon started very early. But was this craving for discovery
primarily a desire to see the world? Hardly. In mentioning
his wanderlust, his memory of trains, his longing to journey
to strange places, he was, in my opinion, expressing a yearning
and a force he could not fully understand. This intense desire
to undertake journeys is rooted in sexual desires.*

Many boys are interested in trains. Behind this is a normal
masculine sexual inclination. But with Nixon there is more
to it. Why was he so preoccupied with the trains going by at
night in Yorba Linda? We can only surmise. Perhaps Frank,
his father, told his son about the time when he was a streetcar
conductor in Columbus and in Los Angeles. And it would
seem likely that in recounting these stories he embellished
them, telling about the glory of driving the tramcar through
the long stretches from Los Angeles to Santa Fe Springs and
Whittier, which took almost an hour. It stands to reason that
much of Richard's daydream about traveling was to no small
extent inspired by his father's talks about his adventurous
work as a streetcar conductor.

In view of Frank's aggressive sexual drive, we may also say
that through his travel, his moving from place to place, he had

---

* Some sixty years ago Hans Blüher called attention to the then popular German Wandervögel (Birds of Passage) Movement as an erotic
phenomenon. Cf. Hans Blüher, *Die deutsche Wandervögelbewegung als
erotisches Phenomenon* (Jena, 1916–17).

found an outlet for his frustrated sexual desires. In his fantasies the son identified with his father. But Nixon went further. He wanted to see the world, not only Yorba Linda, with its population of three hundred people. Unconsciously, he wanted to outdo his father. Being competitive, he wanted to be the best, better than his father, more virile—even to the point (as we shall see) of wanting to replace him as his mother's favorite.

The train that "goes by at night" haunted Nixon. In his acceptance speech at the 1968 Republican National Convention, he talks about "another child," obviously himself:

> I see another child. He hears the train go by at night and dreams of faraway places he would like to go. It seems like an impossible dream. But he is helped on his journey through life. A father . . . A gentle Quaker mother . . . A great teacher . . . A courageous wife and loyal children . . . Tonight he stands before you— nominated for President of the United States. You can see why I believe so deeply in the American Dream. For most of us the American Revolution has been won; the American Dream has come true.
>
> I ask you to help me make that dream come true for millions to whom it is an impossible dream today.

Nixon would like us to believe that his daydreams gratified him; that he continued to dwell on them, however, proves the opposite. Other passages in his acceptance speech catch our attention. He talks about the American Dream in terms of the minority child, but his words seem in part autobiographical:

> He sleeps the sleep of childhood and dreams its dreams. Yet when he awakens, he awakens to a living nightmare of poverty, neglect and despair. He fails in school. He ends up on welfare. For him the American system is one that feeds his stomach and starves his soul. It breaks his heart. And in the end it may take his life on some distant battlefield. To millions of children in this rich land, this is their prospect for the future.

Hadn't Nixon, too, lived in poverty, worked very hard to make a go of it, and still felt threatened by the uncertain future?

In another daydream Nixon had as a child, he unconsciously follows the same longing. In *A Self Portrait* he recollects:

> . . . after I got over wanting to be a railroad engineer and to travel all over the country in that way . . . I suppose if at that time space had been the thing, I would have been one of those youngsters going around wearing a space helmet, but at that time, you didn't think in those terms. But after I got over that . . . then at a very early point, I became rather interested in the whole world of politics, the law and the law as a possibility of developing the abilities which might lead to a political career.[5]

It is noteworthy that even though the content of his daydreams had changed somewhat, being replaced by an ambition to become a politician, we find a common thread. In his first fantasy we learn "I wanted to see the world." This wish is amplified in the second statement, to include "the whole world of politics." Nixon's ambitions are by now great. He didn't talk about his own country—the United States—or about its people. He was concerned with the *world*. These ideas sprang from his unconscious, emerging more and more into his consciousness as he became more adept at articulating his need for mastery and power. But we must try to keep in mind that his daydreams about participating in the world were as primal as his desires to replace his father, of becoming a man.

That a child daydreams about becoming important in the eyes of others and himself is a quite natural innate narcissism. This desire is deeply embedded in his search for manhood. When a child dreams about wanting to see "the world" and at a very early age becomes interested in "the whole world of politics," his ambition seems unusually strong, like that of the great conquerors. Such ambition presupposes a great deal of competitiveness, a trait strong in Nixon. What he lacked in making his personality attractive and convincing, he made up for in fierce competitiveness. In *A Self Portrait,* he tells us more about himself in this regard:

> INTERVIEWER: Being competitive is not a characteristic of yourself you are ashamed of then?
> NIXON: Oh, on the contrary. As I look at this nation and I look at its people, what has made America a great

people and this nation is a great people in the broadest sense of the word . . . is that we have been competitive. We're a very proud people. You look to the history of nations and those nations that have reached the heights of greatness have had people that were competitive.[6]

His answer is interesting both for what it reveals about Nixon's ideas of what makes America great and how it is phrased. While he is unashamed of being competitive, he seldom reveals his own feelings about himself. Instead, as an evasive tactic he cleverly puts himself outside the scope of his own competitiveness by talking about it as a trait of the American people. This way of depersonalizing ideas is conspicuous in Nixon. He answers in a generalized manner to avoid giving himself away. He liked to describe himself as being a very private person. His words in *A Self Portrait* are detached, impersonal, somewhat philosophical:

. . . go back to the early people who founded America. We look at our Europeans who came to these shores and there were the Spanish and the French and the British, all competing among themselves and between each other to see who could find the new world and that competitive drive determined which became the great people of that time. This doesn't mean competition in the destructive sense and as far as America is concerned, I think one of our great features today is that as distinguished from the great societies of the past, we don't have any expansionist ideals at this point.[7]

The "competitive drive" is the reason for the country's greatness. Further, the person with the greatest competitive drive will be the strongest. He thought of himself as the most powerful man. He didn't understand the difference between normal and excessive or ruthless competitiveness.

This is a frightening concept. Competition connotes the idea of doing battle against others; it is a strong drive based on the need to excel, to become the best. In his statement, Nixon reminds one superficially of Teddy Roosevelt (also a sickly child), who personified the concept of rugged individualism and was a staunch apostle of competition.

Nixon does reveal himself when he says:

Whenever you take the competitive spirit out of a people or when you take it out of an individual, you lose something in a country. That spirit has been the great driving force of America . . . its leaders, its people, in all walks of life. I suppose that's one of the reasons why politics appeals to me. It's of course a subsidiary reason, but a very strong one. Anybody in politics must have great competitive instinct. He must want to win. He must not like to lose, but above everything else, he must have the ability to come back, to keep fighting more and more strongly when it seems that the odds are the greatest. That's the world of sports. That's the world of politics. I suppose you could say that's life itself.[8]

Though, so far as I can determine, this is the only time Nixon mentions an "instinct," competitiveness was such an integral part of his whole being that it was indeed an instinct. It became a motivating drive that compelled him to fight ruthlessly in order to be assured of victory. And fighting, in Nixon's view, was "life itself."

It was, I submit, his early daydreams that expressed the unconscious drive to excel and be recognized. And this urge to make other people take heed of him, coupled with his own need to be self-important, was decisively influential as he became a man.

Nixon had such an overwhelming need to be a leader, to be recognized, that he seemed to be saying, "Don't leave me out." We suspect that his competitive drive came from a sense of childhood rejection. In an interview in 1967 his mother admitted as much:

> She [Hannah] said she regretted she "didn't take time enough to sit down and read to the children. There were many things to be done—so many bread-and-butter problems." [9]

Hannah was not given to talking about herself. It is therefore more than likely that she felt particularly guilty about having neglected the children. The important fact, though, is that young Nixon *felt* rejected, whatever the validity, real or imagined, of his mother's statement. His sense of rejection was significant, because it was an emotional element that impelled Richard to make a lasting impression upon people.

His compulsive, constant desire to make himself felt was greater than meets the eye, because beneath it was an effort to overcome his conflicting self, his inner conflict which later was to play an important part in the maturity crisis.

One basic element that shaped his pattern of feelings stemmed from his strong relationship with his mother. We previously have shown that Richard was much closer to his mother than to his father. His aunt Rose Olive Marshburn told me that "as a child Richard wanted his mother alone to do things for him, and he asked her rather than his father." We have noted earlier that he resented and disliked his father, although he was careful not to act openly against him.

To escape Frank's violent temper, Nixon and his brothers sought the love and protection of their mother. "Hannah," Jessamyn West told me, "had to smooth over the damage Frank through his volcanic temper had done to the customers in the grocery store or to his children." Her way of dealing with life was many-sided: she was ambitious for Richard; she manipulated her husband; she was conciliatory and, at times, gave in to her husband.

Nixon was an observant student. In learning to use and adopt his mother's attitudes, he also had to learn to repress his anger toward his father. And yet these hostile feelings remained buried in his mind. A boy who completely represses his hostility toward his father cannot get rid of his hate. Behind repression lie aggressive feelings and actions which break out when the pressure becomes too strong.

This childhood opposition to his father, however, made Nixon very calculating and suspicious of others. Unable to trust anyone, he felt that he had to control everyone. He had to be careful to plan everything in detail. These anal traits, having their origin in his "withholding" or "holding back," had become fixated and were prominent in Nixon's behavior. In college he was called the "iron butt."

A more humorous expression of his anal orientation was his slogan for the college club he claimed to have organized: "Beans, brawn, brain and bowels." Interesting to me was the custom whereby each student would collect things that could be burned and bring them to the site of the annual bonfire, a mound of earth called Fire Hill. As chairman of the traditional festivity in 1933, Nixon was to throw in the last object, and it was important that he select something which could enhance his status as a leader. Mazo tells us:

Normally the bonfire was topped by a one-holer. Occasionally a really superior chairman would drag in a two-holer. In 1933 Richard Nixon established a record that still stands. He produced a four-holer.[10]

Thirty years later, in 1962, when he lost the election for the California governorship and after he had given his famous remark that the "press wouldn't have him to kick around any more," he told his press assistant rather gleefully, "I gave it to them right in the behind."[11]

More than forty years later, we find similar language in Nixon's verbal attack against John Dean during the Watergate scandal after Dean had begun to talk to the United States prosecutors. "He's going to do anything to save his ass." At a later meeting he said, "I have broken my ass to try to get the facts of this case."[12] Equally representative is his remark in the White House tapes when discussing the economy of Italy; he said, "I don't care a shit for the lira."

While these scatological, anal expressions may not seem important, they represent a strong pattern particularly noteworthy in a man so repressed and outwardly proper. With such an anal fixation, coupled with his oral fixation, there could be little or no emotional growth. It must have been confusing to Nixon to feel unloved, like a stranger, and unable to give love. Only toward his mother did he feel a strong bond—but only secretly, because his ego could not accept such a tie.

A culminating and major crisis in Richard Nixon's adolescence was the death of his brother Harold. It is, I believe, remarkable that there is so little reliable information about Harold, who was born in 1909 and died on March 7, 1933, at the age of twenty-four. Nowhere have I found any written description of the kind of child and boy he was or a full description of the history of his illness.

From interviews I have had with people close to the Nixon family it has been possible to reconstruct an impression of Harold and his illness which seems valid. Whatever the precise facts, the traumatic effect of his death on the family, and Richard in particular, is clear. Jessamyn West told me:

When Harold became sick, my brother Merle brought

him [possibly in 1931] to the sanatorium where I was staying.* Other patients told me, "You have a 'lunger' in there." They could see that Harold was gravely ill with tuberculosis. Harold didn't take care of himself. Despite his illness he got himself engaged to a girl. He told Merle that if he was going to die he might as well have a fling. . . .

Harold was older than Richard and much more of a swinger with the girls than his younger brother. As is well known, the second child always has a more difficult role to play than the first one. . . . Harold was taller than Richard, more outgoing, more of a man.

Rose Olive Marshburn also told me:

Harold was much more outgoing, much more inclined to be friendly. He was not a keen student. Rather, he wanted to have a good time. Richard was more serious. Hannah wanted Harold to go to another school because the public school in Whittier wasn't very good. Then also she felt he needed discipline.

Probably around 1925 he was sent to northwestern Massachusetts—three thousand miles away—to the Mount Hermon School,† which was known to have high spiritual and moral standards.‡ He stayed there for a year. He then returned to California and came down with a sore throat, coughing, and tonsillitis. Rose Olive Marshburn has told me that Harold "contracted a bad cold at Mount Hermon and was never too well after that."

These symptoms marked the beginning of his tuberculosis. Merle West, who went to school with Richard during the early years in Yorba Linda, knew the family very well. He believes that Harold became ill in 1927. In 1931 or 1932,

* Miss West suffered from tuberculosis and was in a sanatorium for two years, between 1931 and 1933.
† I have not been able to learn for certain how the Nixons, who seemed always short of money, financed this. Rose Olive Marshburn told me that they may very likely have obtained a scholarship.
‡ The Mount Hermon School was founded by Dwight Moody, the evangelist. Boys took cold showers at five-thirty in the morning, and on really cold mornings, unless they moved quickly, they arrived at breakfast with icicles in their hair. Prayers or Bible study before breakfast was part of the program.

Merle rented the gasoline station from Frank Nixon, who claimed he was too busy in the store and no longer able to service the cars. However, in view of how cantankerous Frank was, and how rude he could be with customers, it is probable that Frank had to be kept away from the store as much as possible. This, in turn, meant that Hannah had to run the store virtually alone. And during the time she also had to care for Harold, who was sick, in 1930, at the age of forty-five, she gave birth to Edward, her fifth son. We may surmise that Nixon's reaction—he was seventeen—may have been one of discomfort and humiliation.

We learn also from Merle West that when Harold walked a hundred feet up the hill to the service station he arrived exhausted and had to sit down to rest. Merle played checkers with him, and remembers him as a delightful fellow, but not robust. He also recalled that Hannah took Harold to Prescott, Arizona, and then "came back for a little while and then stayed there again." But he doesn't remember the precise dates. Keeping in mind that Harold became sick sometime between 1925 and 1927, we may conclude that in all probability he became ill not long after Arthur died.

The fact that Harold was sick for some years is confirmed by Nixon, who wrote in his *Self Portrait:*

> . . . my older brother, oldest brother Harold had tuberculosis. He was sick for five years and my mother for three years stayed with him in Arizona. Those were the days, you know, when it was thought you had to take somebody to a warm climate or a dry climate. And so that was a period when my father in effect was the . . . took care of us all. He did the cooking, we all helped out and then in the summertime we would go over to Prescott, Arizona, to visit my mother and my oldest brother. It was a rather difficult time actually, from the standpoint of the family being pulled apart, but looking back, I don't think that we were any the worse off for it, because we learned to share the diversity and you grow stronger from having to take care of yourself . . . not having your mother to lean on. We all grew up rather fast in those years, those of us who remained home.[13]

It would seem, then, that from 1925, when Arthur died, until 1933, when Harold died, the Nixon family lived in a state of almost perpetual emotional and financial crisis. In order to meet the added medical expenses, Frank had to sell half his property. Hannah took Harold to Arizona, and therefore had to leave the grocery store, which was a great loss to the Nixon family since she took almost full responsibility for running it. We do know that Nixon spent two summers working in Arizona, at a rodeo, as a wheel-of-fortune barker; his pay was reduced from one dollar to fifty cents an hour during the second summer because the Depression had set in. We can assume that he probably spent two or more summers there. A friend of the family, who wishes to remain anonymous, told me:

> Hannah had to leave the grocery store to go to Arizona, hopefully to save Harold [in 1930]. That was when Richard was graduating from high school and going to college. In addition to looking after Harold, in order to make ends meet, she had to take in other tubercular cases. You can imagine the danger she was running herself.* I interviewed some of her neighbors. I interviewed members of the family who let her rent the land. Frank built a little shack there. I cannot imagine any mother, whether she is Quaker, Latin, or Anglo-Saxon, putting up with that . . . she was a hard character in that you got the impression that inside this frail, skinny woman on the outside who might be depicted as a typical Anglo-Saxon cold person, inside was pure steel, pure steel. She was a true Quaker. People said that they wouldn't give two cents for Frank Nixon. They hated Frank and they hated Richard. But Hannah was the exception.

When queried further about Hannah's attitude toward her children, the friend responded:

> She was compassionate. Like St. Francis of Assisi, who true to his faith gave up worldly pleasures and went out begging like a hippie . . . she left her other children. She left them in this sense. She had to leave Richard and Donald behind because she could not

---

* Rose Olive Marshburn confirmed that Hannah took two tubercular roomers into her apartment in Prescott, Arizona.

afford to take the whole family with her. Harold had to go because his life had to be saved. Why wasn't his life saved? From all accounts he was a headstrong, devil-may-care Irishman who at every turn did just the opposite of what his doctor and his parents told him to do. He did just the opposite. He was a wild, red-haired boy—a Kennedy you might say. . . . Harold worked. For whom did he work [in California]? This gentleman hired Harold Nixon. His job was to fumigate the citrus groves. Very dangerous work. People died. So Harold was his employee.

He wasn't supposed to fool around with airplanes, but every opportunity he would run off to the airport. Flying airplanes was his passion. He always was hanging around airports very much against his father's orders.

Up to the time he died he was disobeying orders, doing this sort of thing.

According to Earl Mazo, Hannah left her husband and other children in Whittier to fend for themselves.

It was a period of extreme hardship for the whole family. In Whittier the father, Richard and the other boys took turns preparing the meals—usually canned chili, spaghetti, pork and beans, soup, and at least half the menus consisted of either hamburgers or fried eggs. "Odd as it may seem, I still like all of those things," Nixon admits. "There were many mornings when I ate nothing for breakfast but a candy bar." [14]

Hannah was in Arizona, on and off, for two or possibly three years, from 1929 to 1931, a long time to be away from her family—particularly since it was during the Depression. She may have left because she felt guilty that her oldest son had become afflicted with tuberculosis and was afraid that unless proper precautions were taken her other children might be afflicted. It also may have been that in taking Harold to Arizona she could control him better, for he was not easy to deal with.

Harold was very outgoing, friendly, and lighthearted. He was a "swinger"—just the opposite of Richard, who was serious-minded and studious. Afflicted with tuberculosis,

Harold proved to be self-destructive. Flying in those days was dangerous, and the job of dusting citrus groves was particularly so for a man with tuberculosis. Since he was disobeying orders until he died, we must conclude that this trait did not appear suddenly, but was an expression of rebelliousness which was evident before he became ill.

Mrs. Marshburn wrote me:

> In a little pamphlet prepared after Harold's death, containing a few snapshots and a little memorarium [we learn that] he loved nature, music and beauty in all its forms. . . . His desire to create things in these preparatory years manifested itself in his having written many lovely poems to his family and friends. Harold accomplished as much in his short life in an exemplary way as many others who live their allotted span. His cheerfulness, patience and fortitude in the years of invalidism battling against disease were a constant challenge to those with whom he was in daily contact.
>
> One of the last remarks he made to his mother was "Though I do so want to get well I am so glad I am at peace with my Maker and all is well." [15]

Hannah was a woman of high ambition who wanted the best for her sons; her insistence that her children be well educated was possibly a projection of her shortened education. And yet, does this explain why two of her sons were sent away for various periods of time, Richard to his aunt's home and Harold to a private school in Massachusetts? Besides the earlier mentioned reasons it is my impression that having Harold and Richard around the house was more than Hannah could emotionally deal with. In order to have the energy to maintain the long hours of work at the store, she had to have as few distractions as possible. Family survival depended upon the success of their store. Her ally in times of stress was her sister Rose Olive, who informed me that often either she had to go over to Hannah's house to help out with the children, or they would come and stay with her. One time she remembers in particular was while Frank was building a house in Whittier and they all stayed with her for several months.

The picture we have of Richard Nixon's childhood home

is that it was disorganized. The only steadying force was Hannah, who had to contend with a brutal man who, we learn from the family friend who prefers not to be named here, "could be hard and he could be beastly . . . like an animal. He could be very hard on the children—spank them freely and give them cracks."

What we see is a family in which there was almost unceasing anger, either repressed or expressed. By sending her two children away, which they may have felt to be rejection, Hannah tried to protect them against their father and against their being infected with tuberculosis. She had struggled to keep the home together, believing that "one should stand on one's own two feet." Nevertheless, she had to seek help. Her sister says, "We were always a close-knit family." But in this case it appears that Hannah usually had to stand alone against the crises that threatened to divide the family.

In order to understand the origins of Nixon's emotional turmoil, we must keep in mind the repressed, anger-filled, discouraged mother and the explosive father, and their desperate financial situation, all of which led to a disorganized home.

And Harold's death—when Nixon was in his third year at Whittier College—served further to deepen his guilt and fear of death.

6

The month Richard Nixon entered Whittier College in 1930, he was elected president of the freshman class. He turned out for freshman football, although he was too slow for the backfield and, at 155 pounds, he was too light for the line. He also formed a social club, the Orthogonians—straight shooters—of which he became president. The Orthogonians, in contrast to the Franklins, the existing men's club (who were photographed in tuxedos), were informal. Membership in the Orthogonians consisted of those who played football or were interested in it.

Nixon, who was on the football team, rarely played in a game. "He was on the Whittier squad for four years, never advancing beyond second string." [1]

Clinton Harris, one of his former teammates, told me the same thing he had told Jackson:

> At Whittier College I saw Nixon and admired him a lot as a fellow freshman and as a football player. He wasn't a good football player but he had terrific motivation. He just wasn't big enough. For example, I weighed 210 pounds and had stayed out of high school and was twenty years old; he was seventeen and weighed 155 pounds, so you can imagine the competition he had. And there were other fellows as big as I was.

Nixon's view of playing football was strongly connected with the desire to win, which dominated all his activities. Some thirty years later he spoke with admiration and delight about his football experience at college:

> Well, there's nothing that makes character more than losing, I can assure you. I must say that I don't

78

prefer it. I've won some and I've lost some and winning is a lot more fun. I think I probably got my attitude about winning and losing, at least I was strongly affected in my attitude about winning and losing during my college years when I went out for sports. Our coach was Chief Newman. He was a great football player at the University of Southern California, an American Indian, proud, strong, vigorous, one who didn't rush out to the sidelines when a player had made a good play and was coming out of the game and shake his hand. He didn't believe in that kind of . . . sort of display, but one who had the fierce loyalty of all of his players because they knew he was a strong man and one who treated everybody fairly. But the chief always used to say to us in those days at Whittier before games or after we'd lost a tough game . . . he'd say, "Now look here. I don't believe in this business about being a good loser." He said, "You've got to hate to lose and that means that once you lose, then you fight back," and I suppose that's my evaluation of life generally.[2]

For Nixon, it was unthinkable to lose. Winning in football was a highly personal matter. We discover here an important element in Nixon's psyche; in losing, he felt threatened. Not winning meant loss of manhood; he would feel degraded, without virility. These were feelings he couldn't ignore. Through his tenacious fighting there became instilled in Nixon's mind the idea that he could overcome everything to achieve his goals. To some extent he had been right.

He had become an excellent debater and had won many debates, for which he had received much acclaim. He worked hard and the angels seemed to smile on him, so that we may say there was some foundation for his belief that, ultimately, he was a winner. But would he always win? He may have thought that if only he worked hard enough, he would win, that by his willing it, he could overcome everything. And this may have been a reason for his fighting so hard to be on the football squad regardless of his physical and emotional shortcomings. Richard had the misbegotten idea that by fighting tenaciously he could overcome his inadequacies and become a first-rate football player. He overestimated his ability, and this highly incorrect overassessment became crucial to him, strongly coloring his behavior pattern. He believed that through his will he could overcome his shortcomings in everything, but in football he failed miserably.

Another reason for Richard's zealous efforts on the football field was to prove that he was physically well, in contrast to his older brother, Harold, who was an invalid. Although football was an important and therapeutic way of giving expression to his aggressive inclinations, much of his effort to win glory in football was an overcompensation for his lack of muscular coordination. His muscles and his coordination couldn't keep pace with his ambitions.

Wallace Newman, the coach, says, "We used Nixon as a punching bag. If he'd had the physical ability he'd have been a terror . . ." [3] Richard showed that he could take it and this impressed the team. One must surmise that when he took this physical punishment—taking punches which gave him no rewards—he must have felt it severely, suffered, suggesting in him a masochistic streak, which always seeks its counter-balance in sadism. Almost anyone else would have given up football after trying for a year to make the regular squad. But not Nixon. Unable to estimate correctly the reality of his situation, he persevered through four years in his attempt to make the first team.

Nixon's lack of success on the football field, however, did not keep him from excelling in other activities. As a debater he traveled over the western part of the country, talking about free trade and why the powers of the President should be increased. As his history professor, Paul Smith, recalled, he was "an achiever. . . . He was out to win." [4] His classmate Ed Wunder, who later became Nixon's first financial adviser, remembers that Richard's big outlet was in "the fun of being in things, planning things." [5]

Self-discipline was perhaps his most distinguishing characteristic during these years. And almost as important was a compulsiveness to be highly visible, to be "in the middle of things."

In his first play, in his senior year in high school in 1930, Nixon had met Ola-Florence Welch. Based on Virgil's *Aeneid*, the play was presented by the Latin students. Ola-Florence later said that Richard was "the first boy I ever went with. . . . He played Aeneas and I was Dido and from then on we went together." [6]

Aeneas was candid and sincere. He combined a goodness of heart with deep affection for kindred, friends, and country. Aeneas fell in love with Queen Dido. Ola-Florence recalls that at the end of the play Queen Dido dies and "he throws himself on her bier. It was very romantic." [7]

At Whittier College he continued to act.

> He acted in several school plays. In *The Price of Coal* he was "Jock, a young miner." [His leading lady was Ola-Florence Welch.] The play was marred, the school paper reported, when "the electricians made several errors." In *Philip Goes Forth*, he was Philip's father, who wished his son well when, at the third act curtain, he went forth. In *Bird in Hand* he was "Thomas Greenleaf, a typical Englishman of yeoman stock." The paper noted that in *Bird in Hand* "you will see, no extra charge, Dick Nixon trying to light a pipe . . . and the first bedroom scene ever enacted on the Whittier campus." He generally played older men. "He had a deep voice and an older man's face," a fellow actor remembers, "and he seemed to have physical substance. The effect was more maturity." [8]

That Ola-Florence Welch and Nixon kept company for six years is significant. And yet analysis of their association has been lacking. Even Nixon's most friendly biographer mentions her only once, in connection with her role in the *Aeneid*.[9]

In reconstructing facts concerning their relationship I have necessarily relied on the work of several reliable people who interviewed both Ola-Florence and Whittier College students who knew them at the time. They are, of course, not responsible for my conclusions. In this connection, I have also interviewed members of Nixon's family, Ola-Florence Welch, and friends of hers who were and still are close to her. It is a strange story.

Lael Morgan, writing in 1970, reported:

> They were considered an odd match. Ola-Florence was vivacious and popular, the daughter of the Whittier police chief. She had her pick of beaux and

many were so honored by her attention that—30 years
later—they're still boasting they dated her.

While Nixon was roundly respected, no one has ever
accused him of being a swinger. "Let's face it," laments
one of Ola-Florence's close friends, "he was stuffy!"
"The girls used to say, 'Why do you go out with him?'
[Ola-Florence replied:] I just thought he was the
smartest man that ever was."

Like Nixon, she was an eager student, a doer and an
organizer. She also had an unusual interest in politics.
"We'd have marvelous arguments and talks. We used
to argue politics constantly. He was a Republican. I
thought Roosevelt was wonderful and he detested
him."

She soon discovered there was no hope of converting
her beau to the Democratic Party so she concentrated
on adding a little levity to his life. "I loved to dance
and I pushed him into it. Finally got him to take dancing lessons. I don't think he was ever very happy about
it." [10]

Donald Jackson says that Nixon "took dancing lessons,
appearing at her house one night with the announcement, 'I
can dance,' and immediately set about proving it." [11]

Following this apparent success, Nixon became more
popular when, as president of the student body, he advo-
cated dancing, which was forbidden at the college.

This decision to learn how to dance was undoubtedly
made to please Ola-Florence. Several classmates, however,
have shared a more cynical view of his decision. Nixon, they
claimed, didn't care much for dancing—he didn't really
have time for it. In their opinion, he learned how to dance
to increase his popularity. It was, they concluded, an early
sign that "he was a politician."

That Nixon worked hard for the introduction of dances at
Whittier may also have been an act of rebellion against his
mother. Through this effort he unconsciously may have
wanted to show Hannah that he could be independent and
defy the restrictions of her religious code.

What is unusual about Nixon's using dancing as a means
of expressing his rebelliousness is that he didn't like to
dance. As Ola-Florence admits, "I don't think he was ever
very happy about it." Dancing made him feel uncomfort-

able. His awkward body movements became even more noticeable on the dance floor.

His difficulty in learning to dance leads one to suspect that there were underlying barriers. Dancing, according to his mother's beliefs, was sinful. To dance meant breaking her code of morals. Complicating the matter was Nixon's fear that this sinful activity would bring him into an even closer relationship with a gay, fun-loving woman, the antithesis of his mother.

Nixon's father, Frank, didn't dance because dancing aroused his amorous inclinations, which he was unable to control. A similar fear may have been at work in Nixon, for we suspect he shared Frank's strong sexual drive. In Nixon, these strong inclinations, while essentially predominant, became inhibited. Having been taught by his mother to curb them, he consciously set out to do so. But, as with all sexual aggressions, he couldn't master them. Repressing sexual inclinations led to a strange and unfulfilled relationship with Ola-Florence, and gave rise to an ambivalence between his aggressive behavior and his passive emotional state. The repression of his sexual desires made him unknowing of himself to the point where he became secretive.

This need for secrecy is very evident in Nixon's strong tendency to keep things to himself and to trust only his own counsel. What he did not know was that unconsciously this secrecy was closely associated with the need to keep his sexual life secret. He wanted no one to know his innermost desires; no one was going to know about Nixon the man.

This psychological process is well known. Those who repress sexual desires are unable or find it very difficult to tell anyone anything about themselves because this would be the same as betraying their inner selves and their deep sexual needs.

The six years that Ola-Florence and Nixon went together began with their senior year in high school, and continued through four college years and one year while he was studying law. "Quite a long time," says a friend (who prefers to be anonymous). Although the relationship between them obviously had a sexual dimension, Ola-Florence was mostly attracted by Nixon's mind. This is also borne out by the fact that Ola-Florence said years later, when Nixon was elected President, "I knew he'd be famous, but I thought he would be Chief Justice of the Supreme Court." [12]

Why, then, did Ola-Florence decide not to marry Richard Nixon? One of her friends (who does not wish to be identified) gives us more information about their relationship.

> Richard Nixon was serious; he had a good mind, but was introspective, stubborn, and had a temper. Asked whether they were much in love, she answered: "I thought they were going to be married, until the last year."
>
> "What then?"
>
> "I think," she answered, "Ola-Florence had found out that her views were entirely different from his. She had very definite views and I guess she couldn't put up with him any longer."
>
> "Was he more after her than she after him?"
>
> "He felt comfortable with her, and didn't want to start any new relationship. . . . He was stiff." [13]

Donald Jackson says:

> [Nixon] and Ola-Florence went together fairly faithfully, though rather more faithfully on his part than hers. Occasionally they would tiff: "He'd be harsh and I'd cry; then we'd make up." Some of the other girls thought him stuffy and standoffish. "He didn't know how to be personable or sexy with girls," one says. "He didn't seem to have a sense of fun, you know? I felt a kind of amused affection for him, like 'Oh, Dick, come off it.' " [14]

While some contemporaries saw them as "being in love," others viewed them as an "odd match." Their personalities were opposite: he solemn, serious, preoccupied, standoffish, respected but not well-liked; she friendly, warm, fun-loving, gay, and extremely popular, possibly the most popular girl on campus.

During Nixon's college years, Harold was seriously ill with tuberculosis and he died in March of his third year. Nixon's realistic fear that he too might be stricken with tuberculosis was a very private one; he mentioned it only once to Ola-Florence. But we can be sure that his anxiety served to make him even more introverted, more serious. The picture Ola-Florence gives us is that of a loner:

He seemed lonely, and so solemn at school. He didn't know how to mix. He was smart and sort of set apart. I think he was unsure of himself, deep down. Sometimes I think I never really knew him, and I was as close to him as anyone. I still feel some of that—he was a mystery.[15]

This view is further confirmed by Bela Kornitzer:

Even in school he was a "loner" and, though he was respected and even liked by his classmates, his stock with the girls was not too high. . . .
"Oh, he used to dislike us girls so! He would make horrible faces at us. As a debater, his main theme in grammar school and the first years of high school was why he hated girls. One thing was strange, though. He said he didn't like us, but he didn't seem to mind arguing with us." [16]

He certainly didn't distinguish himself as a ladies' man. He saw girls only as objects, as is indicated by the way he argued with them in debate. While hostile toward them, he didn't avoid them. He dealt with them in an impersonal or indirect way.

Behind this aggression was fear of being overpowered by them, the same feeling he may have had about his mother. Consciously and unconsciously he had to dominate the girls, and one way to do this was to defeat them in debate. If he could not dominate them, he feared people would get the idea that he was effeminate. This fear suggests that he doubted his own masculinity.

Whenever a boy doubts his own masculinity he feels a morbid anger against his father. If he represses these hostile feelings he will, when older, attach himself to people who remind him of his father—father representatives—and develop an angry relationship with them whether or not the anger is deserved. The anger need not be provoked; there need not be any outside cause for it. The cause lies in the man's need to express his anger. Should he also have a legitimate reason for the anger, his reaction will be one of violent outbursts completely out of proportion to the situation. This man will also have difficulty in maintaining friendships with his equals, and will find it almost impossible to cooperate with those he feels are superior to him. He will, in fact, hate them. This same pattern of hostility will be directed also against women.

Doubting his masculinity, which widened the differences between him and Ola-Florence, made a deep relationship between them impossible. Nonetheless, they spent a great deal of time in each other's company, going to the beach, to the movies, to off-campus parties and dances. And they often talked about politics. She was strongly liberal; he a conservative. He resisted giving in to her or her parents, who had been Democrats for generations. Ola-Florence eagerly accepted and defended the political views she had been brought up with. Did this difference also serve to drive them apart? Rose Olive Marshburn told me that this was not a serious factor, although she admitted:

> Politics were more important in her family than in his. I know that her mother and father felt strongly that way. I read in an interview that had something to do with it. Her mother didn't like Richard very much.

This last point is also confirmed by Lael Morgan:

> Ola-Florence's mother didn't like Nixon. She deplored his habit of driving up to the Welch home and blasting his horn, and he showed other traits that she considered ungentlemanly.[17]

In an interview with Lael Morgan, Ola-Florence gave another reason for their parting. What made her angry, in the middle of their senior year, was "the night he took me to the prom and we had a fight. He went home and I had to call my folks to come get me." Also the fact that Richard got mad enough to ask another girl out made her angry, "because we were supposed to be going steady. The Metaphonian formal was coming up . . . I always hated it because you were supposed to ask a boy."[18]

In this interview, Ola-Florence says she invited Gail Jobe, the handsome manager of the campus store. He warmed the bench with Nixon in football, but he was known as quite a ladies' man. Jobe immediately announced his good luck to Nixon, who got "huffy" and declared that he wasn't going with Ola-Florence anyway. So she went to the senior prom with Jobe and Nixon took Marjorie Hildreth, one of Ola-Florence's friends. "There were no hard feelings," Marjorie recalls. "I had my arm in a cast and I don't believe I saw much of him after that." [19]

Still, they continued their "on-and-off" romance. It was in May 1934, in his senior year at Whittier, that Nixon learned he had won a scholarship to Duke University Law School. Ola-Florence told Donald Jackson:

> He was so excited . . . the night he found out about the scholarship—oh, we had fun that night. He was not only fun, he was joyous, abandoned—the only time I remember him that way. He said it was the best thing that ever happened to him. We rode around in his car (he had bought a 1930 Ford in his junior year) and just celebrated.[20]

When Nixon went to Duke Law School he wrote her faithfully from Durham, North Carolina. A friend of hers told me: "If she had married Nixon, his life would have been entirely different. She remains one of my great friends." [21]

Everyone Lael Morgan spoke with seemed to take it for granted that Nixon would marry Ola-Florence when he finished law school.

> "It was a foregone conclusion they would get married," Dick Thomson said. "It ended abruptly. We never figured out why." Stories conflict. "We just drifted apart," Ola-Florence says evenly. "That really shouldn't have happened," says Mrs. Keith Wood, Whittier '36, who married one of Nixon's classmates. "They were a great couple." [22]

They continued to correspond. But then, one time when he came home from law school, he called Ola-Florence for a date. Jobe was at her house. Nixon got furious and told her: "If I ever see you again, it will be too soon." [23]

Yet he kept writing to her.

"How did the relationship end?" I asked one of her friends. "Did Ola-Florence break with him?" "I know that she did," the friend answered, "because of the letters he wrote her. He wrote many, many letters to her and she has them all. I saw only one, and it's a long time ago, so I don't remember exactly what was said, except that I know he was very upset about the break-up." [24]

This strong emotional outburst and rejection offers insight into Nixon's personality. Nixon felt threatened by Ola-Florence's warmth and her ability to reach out to others. At best, their relationship was inconsistent, and as unpredictable as it was with his own father. Once again, we see in this early romantic relationship an ambivalent play of love and hate, attraction and rejection, like and dislike.

On April 17, 1975, I talked by telephone to Ola-Florence. Even over the telephone she projected a strong sense of warmth and friendliness. She struck me as being sensitive, bright, the kind of person who doesn't like to hurt one's feelings. It seemed painful and embarrassing for her to talk about Nixon. There was an undercurrent of sadness in her voice when she spoke about his fate. She explained her closeness to Nixon as a "young romance" and that they just drifted apart.

In speaking of her personal attitudes and feelings about Nixon, Ola-Florence confirmed the opinion of other contemporaries that he was gifted and intelligent, but difficult to get along with. He kept things to himself and did not like to share his feelings. He could be quite aggressive and combative at times, and had a bad temper. She had met Richard's mother, whom she considered a "very fine woman," who always "controlled herself."

When asked if Nixon talked to her about the illnesses in his family, she replied, "He kept most of that to himself." One of my last questions was "Did he like you?"—to which she replied with a laugh, "I guess so." I followed my query with a more probing question: "Did he ever say that he liked you?" She became flustered. "Do you remember?" I asked. "I just don't remember . . . no, I'm really sorry, I don't know if he did." She laughed as she said this. I pursued the subject. "Are you reluctant to talk about him?" She confirmed that she was. As to Nixon's resignation, she said, "I think it's a tragedy for everyone concerned."

We learn that Ola-Florence considered Nixon a "shy boy friend." The fact that she was far more outgoing and was very popular with her classmates, particularly men, raises some doubt as to her own shyness. We suspect that Nixon, in his need to excel and be admired by others, sought out and pursued a girl who was very much in demand. A close friend of Nixon confirms this point: The President was "nervous on dates. He was no ladies' man. I think he went on dates because it was the thing to do." [25]

We detect that there was little genuine emotion in Nixon's dating, which may explain why he spent six years with Ola-Florence. It may have been that he wanted this kind of relationship because it was not threatening. It may be that he only wanted to *play the role* of dating. He *acted* as if he loved her, but he was never emotionally involved. He didn't really understand what feelings were about. It is possible that he loved her as much as he was capable of loving anyone.

Richard Nixon was afraid of both men and women and had a great deal of passivity in him. He also had a strong oral drive, so that the most significant part of his life was spent in talking, explaining, persuading, and debating. The experiences, circumstances, and occurrences of Nixon's oral period intensified this passivity, a phenomenon we see in all persons in whom oral aggression becomes predominant.

We have seen that when Nixon was an infant he cried and screamed loudly. At the beginning of his second year, he suddenly became surprisingly quiet, indicating that his oral desire had been repressed. We suspect that his cries were stopped by the violent outbursts of his father. Being denied normal satisfaction through his mother, he felt a loss—a loss of love. Having been denied this means of expression, he sought to use it in later years. We see this tendency in his incessant talking. It was an attempt to regain what he had lost in the first year of his life.*

The fact that he had lost what he conceived to be love from his mother had profound consequences on his emotional development. He began to feel sorry for himself, rejected, helpless, and dependent on other people—all on an unconscious level. Nixon's orality augmented his passivity and became a means of keeping people, men and women alike, at a distance.

All of us—men and women—have a bisexual nature. That we have homosexual leanings is a fact that many find hard to accept. Nixon's private feelings about his identity

---

* Other people may express their oral drive through smoking, drinking alcohol, eating, or kissing.

remain his deeply guarded secret. What we do know is that when a strong oral drive is the predominant personality trait, the sexual drive will usually be inhibited and weakened. Nixon's oral period was crisis-provoking, and intensified his feelings of passivity and lack of identity as a man. This was one reason why he was to become so preoccupied with "crises," so evident in his book *Six Crises*, which dealt with his struggle to gain maturity.

It is significant in Nixon's development that this intensification of passivity had a strong bearing upon his relationship with Ola-Florence. It was not the strong passion of first love. Theirs was a relationship in which stress and strain dominated more than joy or pleasure. Nixon's passive personality prevented him from establishing a meaningful relationship with her: he could only act and behave in an indirect way.

This pattern of behavior is shown in Nixon's inability to express his feelings: he was "a good boy," well-behaved, as his mother had taught him to be. Behind this mask, however, he was full of fury. Unable to verbalize his anger, he became cautious in "showing his hand," in making his intentions known. We see this same kind of behavior clearly during Nixon's presidency. One of his staff, who worked in the White House for several years and who prefers to remain anonymous, remarked that he felt that Nixon's outstanding characteristic was "furtiveness and a sort of indirectness." He said that typically Nixon handled a problem by making a quick decision before he had enough information to get a balanced viewpoint. In other words, he had a strong need to be a forceful leader even though he lacked the facts that would have helped make his decisions judicious.

A person who is essentially passive becomes aggressive because, feeling helpless, feeling impotent or castrated, he has to compensate for his passivity. The result is a deep ambivalence. This quality is dramatically shown in Nixon's political and personal style. When asked a question, for instance, Nixon rarely answers at once. He first tries to find out what the inquirer's opinion is and then answers in a fashion which very often skirts the real issue. He evades the question and delivers his answer with such force that he can leave the audience with the impression that in fact he did answer it. This mechanism in "answering" questions is highly defensive. We see this style also in Nixon's interviews. Typically he reverses the roles and becomes the reporter, making the journalist the interviewee.[26] By reversing roles, he is trying not to reveal himself and expose his own political views. This transfer of roles allows him to be in control, to make the person who is asking the question his subordinate.

The fact that Nixon's behavior was indirect and lacked genuine commitment is why we question his motivation in dating Ola-Florence. We may guess that his purpose was to impress others rather than to develop a genuine relationship with her. He was only concerned with creating a good image and was unable to establish a deep emotional relationship.

Impressing others, trying to show that one is better than one really is in order to attract attention to oneself, indicates the presence of hysterical traits. While Nixon tried to hide his intention, he also craved to show off his importance, trying to create a good impression.

This concern with image, rather than reality, may not originally have been conscious, but it developed out of Nixon's desire to be the best, or appear to be the best, which is why he had to do things that would bring approval. Without being aware of it, he had to build an impression of something that in fact did not exist.

In his ambivalent relationship with Ola-Florence, Nixon *acted* as if he had genuine feelings, of which he was incapable. This made it impossible for him to approach a situation or problem directly. He was usually able to avoid the problem and was never forced to grapple with its substance.

Richard's six-year courtship of Ola-Florence is a classic example of this kind of acting. It became a game of keeping up appearances, of acting as if there were human and emotional substance in their relationship. For him, this need to play a role made him more divided against himself. He was unable to act with a full personality. This internal conflict made his actions hesitant and indecisive, and if they sometimes seemed to be carried out forcefully, it was more in compensation for his weakness than an expression of strength. A person who is out of touch with, or disconnected from, an inner emotional base finds a greater satisfaction when he is acting a role, on or off the stage. And Nixon, as we know and as Ola-Florence has said, was the consummate actor: "Richard was an excellent actor." In the words of

Professor Smith, his history professor, "he was out to win. . . . He was a brute for discipline." [27]

Richard Nixon is the kind of man who is able to express his feelings best when he plays the part of the individual he wishes to be or feels he ought to be. What he cannot do in reality, he acts out in fantasy. When he was acting on the stage he could act out fantasies which usually—in real life—were not available to him. That Nixon had two competing sides to his personality, making him a divided self, helped to bring out fantasies in him which he was unable to control.

What is significant is that Nixon's singular success in his early life was debating, and this he pursued with every means at hand. Donald Jackson called my attention to an incident which I have been able to verify. On one occasion a student, Lois Elliott, observed him cheating during a college debate. Sitting in the front row of the gallery, just above where he was standing on the podium, she saw he was quoting facts and figures from a blank piece of paper. She told me, "I remember it clearly. It took place in the spring of 1933. I was editor on the school paper covering the debate. I sat in the gallery, and I saw when Nixon spoke in his rebuttal that he quoted from a blank paper. I told it later to my roommate; it was against all regulations, and very cunning. I remember it well." [28]

Reading from a blank piece of paper was almost like play-acting, and talking to audiences from a stage was also. Acting is a very worthy pursuit as long as the actor realizes that he is only playing a role; when he behaves as if he is indeed the character he is portraying, the problem becomes more serious, because then he has identified himself with an unreal person.

Nixon found himself alive when he was debating.

"Nixon is a rather quiet chap about the campus but get him on a platform with a pitcher of water and a table to pound on and he will orate for hours. Last year he toured the northwest with the debate team, leaving a trail blazed with victories and fluttering hearts," the *Quaker Campus* reported in its "Impressions." And its gossip column added a dash of acid: "Nothing is funnier than to call Richard Nixon 'Nicky' and watch him bristle. I did it once and he was too surprised to speak, if you can imagine Nixon inarticulate." [29]

Another incident, reported to me by Jessamyn West, is worth mentioning. Richard met a cousin who was infatuated with him. He took her out for a ride, and he talked and talked about politics and was completely carried away with what he was saying. "He was," she said, "the slowest driver in the world. I had to listen to him all the time." This was Nixon's way of avoiding any involvement, keeping his distance.

It is not farfetched to say that in college Nixon was on his way to becoming a professional actor. Often those who listened to him began to identify with his fantasized feelings drawn from his unconscious because his imagination was more persuasive than their own.

While his imagination enabled him to be a good actor, he failed to establish a genuine relationship with Ola-Florence because unconsciously he was out of touch with his feelings and incapable of love. Their strange interlude came to an end. He had met her while acting. Later, he would meet his future wife in the same way.

PART III

Public Image: The Divided Self

7

When Nixon was graduated from Whittier College in 1934, he stood second in his class; he had been president of the student body, a football player, an actor, a star debater, a baritone in the men's glee club, and was the recipient of a full-tuition scholarship to Duke Law School. His picture appeared in the senior yearbook, *Acropolis*, nine times. While his achievements were indeed impressive, what is striking is that apparently he had no close friends or real romantic interests. He preferred playing many different roles rather than one that risked a personal emotional involvement.

Bradley Morrah, who knew Nixon well in Nixon's last year at law school, told me that Duke University Law School in Durham, North Carolina, "was newly established, and was attracting students by having a full complement of twelve professors and offering scholarships for students with high academic standing. Altogether there were only eighty or eighty-five students, and as a consequence each student knew all the others. Some of them were completely impoverished. The large number of professors in relation to the student body was intended to raise the reputation of the law school." It was under pressure to excel that Nixon began his law studies.

From Durham he wrote letters that Ola-Florence thought indicated that he was lonely and lost. "He wrote me these sad letters. He sounded like he was close to quitting two or three times." [1] Nineteen of his classmates at Duke had scholarships; many were Phi Beta Kappas. Whittier didn't have a chapter in Nixon's time because it wasn't accredited. Nixon felt threatened by his new, strange, and competitive environment; he was afraid of the new surroundings, fearful of being outdone by his peers. His response, however, was hard work and he soon earned the nickname "Gloomy Gus" because of his moroseness. As one classmate, Lyman Brownfield, recalls, "There was a comic strip character by that name who was always puncturing people's fanciful balloons, bringing them down to earth. That was Nixon. . . . He was shot full of rectitude." [2]

Freddie Albrink, another fellow student, confirms this impression. "Some of us might fudge on the hours we worked at the library. Nixon never would. He was a copybook kind of guy without being obnoxious about it. I mean he was industrious, honest, reverent, all of that." [3] William Perdue told me that he roomed with Nixon from the second semester of the first year until they graduated in 1937, and in the last two years the group included Brownfield and Albrink. Perdue remembered that "Nixon had a quality of intensity in him, worked hard, pretty intense guy—he had a sense of privacy and not terribly strong on humor." Professor Lon Fuller found Nixon to be competent, "though not terribly imaginative or profound. And he was what today we'd call uptight—there was the suggestion of an intellectual inferiority complex." [4]

Nixon's apparent conformity to the law school's rules and regulations is noteworthy. He was "uptight" because he feared that he might become aggressive against authority, which would lead to retaliation—a fear rooted in his own personality, which was divided between marked aggressive tendencies and a high degree of passivity. As we have observed, he had a strong need to turn these repressed and suppressed aggressions outward; otherwise he feared they would be turned against himself. To avoid this inner confrontation and battle, he had to find outside goals and targets for his hostility and aggression. If he attacked authority, in this case the Duke Law School administration, he would antagonize those who had it in their power to thwart him. But he couldn't contain himself, as we shall see.

Nixon was caught in the dilemma he had experienced since childhood. He went through high school and college with excellent or good marks. Yet he did not feel equal to his classmates and tried therefore always to set ambitious goals for himself. He knew, unconsciously, that if he achieved his goals he would not have to act out his aggressions against authority. While he had attained academic success in his college years, Nixon found graduate school competition more difficult. Fear of failure always awakened deep-seated anxiety. The climax to his fears came in 1936 at the end of his second year at Duke. Nixon became increasingly afraid that he wouldn't retain his academic standing as third in his class, which, he thought, would mean the loss of his scholarship. Being compulsively competitive, it apparently didn't occur to him that even if he ranked tenth or fifteenth he still would have kept his scholarship. The important point is, he needed to be the best.

The anger and frustration of not knowing his class rank became unbearable; it was essential to find out where he stood. Together with two classmates, Albrink and Perdue, Nixon became an active participant in breaking into the dean's office. At the time, the three young men carefully guarded their secret. Two of Nixon's biographers, Mazo and Toledano, do not mention it at all. A third, Bela Kornitzer, categorizes the burglary as a "prank," commenting:

> . . . he and his roommates, Perdue and Freddie Albrink, became tired of waiting for the Dean's office to release the grades and decided on action. Since Richard was the thinnest of the three, he was given the precarious assignment of entering the Dean's office through a transom for an informal look at the grades. The mission was accomplished with such finesse that years passed before the exploit became known on the campus.[5]

A second source, Edwin Hoyt, tells the same story. Hoyt told me that Nixon himself had informed him that he had gained entrance to the office and found a key to the drawer and located the records. Stewart Alsop, like Kornitzer, makes light of the story:

> . . . the only youthful escapade his contemporaries recall involved his crawling over the transom to get into the dean's office in law school. But his purpose was not to booby-trap the dean's desk, or some such shenanigans. It was to discover, from the dean's records, where he stood scholastically.[6]

Since Nixon was anxiety-ridden, because he felt his entire future depended on his grades, he may well have been the instigator. Was it, then, a mere "prank" or "escapade," or does his role suggest abnormal behavior?

In the spring of 1936, his class rank was beginning to slip. If he fell too far back, he feared, he would lose his tuition scholarship worth $250 a year, which would have ended his law career. What would his home-town supporters, who expected him to live up to their expectations of success, say? What would Hannah think? Or Frank? And what about the members of the debate squad, the football team, Ola-Florence? His reputation was on the line. He had to do well, or they wouldn't respect him.

To leave law school after his second year would be a crushing defeat, one which Nixon's personality could not sustain. The suspense of not knowing what his grades were became unbearable. He became increasingly frustrated with the dean's office for the delay in making the grades public. While Nixon may have had some qualms about the illegal entry into the dean's office, his anxiety about his academic standing, his rebelliousness, coupled with a conviction he would not be caught, overruled any fear of wrongdoing. It is noteworthy that Nixon discounted any chance of his being caught, which would have meant automatic expulsion. He risked all because he unconsciously felt he didn't deserve success. When, after the break-in, he learned he was no longer in the top three in his class, his fears were confirmed.

When I interviewed Perdue, he told me: "It [the break-in] may well have happened. I don't deny the incident. I simply don't remember anything about it." Later, he added: "I have a legal training." Albrink, whom I spoke with on the same day, told me, "Perdue went first into the office over the transom. It was an open transom, and then he opened the door for us. We just looked over the various records and what we could see, and it would take a computer . . . I don't recall whether any of us had pencils or took notes. As I recall, the class grades were in a drawer, a card for each member of the class." Most likely, he told me, they had looked at the cards. Albrink volunteered, "We made no alterations. We had no intention of making alterations. It was to find out." I asked him how he felt after he had seen the records, whether he felt good or bad. He answered, "No, neither way."

I asked how the break-in came about. "We worked," he said, "upstairs in an office on the third floor, came down the stairway and passed the dean's office on the second floor. . . . Somebody said, 'I wonder whether the grades are in yet'; somebody rattled the door; it was locked. I don't know who got the idea to go through the transom. It could have been any of us. We happened to pass the door on our way home." Asked whether it was Nixon who got the idea, he answered, "This was over forty years ago, and I have no recollection. I just have no recollection. Somebody said, 'I wonder whether our grades are in, they ought to be in now, by this time.'" Asked whether breaking into the dean's office wasn't against all regulations, he answered, "The original three of us are still around, but we never did tell."

This account differs from those of former biographers. Albrink, it appears, is defensive in regard to Nixon and wants to protect him. Significant also is that he mentions that they had no intention of altering the grades. One is inclined to think that this may have been something they had discussed but then decided against. Albrink also implies that the break-in was a capricious act, a spur-of-the-moment affair, which he justified on the basis that the dean's office was slow in notifying the students of their grades. Perdue had repressed the break-in incident, and didn't want to discuss it. They both gave the impression it was a caper, no serious damage done. They saw nothing wrong in it. The protection they extend to Nixon is a further clue to Nixon's participation.

Being compulsive, Nixon was driven by his need to win. The goal of his life was winning, and maybe the other two participants also had this attitude. Fortunately for the three students, the illegal entry was not discovered. Bradley Morrah told me, "The break-in wasn't widely known when I was a freshman."

The three must have moved with some care and dexterity not to leave a trace of their actions. Asked why it took such a long time before anyone knew about the break-in, Albrink told me, "This was the summertime. If you run through a stop light, do you tell each cop you pass? I didn't feel it was a crime; on the other hand, the thing was, they didn't hand them out." Since Perdue and Albrink deny that it was a crime, why did they keep it a secret? Whatever Albrink and Perdue thought, it seems clear that Nixon felt he had fooled the dean, the supreme authority figure.

The secret break-in shows an unmistakable parallel to the Watergate event. Nixon learned from this 1936 incident that, if one is clever and daring enough, the rules can be broken without being discovered. And he also learned that by acting secretly he had the power to defy authority, and that it was possible to gain information secretly. Such a state of mind was familiar to Nixon. It was a belief rooted in fantasy that gave him great pleasure.

We see in this incident two contrary emotional forces—secretiveness and exhibitionism, showing that he had power. It was Nixon against Nixon—a man against himself.

Nixon, however, may not have been aware of his inner conflict, which was also why he had kept compulsively busy in college. He continued his pattern of feverish activity in law school. Even if he was frustrated in achieving the highest academic standing, he went out for the most prestigious student job. He became "president of the Duke Bar Association . . . defeating Hale McCown, now Chief Justice of the Nebraska State Supreme Court." [7] And he wrote a paper for the *Duke University Bar Journal of Law and Contemporary Problems*.*

While academically successful at Duke—he finished third in the class—Nixon experienced a frustrating defeat when he, Perdue, and a third student, Harland Leathers, set about to seek positions with leading law firms in New York. According to Perdue's account:

> We stayed at the Sloane House YMCA and I remember that in our naïveté we went into a saloon and ordered a sandwich. We waited interminably and found out later they had to send out for the sandwiches. Nixon was not charmed by New York . . . he had a West Coast prejudice." [8]

His two classmates were hired by prestigious New York law firms, and Nixon was not. He was particularly interested in Sullivan and Cromwell, John Foster Dulles' firm, which impressed him with its thick carpets.

One reason for his failure was his personality. Bradley Morrah, who knew Nixon well at the time when Nixon was

---

* "Changing Rules of Liability in Automobile Accident Litigation."

seeking a job in New York, told me that at Duke he frequently drove Nixon to lunch or dinner:

> I was one of few who had an automobile. For this service students used to buy the gasoline. I remember Nixon most pleasantly. He was very studious, but retiring, a quiet chap. He would have been the last man I would have thought in his class to go into politics. He was reserved. He was not unpopular. He rarely took part as a participant in the athletic events in North Carolina. He was in a very bright class at Duke, which set a high-water mark for achievement. He was number three. He was not particularly warm to the underclassmen, and did not exude any particular warmth. The great fight was to retain your scholarship. When I look back at his career . . . I always saw him as slightly paranoid for some reason. That is my personal reaction. In those days he was odd, something of an oddball.

Rejected by Sullivan and Cromwell, as well as other law firms, Nixon sought a job with the FBI and was once again rejected, though J. Edgar Hoover was later to call him "one of my boys." To be a "policeman" had a strong appeal to Nixon, since it gave him a legitimate opportunity to investigate and track down people who broke the law. Clearly his fascination with the FBI (and with law) was still present when, as President, he was so concerned with "law and order." This concern may have been a reaction to his own antisocial tendencies, which he projected onto other people and which he felt had to be watched. Once again we see his ambivalence—a wish to break the law, yet a need to safeguard it.

Rejected by the eastern law establishment, Nixon chose to return to California. He took the California Bar Examination, passed it, and was sworn on November 9, 1937.[9] Through a fortunate family connection, he joined Wingert and Bewley, the oldest law firm in Whittier. According to the elder Bewley (who had known Franklin Milhous, Nixon's grandfather):

> He came in to see us to see what the possibilities

were of practicing law in Whittier, and at that time we needed a good, young man to do trial work and general legal work, and I was satisfied at knowing the family. He was the type of fellow I would like to have in the office. He was brilliant. He wanted to do trial work, and we needed somebody badly, so we just made an arrangement.[10]

Working with Mr. Bewley's grandson, Nixon had to handle a number of divorce cases. As Nixon himself said, "I remember when I'd just started law practice, I had a divorce case to handle, and this good-looking girl, beautiful, really, began talking to me about her intimate marriage problems." When Stewart Alsop asked, "And were you embarrassed?"—Nixon replied, "Embarrassed? I turned fifteen colors of the rainbow. I suppose I came from a family too unmodern, really. Any kind of personal confession is embarrassing to me generally." [11]

Nixon worked for Wingert and Bewley from 1937 to 1941. In Nixon's very first case as a trial lawyer, only ten days after he had been admitted to the California bar, he became involved in a court case which proved very damaging to his client and subsequently to his firm.*

As far as it is possible to ascertain, Nixon has never mentioned this particular case. Although some details remain obscure, Irving Wallace's careful research pieced together the jigsaw puzzle of Nixon's involvement.

The details are as follows: Mrs. Maria Schee had loaned $2,000 to Otto A. and Jennevieve Steuer. When they did not repay the loan, Mrs. Schee had to sue them, and hired Wingert and Bewley to prosecute. Nixon was assigned the case. The Steuers owned some real estate which could be sold in order to recover their debt.

In the Los Angeles Municipal Court, Action #457600 was recorded on December 10, 1937. Wingert and Bewley prosecuted the action to judgment, which was rendered April 12, 1938. There was no trial; there was a stipulated

---

* The information about this case (except where other citations appear) comes from Irving Wallace, who has written an account of it which he very kindly has permitted me to use. Wallace has told me that a small newspaper published part of the account, and then ceased publication. A summary of the case also appears in *The People's Almanac,* edited by David Wallechinsky and Irving Wallace (1975).

judgment (court order), which means that there was a complaint and an answer. Judgment was entered for $2,000 plus costs and interest; the total was $2,245.29.*

Following this "Agreed Statement of Fact," Nixon had no authority and was therefore wrong to enter Satisfaction of Judgment. This means Nixon was wrong to record that the order had been complied with. Nixon gave written instructions to the Marshal of the City of Los Angeles to attach the Steuer real estate. Without notifying his client, Mrs. Schee, Nixon had the Steuer property put up for sale on behalf of the client and he bought it on June 29, 1938, for $2,300. He had no authority to do so. Furthermore, since there was no other bidder, he could have bought the property for as little as five dollars. He did not understand the proper procedure. This was not all. Nixon put his client into an untenable position when it was found that there already existed two trust deeds (mortgages) on the property, and when this property was foreclosed—that is, sold to satisfy the debt—Mrs. Schee lost out altogether. Nixon made an error in prosecuting the claim for his client which caused her to forfeit her right to obtain a deficiency judgment to recover her debt. This means she lost the right to be paid the balance of the debt after the sale of the property.

Realizing his terrible blunder too late, Nixon tried to undo it. He filed an affidavit on behalf of his client in which he attempted to justify a course of action he wanted the court to take. The court reacted strongly to his affidavit.

In 1950, a prominent lawyer in Los Angeles, now retired (who prefers to remain anonymous), visited Frank Schwartz, whose uncle David Schwartz had been the lawyer who had opposed Nixon in the 1938 litigation. Frank Schwartz showed the anonymous lawyer (whom I shall refer to as Mr. X) a transcript of the proceedings in the Municipal Court, which he read. Mr. X reported to Wallace:

> My recollection was that Richard Nixon's affidavit was so patently fraudulent that the judge sitting on the case said to him—and this was recorded by the court reporter—"Mr. Nixon, I have serious doubts whether you have the ethical qualifications to practice law in

---

* Daniel A. Knapp, attorney for plaintiff and appellant, Appellate Division, Los Angeles Superior Court, pp. 9, 19.

this state of California. I am seriously thinking of turning this matter over to the Bar Association to have you disbarred."

In 1960, when Nixon was about to run against Kennedy for President, Mr. X reported: "I was anxious to see it [the transcript] again." * Mr. X is certain of his recollection of what he had read in the transcript:

> The thing that surprises me is that it's so clear in my mind. I feel that I can quote the thing verbatim. In fact, I repeated the story a number of times to others as recently as 1968. I have seen the words the judge used to chastise Nixon. Again, I remember them . . .

When Wallace asked Mr. X whether he could have made up the whole story, Mr. X replied, "No, I couldn't. My recollection—the thing that impressed me vividly—was the attack by the judge on Nixon's sense of ethics. In my recollection, it went way beyond near-inept legal work."

After Mr. X spoke to his friend Frank Schwartz, who also has retired and who had seen the transcript in 1950, Mr. X stated:

> I told Frank my recollection, the date, the circumstances, everything, just as I told it to you [Irving Wallace], and he said to me, "Well . . . while you generally have a lousy memory, this time you can rest easy because this time you are accurate." And Frank Schwartz corroborated all I had remembered. He said he, too, remembered that the judge's reprimand of Nixon definitely went beyond the question of professional ability. . . . He, too, remembered the judge's words—the judge saying Nixon's conduct was "unethical" and the part about "I am seriously thinking of referring this to the Bar Association." So that does it.

---

* Irving Wallace writes: "Merton L. Schwartz, who had inherited the firm and whose father, David Schwartz, had opposed Nixon, had once possessed the original transcript. But Merton Schwartz couldn't find it. He says that his recollection was that Nixon just did a very stupid thing. The ethical question didn't stick out in his memory. What he remembers most was Nixon's stupidity in handling the case."

Now there are two of us who independently support the story of what happened.

Unfortunately, no transcript is available of what Judge Alfred E. Paonessa said in Division 14 of the Municipal Court, since proceedings are kept on file for only ten years. We have, however, two eyewitness accounts.

When, early in 1976, I interviewed Mr. X at length, he seemed to have changed his opinion on one point. He said:

> That my law partner's recollection as to the source was different from mine slows me up a little bit. At the present time I couldn't swear whether I saw it or whether David Schwartz told it to us. That one part or the other is true, I am a hundred percent clear. But there is no question in my mind that that quotation comes either from the transcript or from David Schwartz's mouth.

I asked whether Mr. X had seen the transcript in 1950. He answered, "I saw it. I handled it." He repeated, "I handled it several times." Since Mr. X saw it and handled it, it is reasonable to believe that he read it and that it was discussed with David Schwartz.*

We know from documented sources† that after the first stipulated judgment in the Municipal Court there followed two subsequent actions. One action was against Nixon and the law firm of Wingert and Bewley for negligence in what he had done. Nixon's client, Maria Schee, engaged another lawyer, Daniel A. Knapp. Then there was an independent lawsuit against the Marshal of the City of Los Angeles and the Steuers in order to set aside the sale that Nixon had undertaken. Richard Nixon had to appear in court as a witness and give testimony about his connection with the case.

A brief prepared by Knapp and still on file in the Appellate Division of the Los Angeles Superior Court reads in part:

---

* The judge's warning to Nixon was, we assume, in the files of Wingert, Bewley and Nixon of Whittier, known today as Bewley, Lassleben and Miller, 7624 South Painter, Whittier, California. However, Bewley reported to me that all their records are destroyed after ten years.

† In the District Court of Appeals of the State of California, Second Appellate District, Appellant's Opening Brief, Respondent's Brief, Appellant's Reply Brief, 2nd Civil no. 13774.

IV. The Legal Status of Nixon in the Transaction

The testimony of Nixon reads thus (Tr. p. 8, 1. 17):

"I generally attend to outside matters such as sales on execution and motions on behalf of the *firm of Wingert and Bewley*. I believe that on June 28, 1938, Mr. Bewley was ill at home. While *I had no particular instructions* from Mr. Bewley on the date of sale, it was part of my duty to attend to such sale and it was always my understanding that we were to press . . . such sale and not to grant any further continuances. *Mrs. Schee was not present* at the time of sale and I do not believe I ever talked to her myself."

. . .

V. Aside from the alleged implied authority, are the said findings construing the authority therein set forth as *actual* authority, supported by any substantial evidence whatsoever?

Taking the evidence most favorable to defendants, and assuming that . . . Mrs. Schee actually and personally directed the purchase in her behalf of the Steuer property at the time and place of the sale thereof on execution.[12]

The fundamental facts still remain. Nixon did not come out and say that he himself didn't even talk to her. He said, *"I do not believe* I ever talked to her myself" (emphasis added). His remark shows that he could not admit a mistake.

Judge Alfred Paonessa, who sat on the bench during the first Municipal Court hearing, is now deceased. Joseph W. Vickers, the judge in the subsequent hearings in the District Court of Appeals, State of California, Division One, had no recollection of the hearings whatsoever, although his name appears on the printed briefs.

That judges forget the hundreds of cases they handle is not unusual. Certainly Nixon at that time was not a public figure. What is clear, and can be proved with printed evidence, is that he behaved poorly for his client and was subsequently sued by her. What hasn't been proved is that he presented a motion that provoked the judge, who threatened to refer his behavior to the Bar Association, either for censure or for disbarment. There is, however, credible personal testimony in Wallace's essay (which follows) and in my own interview with Mr. X to corroborate this contention.

On November 2, 1972, a man who prefers to remain anonymous called Bewley of Wingert and Bewley, who had hired Nixon in 1937. Bewley remembered the case. He could not remember Mrs. Schee at all. But he remembered they paid off her mother, Mrs. Emily Force, and he remembered her very well.

He recalled all of the case except he did not remember Richard Nixon had been connected with it. When he was read the documents, including Nixon's own testimony, he was quite surprised.

He did not recall that Nixon was bawled out by the judge. He said he was surprised by that since Nixon always seemed to get along with everyone.

Bewley remembers they gave Mrs. Force $4,000 [$2,245.29 plus legal expenses] because his firm had made a mistake in allowing her daughter's property to be foreclosed.

Mrs. Force had proceeded on Bewley's advice, said Bewley. Her daughter, Mrs. Schee, owned the beneficial interest subject to a first trust deed. The owner of the first trust deed moved to foreclose—which left Mrs. Schee with a worthless second trust deed. . . . Mrs. Schee went to her mother, Mrs. Force, who then bought up the first trust deed.

In 1969, when Nixon was President, Bewley remembered him very well. In 1972, just before his reelection, Bewley failed to recall that Nixon handled the Schee case at all in 1937, 1938, and 1939 and had been reprimanded by the judge. He did remember, however, the settlement made out of court to Mrs. Force because his firm (he didn't mention Nixon's name) had made a mistake in allowing the foreclosure of her property.

Nixon was a young, inexperienced lawyer just out of law school; nevertheless, his lack of ethical concern, his feelings of superiority in handling (actually, mishandling) the case, seem to bear out his feeling of omnipotence, his belief that he could make decisions without taking his client into his confidence. That the firm had to pay out $4,000 in 1940 indicates that Nixon had cost the firm a considerable sum of money and damaged its reputation as well.

When Bewley in 1969 said that Nixon was brilliant, we can only react skeptically. The propaganda machine was already at work, clearing him of any guilt. All we see is the image of a man who desperately wanted to appear perfect, above the law.

Nixon's actions in entering the dean's office at Duke and his mishandling of his first case as a trial lawyer in Whittier are, I believe, of very considerable importance. In both instances a young man, successful in many respects, had acted in a manner that threatened his career. If he had been caught at Duke he might well have been forced to leave law school; his handling of the law case might have caused him to be disbarred, or at least to lose his position. Such actions are those of a man who unconsciously feels undeserving of success and acts in a self-destructive manner.

Judging from Nixon's other activities, it does not seem that his inept handling of his court case had inhibited him. In Whittier, he became extremely active in filling his days. He became president of a service club of men in their twenties, the 20–30 Club; president of the Whittier College Alumni Association by 1938 and a College Board Trustee by 1939; president of the Duke Alumni of California; president of and attorney for a company producing frozen orange juice (the company went bankrupt). The list of activities continued to grow. On June 5, 1938, he registered as a Republican.

Although most public figures are as busy as Nixon, his hyperactivity was an hysterical expression, a repetition of the pattern he had established in high school, college, and law school. Often we find that a person who is compulsive wants to hide a personality defect by constant activity and involvement, so that others are not given a chance to see his deeper feelings and emotions.

During the early years of his career, Nixon was stiffly controlled, the master of any situation, who could rule his emotions as if in doing so he would deny them. In 1938 Nixon's life took on a new dimension. As a member of the Little Theatre group in Whittier he met a pretty California redhead, Thelma Catherine Ryan (whom everyone called Pat), when they were casting for *The Dark Tower*. Pat Ryan had worked her way through college. At this time she was a teacher in Whittier High School.

Nixon's uncle Oscar Marshburn, a member of the school board, told me that he had interviewed Pat for her job and afterward spoke to Richard about this pretty young teacher. Nixon took to Pat immediately and asked her to marry him on the first night they met. Startled by his boldness, Pat said that

Frank Nixon as streetcar conductor (c. 1907).

Hannah Millhous at the age of twenty-three, before her marriage (c. 1908).
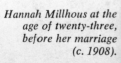

Richard (age two) among pumpkins. Harold in the background, at left.

Richard (age seven) and Arthur (age two) in Yorba Linda (1920).

Harold, Richard, Arthur, and Donald in their Sunday best (c. 1921).

Frank Nixon's gasoline station on Whittier Boulevard in 1923, after a rainstorm. House is at left.

Richard and Harold (date unknown).

Richard Nixon (number 23) with his teammates. Note his serious face, in contrast to the others.

Richard (far right) and Harold (1929 or 1930). The girl at Nixon's side is probably Ola-Florence.

Pat Ryan. This picture is believed to have been taken in 1937, the year she was graduated from the University of Southern California with a B.S. degree in education. (UNIVERSITY OF SOUTHERN CALIFORNIA)

Richard Nixon, air cargo officer in the South Pacific Combat Air Transport Command (SCAT), probably on Green Island (1943).

Seventy-five-year-old Hannah Nixon at her home in La Habra the week before the Republican National Convention in 1960. She told her interviewer, Joe Lewis: "I think Richard will get the nomination but the election . . . it's going to be very, very tough." (WIDE WORLD PHOTOS)

Pat Nixon greets guest at distinguished women's reception in Washington on January 19, 1969, the day before Nixon's inauguration. (NEWSWEEK—TONY ROLLO)

When official White House photographer Ollie Atkins was called to the family quarters of the White House on the evening of August 7, 1974, to photograph the Nixon family, he found it obvious that all three women had been crying. This is the photograph he made at Tricia's suggestion. Left to right, with their arms linked: Edward and Tricia Cox; President and Mrs. Nixon; Julie and David Eisenhower. (PHOTOGRAPH BY OLLIE ATKINS)

Nixon saying goodbye to the White House staff on August 9, 1974. (To the right are Mrs. Nixon, Tricia and Edward Cox.) (UPI)

he must be "nuts." Richard was determined to win Pat's hand, to show her that he was a man, "her" man. Knowing, of course, that Ola-Florence had been married in 1936, a hurt which could not easily be forgotten, he did not want to suffer further rejection. He felt it imperative to win Pat's total and immediate allegiance, just as his father had worked quickly to win Hannah's hand. Unconsciously, he competed with his father. Further, by marrying Pat he could erase his memories of Ola-Florence. It was a way to show that he no longer needed her. And to prove that he no longer loved Ola-Florence, he became Pat's ardent suitor.

Furthermore, they had somewhat similar backgrounds. Both came from poor families. Each had had a difficult childhood. Pat was thirteen years old when her mother died, and as a high school student she had to keep house for her father and two older brothers. William Ryan had been a failure, and had spent some time in the Philippines and Alaska before finally coming to South Dakota, where he married a widow with two children, Katherina Halberstadt Bender, a Connecticut woman born in Germany. Restless, he moved on to Nevada, where he became a miner. He and Katherina had three children; Thelma Catherine was their youngest. In 1916, when Pat was four, her mother persuaded William Ryan to move the family to Artesia, California, about twenty miles from Los Angeles. Pat's father developed silicosis, a disease with symptoms similar to those of tuberculosis, which caused his death two years later. Jessamyn West says that Pat "nursed her father, whose lungs, affected by work in the mines, were probably by then tubercular."[13]

Pat Ryan's youth was a struggle for survival. In 1932 she left for New York, driving a car for an elderly couple. There she found her first job, at Seton Hospital in the Bronx. Later she became an X-ray technician. Her choice of work almost certainly reflects her experience with her own father, who had been afflicted with a lung disease and whom she had so tenderly cared for. After two years of hard work at Seton Hospital, she returned to California and graduated with honors from the University of Southern California. Later she worked as a waitress and salesgirl. Apparently she sought a career in the movies, without much success.

Meager as the information about Pat's father, William Ryan, is, he seems to have been as impulsive a wanderer and

111

as unsuccessful as Nixon's father, Frank. They both roamed the country pursuing the fortune which they never found.

In sharp contrast, Nixon and Pat were hard-working, determined to succeed, and somewhat embittered about their disturbed past.

At the beginning of their relationship Pat had her doubts about Nixon and dated other men. But he was persistent. He even drove her from Whittier to Los Angeles so that she could meet other men she was dating. He would wait for hours and then drive her home. What is remarkable is Nixon's determination to be near her, to control her, and serve her in a useful way. Once again, he was playing the role of a faithful dog.

Any careful observer would find his behavior bizarre and conclude that it was a reflection of doubt about his virility and lack of self-esteem. He certainly showed a strong need for self-punishment, which, in turn, demeaned his real emotions. The persistence he showed in waiting for Pat, his prize, for however long it took to win her was the same trait we later see in Nixon's seeking the presidency of the United States. Once he set his sights on a goal there was nothing that would stop him from achieving it.

We receive the impression that Pat also had a mind of her own, that she was strong and self-disciplined. A school friend remembers her as "very controlled."[14] Even on the most emotional occasions Pat never broke down or let her emotions dominate her behavior. This friend goes on to say, "I saw her at her mother's funeral. She was smiling. She came over to me and said, 'Wasn't mother beautiful?' "

Pat was described as being very pretty, and she still is. Nixon's mother, who met her for the first time after a performance of the Little Theatre group, said, "She was such a beautiful girl. She looked kind of frail to me, but I soon learned that she was a dynamo of energy."[15]

Nixon knew no bounds in trying to win Pat. Since she was fond of ice skating, he was determined to learn to skate, just as a few years earlier he had learned to dance so that he could please Ola-Florence. "But," as a friend recalls, "poor Dick had never skated before. He would go along and hang on the railing. He was serious about it."[16]

We do not know what he told her about his law case. Knowing what its consequences might be, it may very well have been one reason that led him to go to Cuba in 1939 with the

112

idea of establishing a law practice there. But he changed his mind and returned from Cuba to testify as a witness in the Marie Schee court case, which had not yet been settled.

Two years after he and Pat met, she finally made up her mind to marry him. The wedding took place in June 1940 at the Old Mission in Riverside, California.

Why, in view of what we know about the emotional dynamics of Richard Nixon, was he so intent on marriage? His response to Pat was impulsive. She was young and pretty, hard-working and disciplined. She also understood deprivation and shared his seriousness. And Nixon must have been very aware that marriage was expected of young men.

The fact that Richard pursued Pat so relentlessly was no accident. Often a man will marry a woman who physically or emotionally is similar to his mother. Hannah was inwardly strong and controlled, a disciplinarian, and the same was true of Pat. Unconsciously, Nixon established a transference with a young woman similar to his mother. And this choice was different from Ola-Florence, whose gaiety and fun-loving instincts were alien to him. Dating Ola-Florence was a way of rebelling against his mother. Yet unconsciously Richard felt guilty about his feelings for Ola-Florence. How much easier it must have been to pursue Pat, who resembled his mother. Physically Pat was attractive, with her green eyes, red hair, and controlled facial expression. She and Hannah shared many personality traits. Once Nixon said that "Pat is a shy and modest person," but her modesty conceals an iron will and an indomitable spirit.[17]

He might just as well have said this about himself. Even this modesty—a passive quality—is similar to his own reserve and need to provide a check on his aggressions. Like Nixon, Pat was proud, self-disciplined, and not inclined to self-indulgence. Her comment "Even if I were dying, I wouldn't let anyone know"[18] is indicative of her façade of defiance. It also indicates some arrogance, but above all a profound feeling of having been rejected.

Apparently Nixon sought to marry a strong woman who could sustain him, as at times his mother had sustained him. Nixon said of Pat on her fifty-ninth birthday that she is a woman "of great strength of character" and superb sensitivity whose "passion for privacy" prevents her from enjoying all aspects of her role as a First Lady. He also called her a strict disciplinarian.[19]

Pat was a perfectionist and a fighter. And so was he. These qualities appealed to Nixon. They were invaluable traits for a career in politics. Just as Nixon was neat, orderly, exact—perfect—so was Pat.

When interviewed by Jessamyn West, Pat stated that she had never been tired, never been sick, never afraid. When Jessamyn West suggested she must have been completely fatigued after a long trip to Ireland, Pat did not answer, and instead instructed her to write about all the dinners they had attended. Miss West replied that she was not interested in statistics. Pat then snapped, "How can you present me as anything less than perfect?" Her outward appearance seems to confirm Jessamyn West's observation to me: "Pat is hard as nails."

The fact that Nixon married a woman similar to Hannah, a woman described as "hard as flint," tells us much about his psychological needs. Not by nature a warm person capable of sustaining loving relationships, Nixon had been threatened by Ola-Florence's need for love and support. Pat was different. Being in total control of herself meant that she consciously or unconsciously could hide hurt feelings. Like Nixon, she was a performer, an actor—much of her life became a series of performances. Like Nixon, she plays a role because too often she seems to be incapable of spontaneous emotional expression. One has the impression that her face is sculptured—impassive—as if it were a means of protecting herself from dealing with hurt feelings and painful memories of her childhood which have been pushed deep into her unconscious mind. Her smile, appearing fixed, unnatural, seems artificial, something produced for an occasion.

Her anger surfaces rarely. When Gloria Steinem interviewed Mrs. Nixon during the election campaign in 1968, Pat became annoyed by being questioned about her childhood and replied indignantly, "I've never had it easy. I'm not like all you . . . all those people who had it so easy."*[20]

Steinem later told interviewer John Brady:

> I think she was regarding me as part of that world, so when I was asking her questions about her childhood, she was talking about a difficult childhood she had.
> I spent an enormous amount of time telling her also

---

* Nixon used almost the same words in describing his childhood.

about my childhood, trying to connect with her, trying to make it clear to her that we hadn't grown up that differently. I was trying to make some human contact with her . . . So I tried that for quite a long time, which I probably didn't record, and it just didn't work. She just wanted to be the person who had suffered the most. Finally I just let it go. I missed a lot of it also because she got angry.

I think that she was angry because I was asking her what her hopes were, what her dreams had been when she was young, what she wanted to do. She started to say that she hadn't had time for dreams and had always had to work too hard—this whole kind of stream of anger and resentment came out.[21]

Unable to cope with the internal pressure, his need for success, to be on top, to be the star, Nixon, in courting Pat, reverted to an earlier emotional level. He chose a young woman who inwardly was much like his mother, which was a way to repeat his childhood pattern of dependence on a woman. It is not surprising that his pursuit of Pat created conflicts in him. The fact that he sought out an authority figure modeled after a strong and controlling parent who would be strict and single-minded drove the wedge even deeper into his divided personality.

While he *could* have chosen a more relaxed, outgoing woman who would have helped him to develop, he could not exercise a choice, since his pursuit of Pat expressed his unconscious needs. He pursued the girl who satisfied his childhood need for maternal love. Being twenty-five years old when he first met Pat, the emotional needs of a child were still predominant in him. That is not unusual. To overcome all our childish feelings is most difficult, since they are an intimate part of ourselves of which we are largely unaware. Freud once wrote, "In our innermost souls we are all children and remain so throughout life." Since Nixon clung to his childish desire to be close to his mother, he experienced this need as an adult by choosing someone who was much like Hannah. His choice wasn't clear-cut, for it was accompanied by fear and anxiety that Pat might not accept him; he doubted his own manhood; he was depressed, preoccupied, as he had always been.

Childhood anxieties, excessive daydreaming, frustration, fears and anger, depression and brooding, loneliness and need for revenge, do not disappear suddenly, or even little by little, unless there is an overwhelming change in one's personality. But even when these anxieties are overcome the personality may remain blocked. Psychoanalysis offers one means of dealing with these negative emotions. But the success of this process is dependent upon the commitment of the patient to deal with difficult emotions that often have been repressed since childhood. Nixon, up until the time he had married Pat, had neither changed nor undergone psychoanalysis or any other psychiatric treatment.

We see little change in Nixon's personality from his early years in school until his marriage. In 1940 he was still hyperactive, obsessed with oratory, in his legal profession and elsewhere. And he was still acting in the theater. When Pat finally consented to marry him, two years after he had proposed, it was a great personal victory. The fact, however, that he had won her by playing the role of watchman when she went out on dates showed a kind of brutal tenacity—a way to protect what he had come to regard as his own property. He also wanted to protect himself because he feared peer competition; he needed to remain in control of Pat.

It was more important for him to possess someone than to establish an emotional relationship. Because of the great distance, the great disparity, between his ego and his emotions, there were too few feelings to generate genuine affection. After their marriage, Richard and Pat presented the image of the happily married couple. Yet we suspect that he still felt troubled that he might lose her, just as he once had been rejected by Ola-Florence. He was preoccupied, brooding and trying to figure out how to assure his continued mastery over her. We suspect that there was little spontaneity or joy in Nixon's personal life.

Putting Nixon's emotional experiences in perspective, we see a basic inability to express and give love and to receive it. As a child, he felt deprived, alienated, and disillusioned. Having experienced several serious childhood illnesses and accidents, he resented his suffering. He was bitter about the improvidence of his father and the fact that he was compelled to help his mother. What particularly frustrated Nixon was that he had been a "good boy" and yet, despite his academic successes, he felt deeply that he had not been rewarded for his virtue or morality.

The fact that he had done the right thing, like a little boy in his mother's world, made him feel innocent as a man. As the years passed, carrying him from childhood to adolescence and into adulthood, he became increasingly preoccupied with his importance. As he withdrew into the shell of his daydreams, he discerned more evil in others than in himself.

His feelings of being abandoned made him depressed and brought him to the point of despair, where he felt he might just as well overturn the tables, as if to say "the hell with it." For example, when stress became too intense, Nixon panicked and overreacted by vowing, while at Duke, to give up the study of law.

In Nixon, we see a person totally lacking in joy or spontaneity—a sad, depressed individual. He seemed dissatisfied with himself and those around him. He is unhappy in a way I would define as being devoid of happiness.* This kind of unhappiness means being mirthless, cheerless, glum, which probably accounts for his college nickname, "Gloomy Gus." While there may have been moments when Nixon's face showed gaiety, his eyes still reflected cheerlessness and sadness, an expression of his basic emotional state. The *form* of Nixon's unhappiness is that, rather than living in a state of unhappiness, he existed in a void of happiness—in a state of happylessness.

Nixon's deeply buried feelings that his father, and to a lesser degree his mother, were against him had aroused in him a feeling of hate, against both them and himself. He felt that they had rejected him and that he was unworthy of their love. It was this attitude toward his parents that made Richard doubt himself and the motivations of others. It also developed in him a deep mistrust of authority or authority figures, while at the same time he wanted to conform to their dicta.

Feeling neither loved nor likable, Nixon was unable to form a healthy relationship with anyone. Yet wanting also to conform because of his passivity, he desired relationships with others without knowing how to go about it, or how to respond emotionally, spontaneously, to a woman.

The deep gulf between surface and depths, between surface-love and depth-hate, remained within Richard Nixon. It tore

---

* The German word *glücklos*—without happiness—is more descriptive than "devoid of happiness."

117

him apart. It was Nixon against Nixon. Only on the surface
and for a time did he seem to weather his own turmoil. But
the storm which he could neither fathom nor resolve was to
remain within him. Its consequences were to be tragic.

8

"When the war began," Nixon said in *A Self Portrait,* "I enlisted in the Navy and was sent to Quonset Point [Rhode Island] as an officer . . . for officer's training."* When asked why, Nixon answered:

> It seemed to me to be the right thing to do. I could have been a conscientious objector of course, very easily. I say easily because I was a Quaker, a "birthright Quaker" as we are called and I had no . . . I would have had no legal problems whatever and then I could have engaged in other activities during the war such as my uncle [Oscar Marshburn] and others had during World War I, Red Cross and other activities. But I just had a different attitude toward the great problems that we confronted at that time. I was a student of history in my own right. I didn't just take everything from my mother and my grandmother and my father and their ideas and I was convinced that with this great threat of worldwide aggression across the globe, that no one could stand aside.[2]

Actually, in January 1942, Nixon went to work for the Office of Price Administration in Washington, D.C., for half a year until he apparently became disgusted with the bureaucratic machinery of government and with the tedious job of tire rationing. It was only at that point—in either June or August 1942,† not "when the war began" in December 1941

* It may well have been that his distaste for the bureaucracy had grown so great, and also because he was angry at those people at the top who had carved out business for themselves, that at the time he gave his *Self Portrait* he had completely forgotten about his job with the OPA.[1]
† *The Daily News* of Whittier, November 2, 1945, reported that he enlisted in August 1942, whereas the official Navy files quoted below give the date as June 15, 1942.

—that he enlisted in the U.S. Naval Reserve.[3] His campaign version had more appeal, both from a political and public relations point of view. To say that he joined the Navy in response to the "call of duty" instead of mentioning his previous OPA job made him appear patriotic.

Nixon the politician wanted to put himself in the best light, but his explanation is hard to accept, particularly his statement that "no one could stand aside." Nixon was incapable of making a firm commitment based on personal conviction.

But Nixon's duplicity went further. When he says in his speech, "I could have been a conscientious objector," and adds: "of course, very easily . . . because I was a Quaker, a 'birthright Quaker,'" we must question his true belief and attitude. Nixon married a woman who, although of Catholic heritage, was without religious affiliation,[4] and their wedding did not take place in the East Whittier Church, where it was traditional for Quakers in the community to be married. Nor do we know whether the marriage was approved by the members of the Friends, a prerequisite for any devout Quaker. Nixon's commitment to Quakerism is open to question.

Yet Nixon, like many others, may have been afraid to enlist in the war and risk death. Since his two brothers had died from tuberculosis, his fear of death was, I believe, uncommonly strong. He was in good health; yet he feared death. As Ola-Florence had once mentioned, Nixon was afraid that he too might get tuberculosis, which he suspected would be fatal. That he was abnormally afraid of dying we can also conclude from his preoccupation with crises and the ways to solve them, as he describes in *Six Crises*. A man's crises are keys to his personality. People don't usually think about "crises" unless they are afraid that something serious might happen. And the conscious and unconscious fear of death is worse than anything that might actually happen.

Nixon felt ambivalent about going to war and did not engage in direct combat. The official U.S. Navy report on Nixon's war record provided by the Navy Office of Information, dated May 21, 1969 (after Nixon had assumed the presidency), states in part:

On June 15, 1942, he accepted an appointment as a Lieutenant (junior grade) in the U.S. Naval Reserve, and was promoted to Lieutenant, October 1, 1943; and to Lieutenant Commander, from October 3, 1945. Since the war he has been promoted to Commander to date from June 1, 1953.

Following his appointment in the U.S. Naval Reserve in 1942, he had aviation indoctrination training at the Naval Training School, Naval Air Station, Quonset Point, Rhode Island. Upon completing the course there in October 1942 he had duty until May 1943 at the Naval Reservè Aviation Base, Ottumwa, Iowa, as Aide to the Executive Officer. He then reported to Commander Air Force, U.S. Pacific Fleet, and was assigned as Officer in Charge of the South Pacific Combat Air Transport Command at Guadalcanal and later at Green Islands.

For this service he received a Letter of Commendation from the Commander South Pacific Area and South Pacific Force for "meritorious and efficient performance of duty as Officer in Charge of the South Pacific Combat Air Transport Command. . . ." The citation continues: "He displayed sound judgment and initiative in organizing the South Pacific Combat Air Transport Command at both Bougainville and Green Islands. He established the efficient liaison which made possible the immediate supply by air of vital material and key personnel, and the prompt evacuation of battle casualties from these stations to rear areas."

Between August and December 1944 he was assigned to Fleet Air Wing Eight [in Alameda, California], and thereafter until March 1945 was attached to the Bureau of Aeronautics, Navy Department, Washington, D.C. He next served as Bureau of Aeronautics Contracting Officer for terminations in the Office of the Bureau of Aeronautics General Representative, Eastern District, headquartered in New York, New York. Released from active duty on March 10, 1946, he was transferred to the Retired Reserve on June 1, 1966.

In addition to the Commendation Ribbon, Commander Nixon has the American Campaign Medal; Asiatic-Pacific Campaign Medal; and the World War II Victory Medal. He is entitled to two engagement stars on the Asiatic-Pacific Campaign Medal for (1) supporting air action in Treasury-Bougainville operations (October 27–December 15, 1943) and (2) consolidation of the northern Solomons (Bougainville) (December 15, 1943–July 22, 1944).

The same Navy Office of Information record describes Nixon from January to August 1942 as an attorney for the Office of Emergency Management in Washington, D.C. As we know, he was working for the OPA.

I have been provided with different information about Nixon's war record from Philip Mayher, who served as senior lieutenant at Ottumwa, Iowa, from about the beginning of February 1943 to about January 1944. Mayher remembers that Nixon, a junior lieutenant, was an aide to Lieutenant Commander Turner, and that Nixon was still there when Mayher received his orders to go overseas in January or February 1944. According to this information, Nixon cannot have left to go overseas before the beginning of 1944. Another person, who prefers to remain anonymous, believes Nixon came to the South Pacific islands in October or November 1943. Although my informants differ by about two months, in any event Nixon cannot have been in the South Pacific area in the late spring of 1943, as he and the Navy release claim. My unnamed source told me that Nixon could not have been in Bougainville at the time he has given since he was with Nixon at Vella Lavella from October or November 1943 until February or March 1944. As to the medals Nixon received, the same informant told me that "they gave them out in carloads." [5] Although Nixon has claimed that "he was there when the bombs fell" on the Green Islands, the fighting had been over for six weeks when he arrived.* As a matter of

---

* Accounts of the fighting in the area demonstrate this:

Warned by a search plane that the Express was en route, Moosbrugger's destroyers entered Vella Gulf from the south at 2200, August 6 [1943] . . . A little before midnight, four enemy destroyers, three of them crowded with troops for Vila, entered the Gulf from the north and soon registered themselves on American radar scopes. . . . Just as the torpedoes struck their targets, both American divisions opened up with gunfire. Under this neatly timed triple blow, the three troop-carrying destroyers exploded, hurling 1,800 soldiers and sailors into the water and creating such a pyrotechnical display that PT boatmen 30 miles away in Kula Gulf thought a volcano had erupted on Kolombangara. . . . None of the American vessels were damaged.[6]
Further:

In mid-August the Third Amphibious Force, now headed by Rear Admiral Theodore S. Wilkinson, by-passed heavily reinforced Kolombangara and landed 6,000 troops on lightly held Vella Lavella—under cover of Airsols fighters operating from the newly captured airstrip at Munda. . . . On November 1 Wilkinson by-passed the complex of enemy bases on and near southern Bougainville and landed 14,000 troops halfway up Bougainville's weakly defended west coast at Cape

fact, Nixon never saw any fighting. Even his favorite biographer, Bela Kornitzer, says that Nixon's group "was not exactly a combat unit." [9] He was assigned to move from island to island with supplies behind the advancing line. The statement he later made to the Republican Committee in Whittier in 1945 about talking to many GI's "in the foxholes" was a fabrication. There were no foxholes for him. One of his fellow officers in the Pacific says that the work was "so much of nothing. It was very boring, the air filled with mosquitoes and awful humidity. In the evening the land crabs crept over the roads so the cars skidded on the roads."

According to one of his peers, Richard Nixon, when he was in the Navy "was a solitary type, a loner. He isn't the type to have friends . . . he cannot open up. . . . He didn't talk about his family, his wife; it was as if all this was a matter of great secrecy, keeping up a front and not getting too close to anyone . . . he was afraid of becoming involved with anyone, even as a friend because then he would have to reveal something of himself."

Since life in the South Pacific, as Thomas Heggen described it in *Mister Roberts,* was for the most part inordinately tedious, possibly Nixon's most significant wartime activity was poker. He had learned how to play the game in college; he also played at Duke Law School and became a skillful gambler. A man who served in the Pacific with Nixon and who wishes his name withheld describes Nixon as a superb player:

> He was one of the best poker players I have ever seen because of his very personality. He had a poker face, he had extraordinary self-discipline which, being the type he was, would be quite logical with his personality. Poker is a game of strategy and discipline. His great poker games were on the Green Islands.

His ability at poker should not surprise us. Able to con-

Torokina, in Empress Augusta Bay.[7]
Following the occupation of Bougainville, the Green Islands were invaded on January 10, 1944. The Green Islands "were inhabited by some 1200 Melanesians, who were so friendly to us and so hostile to the Japanese that in the operation plan the usual preliminary naval and air bombardment was omitted." The "last air opposition encountered by the Green Islands landing force, except for single night bombers," occurred on February 15, 1944.[8]

centrate and to bluff, he won every night. He began to smoke cigars and had one or two drinks in the evening. One evening he bluffed when he was holding only two deuces and won fifteen hundred dollars. He confided to my informant that he had won about seven to eight thousand dollars in the Pacific, a substantial amount, which he later used in the 1946 congressional campaign.

Bluffing in poker is a laudable skill. Certainly Nixon had come a long way from his strict religious home, where drinking and card playing were considered sinful and forbidden. Even if he disliked or disapproved of poker, there was one aspect of it which had inordinate appeal to Nixon—winning. The money—a little godless, perhaps—was good, very good. But to win, to be the best, was a yearning that he had had since childhood, and he felt emotionally gratified to be the best in poker. Nixon had a compulsion to win at poker which took precedence over his rigid, religious upbringing.

Yet we suspect that Nixon may have had conflicting feelings about the game, since playing cards, especially for money, was gambling. Only "tramps" and "bums" did it—words he must have heard time and time again from his grandmother, Almira, and his parents. Nixon says of his grandmother, Almira Milhous (who died in 1943 at the age of ninety-four), that she had "great concern for people who were less fortunate. It was often said . . . that no tramp ever came to the door and got turned away."[10] Tramps were destitute persons. "Tramp" and "bum" were names Nixon had been called by his impulsive father. These scolding, hostile expressions Nixon would use repeatedly against students and others who between 1967 and 1971 vigorously protested and demonstrated against the American involvement in the Vietnam War and the invasion of Cambodia.

It is clear that Nixon, from early childhood, was at war within himself. Even when he played poker at Bougainville, he felt guilty about winning money by bluffing. Since he had a strong need to be considered "one of the boys" he smoked, drank, played cards—he assumed their values, more secular and profane than his own. He attempted to identify with them, to break away from his mother's binding influence and to become, so to speak, "his own man."

Through card playing, Nixon was able to work off some of his aggressions. It was also lucrative. Gambling, although Nixon surely didn't realize it, may have served as a form of psychotherapy. But the most conspicuous benefit was that it made him a "big man." People looked up to him, he became the focus of attention, and this brought satisfaction. We suspect, however, that Nixon was disturbed by his success at poker. He felt trapped between a need to excel and to be a "bad boy," and an equally strong need to be a "good boy," following Hannah's dictates.

Still caught up in this childhood conflict between repression and the need to be the center of attention, Nixon's instinct was to remain secretive. Yet his ego pulled him in the opposite direction. His need to be outwardly a "big man" later—a politician—came to affect his passive feelings. Once he made the choice to become a public figure, he became, as he himself said, "an introvert in a highly extroverted profession."

I have used the word "choice" with reservation. Did Nixon really have a choice? I think not. His need to call attention to himself had developed from a deep-seated oral complex which made him crave control and power through the use of his mouth. Becoming a politician was an instinctive and almost inevitable response to a deep oral need that was a predominant feature of his personality.

Nixon described his first political step in *A Self Portrait:*

> When I was stationed in Middle River, Maryland,* I was settling the contracts, the huge Navy contracts for the Martin Mars . . . that was the big flying boat . . . at that time I received a wire from an old friend, the banker in our home town of Whittier, California, who had incidentally gone to college with my mother at Whittier, saying we're looking for candidates to run for Congress. Would you like to come out and appear along with several others before a committee that's trying to endorse a candidate? And I flew out there, made a ten-minute speech before the committee, flew back to Middle River, Maryland, and within a week they informed me that I had been selected from among the candidates to receive their endorsement and I was off, and from there it was all just smooth sailing, almost.[11]

* The official Navy record reports that he was stationed in New York City, although he may have been assigned to work in Maryland.

Considering that Nixon was withdrawn, hostile, and unable to get along with others, it might seem remarkable that he sought a career in politics. Even Kissinger, who has known Nixon for a long time, has said, "I have never understood how he became a politician."[12]

It stands to reason that Nixon's overwhelming desire to become a politician was based not only on his oral fixation but also on a need to control external events and situations. Politics would help him get away from his inner conflicts; it made it possible for him to believe that he would thus be able to escape his emotional problems. He could assume a public role without having to deal with the private self.

When Nixon says that he received a wire from an old friend, we suspect that he played a role in being sent this invitation. The fact that the offer to run for public office came from a college friend of Hannah's suggests that she too may have had a hand in the matter; she was a controlling parent and had strong ambitions for her son.

The Daily News of Whittier tells of Nixon's meeting on November 2, 1945, with the Republican Candidate and Fact-Finding Committee to propose a candidate* for the Twelfth Congressional District:

> The final speaker was Lt. Richard Nixon, of this city, who appeared in the uniform, since he is now on short leave from the navy. He expressed his appreciation for having been given an opportunity to address the committee, and outlined two definite opinions now held as to what constitutes the American system. "One advocated by the New Deal is government control in regulating our lives," said Mr. Nixon. "The other calls for individual freedom and all that initiative can produce. I hold with the latter viewpoint. I believe the returning veterans, and I have talked to many of them in the foxholes, will not be satisfied with a dole or a government handout. They want a respectable job in private industry where they will be recognized for what they produce, or they want the opportunity to start their own business.
>
> "If the choice of this committee comes to me I will

* The specifications for the candidate were: "He must be a veteran, young and personable, with some education. He must be a Republican in favor of state owenrship of Tidelands . . . and opposed to government controls and other forms of 'New Deal Socialism.' "[13]

be prepared to put on an aggressive and vigorous campaign on a platform of practical liberalism and with your help I feel very strongly that the present incumbent can be defeated. Anyway I would welcome the opportunity to have a part in returning this great district to the Republican party."14

Nixon, on short leave from the Navy, appeared in uniform at a time when the war had been over for three months. The uniform may have helped him to make a good impression on the committee. We know that his reference to "foxholes" is specious. The importance, however, of his presentation was that it revealed Nixon's uncanny ability to dramatize himself and thus to create the desired political impression. It was a calculated effort to manufacture an image of himself as a patriotic, virile figure. And he had added, "I will be prepared to put on a vigorous and aggressive campaign." He was chosen to be the Republican candidate.

It was to be more than an aggressive campaign. Jerry Voorhis, who had served ten years in the House, was his Democratic adversary; he was well-to-do, and Nixon, still resenting his childhood poverty, had one more reason to be angry at the opponent he was chosen to challenge. Using his debating skills against Voorhis to win all the points he could, just as he had done during his school and college years, he considered the victor to be the one who scored the most points. Oratory was his way of releasing aggression. He decided to achieve a total victory in the election against the capable New Deal lawyer who had graduated Phi Beta Kappa from Yale.

He began his campaign attack by charging that Voorhis was a front for un-American elements, that the CIO Political Action Committee, which had campaign funds at its disposal and which, he stated, followed Communistic principles and goals, had endorsed Voorhis. In fact, Voorhis had specifically stated that he did not want any such endorsement—and it had never been offered. Another method of attack he used in the campaign was to telephone thousands of voters in the district and say: "This is a friend of yours but I can't tell you my name. I just want to tell you that Jerry Voorhis is a Communist."15

By using the "big lie," Nixon was able to trick people into believing that Voorhis was a Communist sympathizer; with his dirty tactics, he won handsomely by a margin of 15,000 votes.

In his mind, by defeating Voorhis he defeated Yale University, the eastern establishment, and a man of means. As a result of this vicious campaign, Voorhis was politically destroyed, never to run again for public office. Yet Nixon, with his smear techniques, made himself victim as well as victor. Nixon's resort to falsehoods and slander continued the erosion of his inner self, his ability to judge things objectively, even himself.

For Nixon it was an exciting campaign. He said in *A Self Portrait:*

> . . . And of course that first campaign . . . I've been in many others, but it was the most exciting of all. I remember getting the campaign news when I knew I was elected to the Senate and when I knew we'd won in 1952 and all the rest, but there's nothing like winning the first one.[16]

"Winning the first one," as Nixon put it, reminds me of the way women talk about having their first baby. To Nixon his first election was the most exciting of all elections. It stirred him up, awakened him to the realization that he had been accepted. But there was more to it than that—his being elected was almost like a miracle. He had given birth to a congressman!

During the campaign, he and Pat spent half their money: their wartime savings and, of course, his poker winnings. His gambling had begun to pay off handsomely. This first campaign, like others to follow, reveals Richard Nixon's instinct for the jugular. He viewed political opponents as deadly adversaries. In his campaign against Voorhis he was out for the kill, as if destroying the "man" was his primary mission rather than providing genuine political leadership. It is clear that his repressed hostility against his father and mother made him fight as an adult as he had in his childhood. His political behavior reveals how intense his outwardly directed aggressiveness and hostility were, and how desperately he felt he had to win. His emotional state made it impossible for him to view his opponents objectively; opponents were personal and threatening.

The strategy Nixon used in this first campaign (with the firm and slick guidance of Murray Chotiner) was to destroy the credibility of his opponent by associating him or her with groups and activities that were beginning to be considered "un-American." This strategy, which was to be used again, also served to make Nixon into a political hero, a patriot strongly committed to the preservation of the American system of law and order. The result of Nixon's aggressive and devious campaign was that when he became a freshman congressman in 1947 he had called attention to himself. His hysterical need had brought success. He was a man to be reckoned with. He was appointed to the House Committee on Un-American Activities, replacing Voorhis, who had served on that same committee.

The issue of Communism was especially appealing to Nixon in furthering his ambition to attract nationwide attention to himself as the protector of American democracy. It was an issue that reinforced his mother's staunch ethical code and projected an image of himself as a crusader.

The story of Nixon and Alger Hiss is fascinating, particularly since it again reveals the strategy Nixon consistently used to destroy the reputation of opponents.

In *Six Crises,* Nixon says that David Whittaker Chambers appeared before the House Committee on Un-American Activities on August 3, 1948, and gave the names of four members of his underground Communist group, "whose purpose, he said, was *not* espionage [emphasis added] but rather 'Communist infiltration of the American government.'" He goes on to say, "This was the first time I had ever heard of either Alger or Donald Hiss."[17] This statement, I believe, is untrue.

In a letter dated April 26, 1974, addressed to Alger Hiss, Peter H. Irons, then of the Department of Sociology, Boston State College, Boston, Massachusetts, wrote:

> I'm writing you because my research turned up some material relating to your case which I thought you might not have known. Let me summarize it for you. In the files of Francis P. Matthews at the Truman Library I found material indicating that Matthews, who in the early 1940s was chairman of the Chamber of Commerce's Committee on Socialism and Communism, had secretly hired ([illegible] in 1946) a Catholic priest named Father John F. Cronin to prepare a series of pamphlets for the Chamber to use in stimulating a national anti-communist campaign directed both at the federal government and

businessmen. Father Cronin, who taught at a Catholic seminary in Baltimore and had been involved with CIO labor organizing campaigns in the late 1930s and early 1940s, had been approached in 1941 by two agents of the FBI, one of whom was William C. Sullivan. Sullivan had learned that Father Cronin was collecting data on communist involvement in the labor movement, and he asked Father Cronin to share this data with the FBI. In return, Sullivan offered to supply Father Cronin, on a confidential basis, with FBI material on communist activities in the federal government.

Father Cronin's work led in 1944 to a series of reports incorporating this material, which he circulated to a number of Catholic bishops. In turn, the bishops, through their national body, asked Father Cronin to devote an entire year to preparing a report for them on communism in America and the response of the Catholic church to it. Father Cronin spent all of 1945 preparing this report, which was circulated at the end of 1945, with each bishop receiving one numbered copy. The report, which had never been shown to any scholar until Father Cronin showed me his copy in 1971, included allegations taken from FBI files which were based on the FBI interviews with Whittaker Chambers (although he was identified only as an "editor of a national magazine"). The report identified you, John Abt and Lee Pressman as members of a communist group in the government, and said that Chambers had vowed to "expose" you as a communist agent if you were named as Secretary General of the UNO.

One copy of the report was shown by a bishop to Francis Matthews (later named by Truman as Secretary of the Navy, from which post he was removed in 1950 for advocating nuclear attack on the Soviet Union; his punishment was appointment as Ambassador to Ireland). Matthews, in his role with the Chamber of Commerce, hired Father Cronin in early 1946 to prepare the pamphlet series mentioned above. In preparing these pamphlets, Cronin received additional material from FBI files as well as from HUAC and State Department files supplied by Benjamin Mandel, who had worked in both agencies (spending 1945 and 1946 in the State Department security office and then returning to HUAC). The pamphlets were cited by the FBI in their testimony before the President's Temporary Commission on Employee Loyalty in late 1946 and early 1947 as verification of the FBI's allegations of communist infiltration of government.

Another copy of Father Cronin's 1945 report to the bishops was shown to Congressman Charles Kersten, a Wisconsin Republican and member of the House Education and Labor Committee. *Early in 1947* [emphasis added], Kersten met a newly-appointed member of the Committee, Richard Nixon, who was also, as you know, a member of the HUAC. Kersten has written to me that Nixon asked him early in 1947 to recommend an authority on communism, since Nixon had become interested in Kersten's investigation of the Allis-Chalmers strike (which took place in Kersten's district) and wanted to find a communist angle to pursue on his own. Kersten recommended that Nixon meet Father Cronin and Monsignor Fulton Sheen and set up meetings for Nixon with both of them.

Father Cronin told me that beginning in early 1947 he provided Nixon with much of the data he had received from the FBI, and helped prepare Nixon for the hearings before which you appeared in 1948. He did not tell me directly that he gave Nixon material received from William C. Sullivan and Benjamin Mandel, but left me with that implication. This would account for Nixon's detailed knowledge of your life, in spite of Nixon's claim in *Six Crises* that he first heard of you on the day Chambers first testified before the HUAC in August, 1948. It seems likely to me that Father Cronin either provided Nixon with this data or referred him to Sullivan and/or Mandel, both of whom had access to FBI and State Department files and the interviews with Chambers.[18]

When Nixon innocently said, "This was the first time I had ever heard of either Alger or Donald Hiss," he had either forgotten or he was not telling the truth. It must be noted that as a member of HUAC he had, during the summer of 1948, been investigating Communist espionage in the United States government.

I believe it is not farfetched to say that it was Representative Nixon, not Senator Joseph McCarthy, who first dramatized the issue of Communism in this period of our history. It was Nixon who exploited the issue on a national scale; McCarthy expanded and widened the scope of the fear-mongering.

Evidence of this suggestion is found in the speech Nixon gave before the House of Representatives on January 26, 1950.[19] In it, among other things, he says:

The Great Lesson

The great lesson which should be learned from the Alger Hiss case is that we are not just dealing with espionage agents who get 30 pieces of silver to obtain the blueprints of a new weapon—the Communists do that too—but this is a far more sinister type of activity, because it permits the enemy to guide and shape our policy; it disarms and dooms our diplomats to defeat in advance before they go to conferences; traitors in the high councils of our own Government make sure that the deck is stacked on the Soviet side of the diplomatic table.

Compare this with McCarthy's Lincoln Day speech in Wheeling, West Virginia, two weeks later:

I have in my hand 205 cases of individuals who would appear to be either card carrying members or certainly loyal to the Communist Party, but nevertheless are still helping to shape our foreign policy.

One thing to remember in discussing the Communists in our Government is that we are not dealing with spies who get 30 pieces of silver to steal the blueprints of a new weapon. We are dealing with a far more sinister type of activity because it permits the enemy to guide and shape our policy.[20]

Nixon had personal reasons to arouse the American people to the danger they allegedly faced. He was at that time longing for an issue which could attract and hold the attention of the American public. He needed a dramatic one and found it—Communism. In advocating an anti-Communist drive he was over-arousing, proclaiming and over-proclaiming, debating and over-debating, just as his father had done. He had to be combative like his father, who "was willing to debate anybody, anytime and on any subject."[21]

But there was more to it than finding espionage agents. Nixon accused the Truman administration of providing a cover for agents. What is ironic about this accusation is that he falsely charged the Truman administration with the kind of irregularities that brought down his own administration twenty-five years later. The elaborate attempts of the Nixon administration to cover up its misdeeds showed a flagrant disregard for the law.

There is a significant pattern in Nixon's behavior as a politician. Because of his aggressiveness, a cover-up for his own passivity, which he had to deny at every turn, he felt he had to inject himself into every matter. His low frustration level, coupled with his underlying desire to call attention to himself, brought him into conflict with decency and with the law. Up to the point of the initial indictments on December 15, 1948, one could not be sure whether Chambers, Hiss, or both were to be indicted. That Hiss was indicted by a margin of one vote cast by twenty-three grand jurors leads me to question the credibility of his indictment.[22] Highly disturbed and disappointed about the hung jury in the first Hiss trial on July 8, 1949, Nixon requested on July 12, 1949, that the presiding judge, Samuel H. Kaufman, be impeached because he had been "prejudiced for the defense and against the prosecution," alleging that "the judge's favoritism was obvious and apparent."[23] "The jury's 8–4 vote for conviction came frankly as a surprise to me."[24] Nixon had become both prosecutor and judge; he spearheaded Republican demands in Congress for investigation of the trial judge.

Wanting immediate gratification and deprived of his longstanding desire to "get" Hiss, a representative of the eastern establishment, Nixon was incapable of controlling his anger. Because he wanted revenge, he was anxious to investigate the judge rather than face the fact that the Hiss jury had been unable to convict—to reach the required unanimous decision. Nixon couldn't abide failure. He *had* to win.

He attacked the judge's rulings in Hiss's first trial, and wanted another judge appointed for the second trial. This is an unusual procedure; yet Nixon exerted strong pressure from his congressional seat. And when Judge Henry M. Goddard, who presided at the second trial, ruled contrary to Nixon's opinions, Nixon objected.

At the time of the second Hiss trial in November 1949– January 1950, Nixon had already decided to run in California for the Senate against Helen Gahagan Douglas.[25] She was a member of Congress and was on the Committee on Foreign Affairs. Acclaimed for her beauty, intelligence, and many achievements, she had supported the New Deal and was an ardent admirer of Franklin Roosevelt. Nixon, arguing that state socialism was the same as Communism, viciously distorted her political position (as he had Voorhis'), characterized her as the "Pink Lady," and compared her voting record (printed on pink paper) with that of New York congressman Vito Marcantonio, whom he described as a "notorious Communist party-liner."[26] In the campaign he didn't mention that he himself had voted several times with Marcantonio. In order to smear Mrs. Douglas, however, he suggested that there was a sinister "Douglas-Marcantonio Axis."

Nixon's highly organized and vicious campaign paid off well. He won by more than 680,000 votes out of 3.5 million cast. One somewhat innocuous but revealing campaign device was repeated in several small California towns. Before Nixon began a speech, he distributed ten large placards, each with a single letter, which, when held up by the audience in proper sequence, spelled out I LIKE NIXON. Although the crowds were small, the impact was effective when the audience held up the placards and the slogan "I like Nixon" appeared. Nixon had a compelling need to be liked.

The Hiss case was complex indeed. He was convicted on January 21, 1950, at the second trial, on two counts: perjury and denying to a federal grand jury that he had turned over State Department papers to Whittaker Chambers, a confessed Communist spy courier. Hiss was sentenced to five years' imprisonment and served three years and eight months.*

What concerns us is the decisive role Nixon played in the case. Why was Nixon so hostile to Hiss, so sympathetic to Chambers? We do not know why Nixon identified so closely with Chambers. Chambers, who suffered from depressions, was a poor boy whose parents didn't get along and whose mother, like Nixon's, "began to bake cakes for sale" to earn a modest living. His brother committed suicide. His childhood was traumatic. He was a homosexual. Whether these facts

---

* Although he was disbarred in 1952, on August 5, 1975, the Massachusetts Supreme Court found that he had demonstrated "moral and intellectual fitness" and should be readmitted to the bar.

contributed to their closeness we may never know, but it is clear that Chambers became a means of attacking Hiss.

We know from *Six Crises* that during these months Nixon spent much time with Chambers. He says:

> To avoid any publicity, I made the two-hour trip from Washington to his farm by car. We sat on some dilapidated rocking chairs on his front porch overlooking the rolling Maryland countryside. It was the first of many long and rewarding conversations I was to have with him during the period of the Hiss case, and through the years until his death in 1961.[27]

Why did Nixon want to avoid publicity when he visited Chambers? Why did he keep his conversations with him secret? Why didn't he talk with Hiss, a point brought out in Hiss's book, *In the Court of Public Opinion*? We are left with the impression that at an early point, and without all the evidence, Nixon had made up his mind that Hiss was guilty.*

To understand the relationship between attacker and victim in the two Hiss trials we must be clear about Nixon's role in the events. First, one is struck with Chambers' unusual ability to recall details about documents, rugs, and so forth. Too many events were remembered in detail twelve years after they had occurred. One wonders whether Chambers was not given details, or had his memory refreshed by the FBI, or even by Nixon himself. Chambers kept changing his story, and adding details. Chambers is described as having an excellent mind, but to recall so exactly details about his relationship to Hiss and Hiss's wife is highly suspect. We also are led to question to what extent, if any, mental pathology was present in Chambers' involvement with Hiss.

It would seem that from about 1935 until 1949 Chambers, consciously or unconsciously, pursued Hiss very much like a jilted lover. It may have been that Nixon's unflagging interest was not only to find out which one of the two told the truth but also the *secret* of their association. According to Nixon,

---

* When Chambers took his son to Washington, D.C., to appear on *Meet the Press*, on August 27, 1948, Nixon, somewhat upset by speculation that Hiss and Chambers owned the same property in Westminster, Maryland, introduced the boy to newsmen with the startling announcement: "This is Mr. Hiss's young son."

135

Hiss tried to conceal the truth, a point clearly brought out in *Six Crises:*

> . . . I continued to appraise the testimony of both Hiss and Chambers. I knew that we had reached the critical breaking point in the case. Timing now became especially important.

He goes on to say:

> If Hiss's story about Crosley [Chambers] were true, why had he not disclosed it to the Committee when he first appeared in public session? Why had he first tried so desperately to divert the Committee from questioning him on the facts Chambers had previously testified to? The longer I thought about the evidence, the more I became convinced that if Hiss had concocted the Crosley story, we would be playing into his hands by *delaying**
> [emphasis added] the public confrontation until August 25, thus giving him nine more days to make his story fit the facts. With his great influence within the Administration and among some of his friends in the press, he might be able to develop an enormous weight of public opinion to back up his story and to obscure the true facts in the case. The more I thought about it, the more I became convinced that we should not delay the confrontation. *Only the man who was not telling the truth would gain by having additional time to build up his case* [emphasis added].[28]

Apparently Nixon understood Hiss's dilemma. Unconsciously, Nixon's need to discover the secret tie between Hiss and Chambers became the major reason for his concern with the case.

Nixon felt that Communism threatened the country because it controlled its adherents completely. It was this kind of control which he himself unconsciously wanted to command.

Communism in America was subversive, it worked covertly to overthrow the United States government, just as Nixon himself would do when he became President. Nixon was obsessive in his concern with people whom he thought were

---

* Nixon's remark that timing was especially important is significant in view of the 1974 impeachment proceedings, which he tried to delay.

secretly working against the United States. Nixon was drawn to Communists, fascinated by their secret life, because, like himself, they were secretive and wanted mastery over others.*

Nixon had a hidden side to his life which made him unconsciously identify with political subversives. And Hiss too was that way, he thought, although Hiss had not admitted to it. People work covertly because they are afraid to come out in the open with their thoughts or ideas; they hide their real intentions. They keep them private as if they were embedded in the unconscious. One may ask whether Nixon, by his early and constant preoccupation with probing into suspected subversive people, was probing into his own unconscious mind. Was he, too, somehow subversive in his thoughts or ideas? Psychology tells us that deep down each of us has antisocial or criminal tendencies. Under intense pressure or conflict everyone wishes to act out his hostile emotions by stealing, hurting, raping, or even killing. The need to rebel, to strike back, is very strong in each of us. And this is true despite all outward appearances to the contrary. Our unconscious has its own wishes and desires, its own hopes, fears and hates, and fantasies, regardless of how sharply they are controlled by the conscious mind. Goethe once said that "there was no existent crime the inclination toward which he could not trace within himself."

Nixon's relentless drive against the Communists, the subversives in and outside the government, was not accidental. His anger against them was deeply rooted in his own hostility, the part that was mostly beyond his control, but which nevertheless directed his tireless efforts to destroy the secret enemy. One may well say that in his efforts to destroy Hiss he was also trying to destroy the secret enemy within himself, the secret tendencies of wanting to revolt against all the rules society and authority had imposed upon him and which he had inwardly rebelled against, but with which he outwardly went along.

The reason he was so vicious in his attack on the "subversives" was his fear of them! To a large extent, he feared his own unconscious hostilities against any government. From Nixon's own mostly unconscious and early interest in subver-

---

* It was at this time in 1950 that Nixon was covertly receiving his own secret campaign slush fund which was not made known until September 1952.

sive activities, we gain a clue to his later almost monomaniacal fight against anything he thought was subversive. This position, which he assumed as President, made him feel, however incorrectly, that he was the supreme arbiter of right and wrong.

His fight against Hiss became a crusade against the secretiveness in Hiss, and some twenty-five years later Nixon unconsciously carried on the same crusade against Daniel Ellsberg. It was also a fight to preserve his own secrets. It too was Nixon against Nixon.

In 1950, people were unaware that Nixon had any secrets. In 1952, however, when he was nominated as Vice-President to run with General Eisenhower, the nation's press eagerly sought to find out more about Nixon. The New York *Post* in September 1952 was the first newspaper to reveal the existence of a "secret Nixon fund." The research had been carried out by four reporters

> . . . who had been looking for background information on the Republican vice-presidential nominee. The reporters were Leo Katcher of the New York *Post*, Richard Donovan of *The Reporter* magazine, Ernest Breasher of the Los Angeles *Daily News*, and Peter Edson, columnist for Newspaper Enterprise Association, a feature syndicate belonging to Scripps-Howard interests.
>
> Edson wrote the story after interviewing Nixon the Sunday before the story appeared. "He told me the basic facts and said it was all right to use them," Edson explained later.[29]

Nixon was accused of an illegal act which he had kept secret—precisely what he had accused the Communists of.[30] Nixon shook with rage because he had been caught with "his fingers in the cookie jar."

He wrote about the charges in *Six Crises:*

> . . . [Since 1950 a political fund . . . had been set up by my supporters in California. It was used to pay expenses for travel, printing and mailing of speeches, and extra clerical help—expenses which were strictly political in character and for which, therefore, I could not properly be reimbursed by the government. The fund had been set up after my election to the Senate in 1950. Dana

Smith, my Finance Chairman in that campaign, handled the collections and disbursements as trustee.[31]

When asked whether he had received a $20,000 supplement to his salary, he replied that the speculation was "completely false."[82]

Why were Nixon and his supporters so secretive about the slush fund? Why didn't they make it public if, as Nixon said, the expenses were "strictly political in character"?

His claim that the slush fund was to pay for political expenses was devious. Who could say that the fund was not also to help him personally? Nixon concluded, "It never occurred to me that from such an innocent beginning would grow the most scarring personal crisis of my life."[83]

The disclosure, which questioned Nixon's integrity, threatened his political career. It was like a threat from the overwhelming authority of his childhood—his parents. He had to strike back.

The events are recounted in Nixon's *Six Crises*. He had to appear on television—go to the public—to proclaim his innocence. "I had no choice but to use every possible *weapon* [emphasis added] to assure the success of the broadcast.[34] One hour before the broadcast New York governor Thomas Dewey telephoned to say that the opinion of the party's leaders, including General Eisenhower, was that he should resign as vice-presidential nominee.

> My nerves were frayed to a fine edge by this time and I exploded. "Just tell them [he told Dewey] that I haven't the slightest idea as to what I am going to do and if they want to find out they'd better listen to the broadcast. And tell them I know something about politics too!" I slammed the receiver down . . .[35]

Nixon went ahead with his Checkers speech on September 23, 1952. He hadn't done anything wrong, he maintained. He hadn't used any of the money for himself. His wife didn't wear a mink coat, but rather a good "Republican cloth coat." His oral drive was at work, drowning his secret and illegal acts in a public relations stunt. While he survived the charges against him, he was unable then or later to disprove them. Throughout his speech, in which he combined drama with sentimentality, he was a supreme actor, and turned defeat into victory. And Dwight D. Eisenhower, who had wanted to dump his vice-presidential nominee, lost his battle to remove Nixon from his ticket.

More histrionics followed. When Eisenhower later met Nixon at the Wheeling, West Virginia, airport, the cameras showed Nixon weeping on the shoulder of Senator William Knowland. Dr. Albert Upton, who was Richard's director in the Drama Club when he was in high school, commented that he "knew how to take direction and could cry real tears at each performance."[36] Dr. Upton also said:

> I taught him how to cry, in a play by John Drinkwater called *Bird in Hand*. He tried conscientiously at rehearsals, and he'd get a pretty good lump in his throat and that was all. But on the evenings of the performance tears just ran right out of his eyes. It was beautifully done, those tears.[37]

Nixon had certainly learned how to act. He liked to act and acted well. It may seem strange that such a rigid person could be a good actor, but Nixon acted without any personal emotional involvement. No wonder that Dr. Upton "twinged" when he later saw pictures of Nixon weeping on the shoulder of Senator Knowland.[38]

From his acting Nixon had developed a political asset—an ability to project a variety of emotions. The Checkers speech restored Richard Nixon as a vice-presidential nominee, and temporarily restored his confidence. Even more important, Nixon had learned that by appealing directly to the people, with lies and bathos and whimpering, he could reverse public opinion and win his case.

Later, when it was discovered that Adlai Stevenson too had a personal fund, Nixon complained bitterly about the attention that had been given to his own fund, and he had the answer: it was a conspiracy, the Communists were behind it all.[39]

Almost three years later, at a luncheon given by the Radio and Television Executives Society on September 14, 1955, Nixon, who had been invited to speak, leaned across the lectern and grinned at his audience as he proclaimed:

> "You all remember the 'Checkers' speech, I suppose?" Some of them chuckled at his conspiratorial tone. "Well,

I want you to be the first to know"—he paused so the executives could savor the moment too, the pause also serving to illustrate that he could back up his next three words with talent: "I staged it."[40]

The following day Nixon spoke in New York and proclaimed "the need for sincerity."[41]

In the spring of 1953, when the Army-McCarthy hearings took place, Nixon provided another performance to enhance his political image. Even though Nixon had been one of the leaders, if not *the* leader, of the anti-Communist front since 1947, it is illuminating that he turned against the conservative anti-Communists. Roy M. Cohn (who was McCarthy's assistant) has told me:

> Obviously McCarthy and I were less important to Nixon at that time than was President Eisenhower, whom he was looking to succeed. So when they finally decided to do McCarthy in and do a hatchet job on him, Nixon was the fellow they selected, and Nixon was perfectly willing to turn on his conservative friends and cut their throats—one, two, three. He was the one behind the scenes who first of all engineered the Army-McCarthy hearings by getting Senator Potter of Michigan, a very weak junior senator with no brains, to write a letter which precipitated the release of the Army report which plumbed these hearings into the situation it was. Then when it came to censure, don't forget it was Nixon, the Vice-President, who appointed the committee, including Senator Ervin, the man who ultimately helped Nixon to get McCarthy. So Nixon was a superb hatchet man.*

When I asked specifically whether Nixon had engineered the hearings, Cohn said, "There is no question about it . . . it's a fact." I then pointed out to him that Nixon was very much in agreement with McCarthy, to which he countered, "That was only when that was the way to go, but when Nixon's bread was buttered on the other side and he was playing up to Eisenhower, then he didn't lose a minute's sleep about turning right on McCarthy." Did this mean that Nixon's

---

* It should be added that Cohn has asked me to say that he was and still is an admirer of many of Nixon's achievements.

opinion was for sale, depending on who was the boss? Those closest to the situation feel this was so.

Nixon saw all issues in terms of people, of adversaries, of himself, and was seldom capable of being objective. His attitude was rooted in his difficult and distorted relationship with his parents. His unconscious feelings were continually directed toward displacing his father. An incident in the early 1950's involving Drew Pearson is pertinent. When Roy Cohn asked Nixon what to do about Drew Pearson, Nixon replied, "When you hit a king, kill him." The response suggests Nixon's unconscious wishes or fantasies: Nixon wanted to kill Pearson, for Pearson was a powerful columnist whose accusations and political revelations often dominated the news. He was, to Nixon, tyrannical and impulsive—as Frank Nixon had been. Thus it was difficult, if not impossible, for him to see issues objectively.

Several months before the Republican Convention of 1956, Nixon faced another threat, which he handled with somewhat more control. Nixon writes in *Six Crises* that when Eisenhower was asked on February 29 whether Nixon would be his running mate in the forthcoming election:

> The President evaded a direct reply, saying he could not properly speak out on the choice of a running mate until after the Republican National Convention itself had picked its presidential candidate. In politics, however, not speaking out can be another way of speaking out, and the President's words set off a wave of speculation by the public and a furor among my own friends and supporters. This, in turn, caused embarrassment to me because I still could say nothing before the President spoke.
>
> At the next weekly press conference, on March 7, the President delivered his famous answer: "I told him [Nixon] he would have to chart his own course and tell me what he would like to do." His statement was telephoned to me soon after the press conference in a somewhat garbled version. The impression I got was that he was really trying to tell me that he wanted me off the ticket.[42]

The onus was put on Nixon, who responded defensively:

> I told them [Leonard Hall and Jerry Persons] that
> everyone in politics knows a Vice President cannot chart
> his own course. "It's up to him if he wants me," I said.
> "I can only assume that if he puts it this way, this must
> be his way of saying he would prefer someone else."[43]

Nixon had been rejected. Fortunately for him, the New
Hampshire primary, the first in 1956, took place at that time,
and the voters had returned "a surprising, unsolicited write-in
vote of 22,936 for me as the vice-presidential candidate."[44]
Here was clear evidence that the people wanted Nixon to run
again. Eisenhower, however, still delayed his decision, saying
that he could not choose a running mate until he himself had
been nominated. Weeks went by without a decision.

Faced with the crucial question of whether or not he was to
stay on the ticket, Nixon, according to one report, claimed to
say to the General, "There comes a time in a man's life when
he has to fish or cut bait."[45]

Actually Nixon had said, "General, there comes a time in
matters like this when you've either got to shit or get off the
pot."[46]

Nixon was enraged. This time it was anger against a general, the President of the United States, a father figure. We
know, too, that the President's customary attitude toward
Nixon was one of rejection. Nixon was never invited to the
White House as a friend, nor was he ever asked to play golf
at Burning Tree. Nixon was not even invited to use the White
House swimming pool.*

Nixon couldn't accept the fact that Eisenhower didn't want
him on the 1956 ticket. Despite his statement that a Vice-
President cannot chart his own course, Nixon decided to ask
Eisenhower if he could run for Vice-President. Perhaps for
the first time in history a Vice-President was forced to announce his own candidacy for the vice-presidency long before
the nominating convention. It was a humiliating act, indicating little or no self-respect. Yet Nixon couldn't comprehend

---

* When Nixon became President, he covered over the pool and made
it into a press room, saying that he needed it for staff conferences, a
further expression of his anger against Eisenhower. Information about
Nixon's personal relationship with Eisenhower comes from a reliable
source who wishes to remain anonymous.

the nature of a political partnership. He thought Eisenhower didn't like him because he considered him a personal adversary. Nixon used politics to satisfy his emotional needs, and that marks the difference between a statesman and a man who is still frustrated by a childhood need to be recognized by his elders, his parents.

At the Republican National Convention in 1956, the President told Emmet John Hughes, his speech writer:

> "I've been watching Dick for a long time, and he just hasn't grown. So I just haven't honestly been able to believe that he is Presidential timber." Fully recovered, the President told other friends that Nixon was a young man who managed at the same time to be "too political" without holding a *genuine point of view* [emphasis added]. Nixon had believed that the way to rise politically and to ingratiate himself with Eisenhower was by doing the President's political dirty work.[47]

Garry Wills concludes, "All this did . . . was convince Ike that he [Nixon] was not made for higher things."[48]

Nixon's inability to recognize his own limitations was based on his preoccupation, his obsession with becoming President —a point to which we shall return. During the convention Frank Nixon had become so ill that Nixon had to hurry to Whittier. When he returned to San Francisco, he again learned about the attempts to dump him from the ticket. His father died later, aged seventy-seven, on September 4, 1956. Neither he nor Nixon's mother, Hannah, who for the last two years of her life stayed at Whitmar Convalescent Hospital, and who died on September 30, 1967, were to see their favorite son become President.

For years Nixon had sought to win Eisenhower's admiration and respect, and had failed. In *Six Crises* he could say that Eisenhower "was a far more complex and devious man than most people realized . . ."[49] He could certainly have said the same about himself.

During his second vice-presidency, we observe a Nixon still preoccupied with himself and his status vis-à-vis Eisenhower. Apparently, he must have been so obsessed with placing himself in the best light in the President's mind that everyone else had to be disregarded. One man who worked very closely with Nixon from 1957 to 1960 (and who does not wish to be identified) said he rarely had a chance to talk with him. Their sole means of communication was through memoranda, even though this man worked in the Vice-President's office. Nonetheless, to Nixon he was unimportant.

It is true that except for a few times when Nixon's anger broke through his thin veneer of total allegiance to the President, the Vice-President exercised great self-control, a self-control which went back to his earlier childhood training by his mother and which he had learned to develop in dealing with his father.

What we can see, however, is that Nixon, without realizing it, always perceived politics in personal terms, in terms of adversaries—a viewpoint similar to that found in the paranoid person. Nixon, more than other public personages, always had to keep his guard up, lest he make a wrong judgment. He knew that he had to be on the watch, and that is one reason why he was inhibited in making decisions. As he seriously questioned his own decisions, it may well be that his doubt went so far that he felt innocent about his transgressions.

At the end of his vice-presidency in 1960, Nixon was fighting with himself on all fronts. His inner impulses pushed him in different directions and created a multiplicity of contradictions in his behavior. Always near the surface was gnawing self-doubt. As a result, he never was at rest, he never experienced inner tranquillity. In his political and private life alike, he never walked one road. He walked many roads—low roads, high roads, crossroads. Any road.

9

In the fall of 1960, as Nixon's second term as Vice-President was drawing to a close, he faced a new challenge. His party had nominated him for the presidency. His cherished dream, his obsession, seemed to be within his grasp. He had never lost an election, and in spite of—or perhaps because of—a nature that was enigmatic to some, he had a good chance of winning.

Certainly his rise to political prominence had been meteoric. His essentially conservative position appealed to many. To his followers he was a constructive, hard-working man; some thought him eminently suited to be President because of his long service in Congress and as Vice-President. And yet few of his followers would have called him popular. Nixon was secretive, withdrawn, suspicious. People couldn't get close to him or even feel close. He was serious, seldom humorous, and he gave the impression of a man who carried a deep secret around in his head. He was not comfortable with himself and others were seldom comfortable with him. What many didn't realize was that Nixon's behavior reflected diametrically opposing traits—passivity and aggression. These characteristics were so strong that they made Nixon a contradictory person. Inwardly Nixon was confused and he desperately tried to give the appearance of strength. By giving the impression of being strong, he could cover up his passivity. He could undermine Voorhis and Douglas; he could pursue Hiss; in the future he would attack Ellsberg and bomb Cambodia. He could indeed be aggressive, but beneath this outer show of toughness was an inner life filled with contradictions that had been present since childhood. These contradictions created an ego weakness which desperately needed to be shored up by the power and accounterments of public office. The presidency, if achieved, would make it possible to keep everything under his control.

Whereas Nixon's aggressiveness appealed to many, his opponents saw him in a different light. Many thought him devi-

146

ous and untrustworthy. He was called "tricky Dick," and in 1961 Harry Truman expressed what many had thought when he said, ". . . Nixon is a shifty-eyed, goddamn liar, and people know it." "He not only doesn't give a damn about people; he doesn't know how to tell the truth. I don't think the son of a bitch knows the difference between telling the truth and lying."[1]

Though Nixon later liked to attribute his alienation (read: secretiveness) to the isolation forced on a Chief Executive, the pattern was evident in his earliest years at Whittier.

In the White House, as in his childhood years, Nixon revealed only a small part of his life. His public posture became a façade to mask the turbulent inner life which he guarded jealously because he did not and could not share his feelings with anyone. His remarks about himself when Vice-President, as elicited by Stewart Alsop, are revealing:

> The more you stay in this kind of job, the more you realize that a public figure, a major public figure, is a lonely man—the President very much more so, of course. But even in my job you can't enjoy the luxury of intimate personal friendships. You can't confide absolutely in anyone. You can't talk too much about your personal plans, your personal feelings. I believe in keeping my own counsel. It's something like wearing clothing—if you let down your hair, you feel too naked.

A little later in the same interview, Nixon commented:

> I do meet a great number of people, and part of the image of me as cold or withdrawn is false, I think, partly as a result of the press. But it is true that I'm fundamentally relatively shy. It doesn't come natural to me to be a buddy-buddy boy. When I meet a lot of people, I tend to seek out the shy ones. . . . You know, I try to be candid with newspapermen, but I can't really let my hair down with anyone.
> ALSOP: Not even with old friends, like the Jack Drowns, say?
> NIXON: No, not really with anyone, not even with my family.[2]

The main reason for his secretiveness was his isolated, encapsulated inner life where his fantasies and frustrated ambitions confronted a world he conceived as being hostile. Fantasies or daydreams are private; they are absolutely self-contained. Only the daydreamer knows what he or she is thinking or dreaming of and therefore has an advantage over everyone else. And Nixon was the type of person whose daydreams were an essential, if not *the* essential, part of his private world. His secretiveness was rooted in his fantasy life, which made him more vulnerable to attack as a politician. Nixon was far more cautious than the usual politician who tries to protect himself by playing his cards carefully.

His fantasy was to become President of the United States. He suffered from obsessive-compulsive longings to become President. Unlike others who have yearned to become President, this drive was more pronounced in Nixon because of his compulsive need for ultimate power to control others. As early as 1948, when Nixon was a congressman, a man who knew Nixon well told me that he was struck and much surprised when Nixon talked about his job as if he were President. While many aspire—and work with tremendous energy —to become President, to Nixon, the goal had become an obsession, a fever intrinsic to his emotions. The desperate need to master everyone fed his ambition and encouraged him to seek out larger and larger domains, larger and larger audiences for control.

Nixon, of course, realized that people either admired or hated him in the extreme. This polarization was politically useful because it enabled him to draw dramatic attention to himself. He consciously made himself highly visible so that people could react to him personally, although I seriously doubt that Nixon realized why he was so thoroughly disliked by some.

Why, we ask, did Nixon excite such degrees of love and hate? It was, I submit, a part of his mystique. With Nixon, the more unfathomable he was, the greater the attraction to him. We are fascinated by mystery. It bothers us. It is our human nature to want answers, to see things as a whole, to get a "reading" on a person, to find the man behind the mask. Curiosity helps account for the public's fascination with Nixon.

There was also an odd sympathy for Nixon. Even when he was in public office, and some saw through him, he created sympathy for himself. He was a poor boy who had made good the hard way. He was physically awkward and uncomfortable with people—and his ability to succeed in spite of these obstacles proved attractive to some. The public didn't want to believe the worst. Nixon fostered and played the role of underdog with great skill. Even as President he felt, as many who voted for him did, that he was an underdog. He played up the isolation of public figures and the martyrdom of service. But precisely which factors convinced the American voters to elect him President we can only surmise. Certainly he represented a conservative strain in American life; one can surmise that some voters sought a leader of his kind who would act out for them the hostility that they felt and also tell them what they wanted to hear. Nixon was not elected in 1960, but in 1968 and again in 1972 they elected their man.

In the fall of 1960, he was bitter against Eisenhower and refused his political help in the campaign against Kennedy. He saw Eisenhower as the "bad father" who had let him down. He had been helpful in 1952 in getting Eisenhower his first nomination. Nixon couldn't forget all the traveling both at home and abroad that he had done for Eisenhower; he had placed himself in physical jeopardy in 1958 in Caracas, and had gone to the Soviet Union, where he had his widely publicized "kitchen debate" with Khrushchev. Instead of looking beyond his ego needs, he felt he had to strike back at Eisenhower by telling him that "he was charting his own course." He would do it himself, without his "father." Nixon wanted to have total control of his campaign, exactly the kind of control over himself and others that he had yearned for since childhood, and that he exercised when he won the presidency in 1968.

This need to control had been ingrained in him and became more prominent with time because of Nixon's fear that anything less would subject him to the control of other people. This was a fear he was to live with all his life.

As the 1960 presidential campaign grew more heated, John F. Kennedy challenged Nixon to a television debate. Nixon, the experienced high school and college debater, also remembered the success of his Checkers speech, which had brought him into national prominence and had swept him into the vice-presidential office eight years before. Supremely confident, he accepted Kennedy's challenge. He did not take the advice of his political associates who counseled against the debate, for it never occurred to him that he might not win. As it turned out, the debate hurt his campaign. Nixon appeared haggard and tired alongside his fresh and vigorous opponent. The debate gave wide exposure to Kennedy, who at that time was less well known to the public. He had failed to anticipate these results.

Shortly after his defeat Vice-President Nixon met Kennedy in Florida and, as he wrote in *Six Crises,* he told the President-elect:

> It [the CIA] should continue to have primary responsibility for gathering and evaluating intelligence, in which it was doing a good job. But I said it had been my plan, had I been elected, to set up a new and independent organization for carrying out *covert para-military operations* [emphasis added].[3]

Even in 1960 Nixon had wanted to control events. The seeds of the White House "plumbers" were in Nixon's mind more than ten years before the Watergate break-in.

Despite outward signs of bravery, Nixon's loss of the 1960 election was a devastating defeat to his ego. He had been rejected. He was depressed and angry. There were rumors that he had been seeing a New York internist, Dr. Arnold Hutschnecker, for a variety of symptoms which have been described as being psychosomatic.

These rumors were founded in truth. He did visit Dr. Hutschnecker, but how many times he saw that doctor or what kind of treatment—if any—he received we do not know. Hutschnecker declared in an article in *Look* magazine that he "detected no sign of mental illness in him."[4] Since we must take into account the understandable refusal of the physician to divulge information about his patient, his statement cannot be evaluated. Knowing Nixon's intransigence and deep suspicion of anything akin to psychotherapy we may suspect that any advice that was offered went unheeded.

Still smarting under the defeat by Kennedy, he decided to run for the governorship of California in 1962. During the campaign, in an unguarded moment he made a slip of the tongue, saying he was running for the "governorship of the United States," which meant of course that he still had the presidency in mind.

He lost the election to Pat Brown, and it was early in the

morning, when the returns were in, that Nixon appeared before the press to say, "You won't have Nixon to kick around any more, because, gentlemen, this is my last press conference." Here indeed we see the bad loser, the unsuccessful candidate showing his true feelings—making a politically unwise statement and one that suggested his view of the press and of himself. He was still the little boy who felt mistreated. Certainly he had not grown up.

Although from all outward appearances he seemed to have given up the pursuit of the presidency after his California defeat—he had assured his wife (their relationship was already strained) that he never would run for public office again—he knew himself very poorly. How could he give up his obsession for the presidency? He was of two minds. One pulled him in the direction of being secretive: no one was going to know his real desire to become the President. The other was his dramatic wish to *show* that he could become a President. Nixon was tormented and in conflict with himself.

Most people assumed, following his defeat in 1962 in the race for governor of California, that his political life was finished. Political obituaries of Richard Nixon began to appear in the press.[5]

The years from 1960 to 1968, when Nixon was out of public office, were difficult for a man who had a desperate desire to become President. After his defeat in 1960 he practiced law in Los Angeles from 1961 to 1963 with the firm of Adams, Duque and Hazeltine. However much he disliked New York and the eastern establishment, after his defeat in 1962 he had to find another base for his political activities, which, for the time being, would be mostly covert. And so in 1963 he joined the prestigious firm of Mudge, Stern, Baldwin and Todd in New York. In 1964 he became a partner. (In 1967 John Mitchell joined the firm as a partner.) Nixon was biding his time, waiting patiently for the opportune moment to move again into the forefront of American politics.

He continued, however, to work in the Republican vineyard to enhance his personal and political standing. It was a tribute to his determination to succeed, to regain public confidence, that the press began to write about the "new" Nixon. No longer did he seem the "old" Nixon. Even during his vice-presidency, he had seemed to some to become a "new" person—an impression which the astute political observer Ted

Sorensen also received. Nixon seemed to be pleasant, convivial, concerned, a good sport about criticism, and interested in others. In 1968, before the election, Walter Lippmann wrote, "I believe there really is a 'new Nixon,' a maturer and mellower man who is no longer clawing his way to the top."

Interesting in this respect is what his mother said when asked about the "new" Nixon: "Oh, no. There's no such thing as a new Richard. He has always been exactly the same; even as a boy I never knew a person to change so little." [6]

Despite belief in some quarters that Nixon had changed, he was not his party's choice in 1964. The 1964 Republican Convention nominated Senator Barry Goldwater, who lost decisively to Lyndon B. Johnson. Only in 1965 was Nixon advised that he might be the 1968 Republican nominee for President.[7] It appeared to be a long uphill fight, but, tenacious as always, he had clung to the prospect of the presidency and was nominated in 1968. Since the nation was in the midst of the Vietnam War and consequently tragically divided, Nixon had the opportunity to offer positive new leadership, particularly since his opponent, Vice-President Hubert Humphrey, possibly out of loyalty to President Johnson, identified himself with the Administration's policies. Nixon did have several obvious shortcomings, however, which worried his campaign staff. First, he exploited every means available to obtain his purpose, to become President, a tactic he had used in his previous campaigns. Also he didn't take into consideration the opinions of his staff. He was so self-centered that he wanted to manage his campaign himself. The draft of a speech he was to give during the Oregon primary in 1968 is revealing:

Somebody has once said that in politics there are those who want to win an office so they can be somebody. And then there are those who want to win an office so that they can do something.

Now, I'm not in the first category. That doesn't mean that that makes me better than anybody else. But I've already been everything really that I could be in terms of prestige. If I never have another state dinner or review an honor guard, or get another award or plaque or something, that's fine. Because I've had all the honors, and certainly those honors should be shared, and I would be delighted if they could be. But also I have a unique experience. I'm one of the few people in this country who has experience in the House, Senate, eight years as Vice President. Since that time I've traveled around the world as a private citizen, talking to the leaders of the world, the political and the business leaders. And I think I know something about our problems at home and abroad. I have some experience that many of the other candidates may not have.

With that experience and with numbers of Americans believing, as apparently numbers of them do as indicated by the first two primaries, that's the kind of experience we need, I feel that I have not only an obligation but a challenge to step in there and give it a try. In other words, I am running for President because I want to do something.

The second paragraph, beginning "Now, I am not in the first category," was deleted after a great deal of controversy. Nixon's campaign staff felt it was too self-laudatory, "almost like a lie"; one of his staff who prefers to remain anonymous shuddered. The problem of how to project Nixon apparently became so difficult that several of the staff threatened to resign. Roger Ailes, who worked closely with Nixon during the 1968 campaign, is quoted as saying:

Now you put him on television, you've got a problem right away. He's a funny-looking guy. He looks like somebody hung him in a closet overnight and he jumps out in the morning with his suit all bunched up and starts running around saying, "I want to be President." I mean this is how he strikes some people. That's why these shows are important. To make them forget all that.[8]

Another need was how to show that Nixon had a "human touch." His staff and advisers decided the best way to do this was to make a film depicting Nixon as a warm person. The film, entitled *Richard M. Nixon: A Self Portrait*, proved to be an arduous undertaking. It was made in the course of seven weeks in 1968 in southern California, on Long Island, New York, and elsewhere. The planning and filming proved to be difficult since Nixon was traveling all over the country.

After between $400,000 and $500,000 had been spent on the film there were serious doubts about continuing the project, particularly because Nixon's family felt it was too intimate. However, since Hubert Humphrey was gaining on

Nixon in the polls, the film had to be made usable. And after much discussion, another $25,000 was allocated for the project. There was an urgent need to project a "human" Nixon. When the film was completed, Nixon had a difficult decision to make.

Nixon did not like the finished film and asked Billy Graham to view it. Sick with the flu, Graham managed to crawl up the stairs in a New York City loft to view it. He liked it. He called Nixon from a pay telephone and told him so. It was only then that Nixon approved its use.[9]

The film was hurriedly distributed and shown three times a day throughout the country on the weekend before the election. It became an important part of the Republican campaign. Again we see public relations image makers behind the Nixon victory. Madison Avenue had gone to work to sell the candidate.

I had an excellent opportunity to study Nixon's face when I attended a private screening of *Richard M. Nixon: A Self Portrait,* which lasted twenty-five minutes. The film documented important parts of Nixon's life—still pictures of his childhood, his family, his adolescence, as well as pictures taken of him while he was a lieutenant in the Navy. Most of the film, however, focused on Nixon answering questions about himself and about his aims. Here was the "self" Nixon had consciously and unconsciously managed to create out of his past hurts. Despite heavy makeup his face appeared somewhat lifeless. It was striking to see how irregular his features were. Most predominant was the mouth, which moved up and down—slow and fast—and seemed to fill Nixon's face like a mechanical device. His jaw jutted out aggressively. When he smiled his mouth was fixed and frozen. One could sense that any attempts at humor or spontaneity were studied. A friend of Nixon who had known him thirty years before confided, "For Nixon to smile was a major act. With his frozen grin on his face he was so awkward . . ." His lips were thin and tensely drawn.

Nixon's upswept nose, ponderous eyebrows, and asymmetrical lips seemed to have been randomly assembled. The face lacked harmony. While there is not yet a science of morphology, quite possibly there is some connection between the face and the character. Certainly Nixon's face and mannerisms suggest an inner struggle of considerable intensity. As a young man he gave the impression of being rather handsome—and unusually alert. But when he tried to appear relaxed in the film, his look was highly controlled, grim, described by Stewart Alsop as "the look of a man who rather expects to lose."[10]

When a man is so unsure of himself, unable to get along with himself, how could we believe him when he proclaimed that he was going to "bring us together," to give us "law and order," and to settle the war in Vietnam, possibly the most formidable task at hand? Throughout his campaign he talked about "peace with honor" in Vietnam, that he had a *secret* plan to establish peace. Americans believed Nixon because he told them what they wanted to hear. It is significant that Nixon carried over his ideas for peace from his own fantasies into the world of reality, and from reality back into his world of fantasy. He became inclined to follow ideas in the real world only so far as they fitted his fantasies. As a child he had fantasized about being a hero and he carried this tendency into his adult life as a politician. He was unable to discern clearly the reality of situations because he carried out acts which were in accord with his fantasy life.

Nixon won the election. Like the legendary phoenix, he arose from the ashes. The concept of the "new" Nixon had caught on. As late as January 1971, *Newsweek* spoke of the possibility of still another "new" Nixon.

> . . . true to his own precepts, he seems to have begun weighing the wisdom of his past two years' purposes and examining the strength of his resources—and the result may well be yet another "new" Nixon, softer-voiced, more charitable and as pragmatic as ever, settling into stride for the long run-up to the 1972 elections.[11]

People believed what they wanted to believe, and a majority of the electorate in 1968 was willing to accept the false image. The mask of the "new" Nixon helped him to win and to hide his real personality. Strenuous efforts to transcend the "old" Nixon with public relations helped in 1968. A man had been sold to the country.

But the "old" Nixon wouldn't let go. The "old" Nixon was the real one, his shield against a hostile world, a protection for his inner world. He was comfortable in a crowd because, by becoming part of it, an impersonalization took place where his own inner being could not be attacked or assaulted. He did not have to function on a one-to-one basis. Instead he projected an image.

Many were eager to think that a "new" Nixon had been created, and by projecting a positive image and evoking the enthusiasm and support of large crowds, Nixon could create an artificial rapport. He could respond to adulation, to group emotion, and could speak with fervor and conviction.[12] To a great extent, it was Nixon's image that seduced them.

Those who have observed Nixon at close hand all agree that he is tense and preoccupied when he speaks to one or two individuals. However, when he talks to a group of people his temperament changes, his eyes light up, and he is able to talk and talk as though it were easy for him. The reason for this easy delivery before large, live audiences is that he doesn't have to talk directly to any one person in particular. There is no need for him to involve himself with anyone. Even when he doesn't have a written speech in front of him, he has rehearsed what he is going to say, which may explain his relative ease in front of a crowd, so that his performance becomes flawless, perfect. This behavior is not unusual for politicians in general. In Nixon, though, the performance is more intense. He likes to show that he is in command of the situation, and he is also subtly letting his audience know that he speaks without written notes, another sign that he likes everyone to know he is in control of what he has to say.

But behind his apparent cool, perfect demeanor one senses his anxiety, for his delivery is stiff, cut off, rigid—not flexible or fluid as one would expect from an orator who has given hundreds of speeches. When we remember that he has given a great many speeches we can then recognize how his delivery resembles the awkward movements of his arms, which appear oddly disconnected from his body. Since he is inflexible, intensely preoccupied, his speeches don't flow naturally.

There have been exceptions to this style in Nixon's public speaking, but these exceptions were few and far between. One exception was his acceptance speech at the 1968 Republican National Convention. It was carefully written and perfectly planned, and partisan though it was, it held his audience.

It is hard to be certain whether Nixon was consciously aware of the seductive nature of speechmaking. But even if he had only an inkling of it, this seduction, with its element of cunning, became a means of political as well as personal survival. He could keep a crowd under his spell and simultaneously keep his secrets. He was a good actor.

His own affairs and those of his administration, far from being public, became private, hidden even from many Cabinet members, the leaders of Congress, and most of his White House staff.

According to Robert B. Semple, Jr., writing in *The New York Times*, Nixon proclaimed from the outset of his presidency in 1969 that he would "invest a 'director of communications' and—within reason of course—urge him to open wide the books of government . . . he placed his faith in his own carefully contrived decision-making process."[13] This avowed plan and the contrary action that followed reflected ambiguity and duplicity and caused confusion. The White House came to function as an expression of Nixon's character.

Other factors contributed to the aura surrounding Nixon's administration. People always have been in awe of those who through their own work or inheritance have advanced to a high position in society or who have through the elective process succeeded in becoming a high-ranking official. Names like Morgan and Rockefeller and Kennedy impress people since they suggest not only wealth but also influence and power. The average man admires them secretly and holds them in awe even though he may envy or resent them.

A President occupies a unique position of power. He is foremost in the minds of most people and is regarded almost like a king, a protector. The yearning in people to believe that someone will take care of them like a father figure is projected onto the presidency. Our fantasy bestows on the President a role of omniscience. For the conscious mind this is, of course, not true, but it is for the unconscious. The President lives in the White House, which is like a guarded castle: he is the Commander in Chief, he is the sovereign power.

And so we can easily understand the veneration we have for the President and the power with which he has been imbued. Such power, consciously or unconsciously, makes him both attractive and fearsome. Our uncertainty as to how he makes decisions or what he may do provides the mystique which surrounds the presidency. Nixon had developed this mystique even before he entered the White House. It had paid off handsomely.

Nixon's attitude toward his Cabinet in 1969 reveals his

emotional conflict. Fearful of not being in control of his own government, he felt threatened when confronted by such independent men as Hickel, Laird, Connally, and Finch. He was unable to face his hidden fear of being controlled. Instead of trying to cope with his fear, he avoided it, and one by one the Cabinet members who "threatened" him were dismissed or resigned. The Cabinet members appointed during his second term were men totally dependent on Nixon for their power and prestige—the major exception being Kissinger.

His inability to get along with strong Cabinet members also arose from a compulsive need for total allegiance from anyone who served him. This need originated in the ideal of loyalty he felt he had received from his mother; it was, however, more her loyalty to him than the other way around. And Nixon similarly required unquestioning loyalty from his White House staff. The fact that he could not differentiate between disagreement and disloyalty became a significant cause of the Nixon tragedy. Ironically, Nixon believed that nobody could be trusted. To compensate for his inability to give loyalty, Nixon demanded it from others. It was to become one of the cornerstones of his presidency.

Just as he was angered by anyone in his administration who seemed to defy his wishes, he became furious with the North Vietnamese when they defied his peace demands. Unable to tolerate what he considered intransigence, he took Hanoi's position personally. He felt terribly guilty over his secret and illegal order to invade Cambodia during the last days of April 1970, which he belatedly announced during a nationwide telecast on April 30.* Long before that, however he had ordered the secret bombings of Cambodia—a neutral country. Threatened by huge and serious antiwar demonstrations that ravaged the country, he saw them as a personal assault.

The morning after announcing the invasion of Cambodia, in a speech to Pentagon employees he characterized the war protesters as "bums." [14] Although William Safire tries to minimize the importance of Nixon's use of the word, there can be no doubt that this is just what he meant. Why else did the former President become so enraged when from his White House window he saw a young demonstrator carrying an anti-

---

* One of the reasons given for the 1970 Cambodia invasion was to find COSUN, the enemy communications headquarters, or underground Pentagon. When only reserves of arms and rice were found, the government announced that it had "achieved its objectives."

war placard that he ordered a White House aide to chase him away? And why was he so angry, disturbed, almost irrational about the "bums" if he didn't identify with them and didn't feel that he himself was a "bum"? The demonstrating rekindled memories of his father, who often mistreated him and his brothers and had called them "bums."

On May 4, 1970, at Kent State University, four innocent students were shot to death and eight were wounded by National Guardsmen. President Nixon, confronted with a cry of anguish from most Americans, could only say, "This should remind us all once again that when dissent turns to violence, it invites tragedy." The students were not armed; the National Guardsmen were.

Nixon was tremendously affected by the violent attacks on him in Congress and in the media. The emotional climate of the country was charged with a frenzy that had severe repercussions on Nixon's mind. A revealing incident took place at the Lincoln Memorial early in the morning on May 9, 1970. The previous evening Nixon told William Safire in a telephone call:

> If the crazies try anything, we'll clobber them—relax, whenever I say anything like that, it drives people up the wall, I know. The country's been through a terrible experience this week [the Kent State tragedy].[15]

Nixon was restless, troubled, and angry about the war and the Kent State deaths, and spoke almost incessantly on the phone, from 9:22 P.M. on May 8 until 4:22 A.M. the following day. The telephone log [16] shows that he made fifty-one phone calls, of which only one was to Mrs. Nixon, at 10:39 P.M. There were eight to Kissinger; seven to H. R. Haldeman; four to Rose Mary Woods; and the rest to Dr. Norman Vincent Peale, the Rev. Billy Graham, Helen Thomas of the UPI, and members of his Cabinet and his staff.

As Safire says:

> He finished on the telephone at two-fifteen and went to bed. He "slept soundly until shortly after four o'clock," as he later put it—actually, it was three-fifteen —and went into the Lincoln Sitting Room off his bedroom. He put a record on the turntable: Rachmaninoff's

First Piano Concerto, Eugene Ormandy conducting the
Philadelphia Orchestra, Philippe Entremont, soloist.[17]

Standing at the window, Nixon saw students beginning to
congregate around the Washington Monument. Later, becoming more and more disturbed, he drove out to the Lincoln
Memorial, where he talked with a group of students about
stopping the war in Cambodia and Vietnam. Nixon talked
about Neville Chamberlain and about Prague until he was interrupted by a young woman who told him that she wasn't
interested in Prague. What she was concerned about was what
life was going to be like in America. He ignored her question. He talked about the many hundred million people living
in China, then talked about the war and football. One student,
although she had heard only part of Nixon's remarks, said
that "most of what he was saying was absurd. Here we had
come from a university that's completely uptight—on strike—
and when we told him where we were from, he talked about
the football team." [18]

Nixon was not depressed about the war in Indochina itself,
the people of Vietnam, American demonstrators, or what the
conflict was doing to America's reputation. He was angry because he couldn't have his own way. He was not a "pitiful,
helpless giant." What he feared was national defeat, which unconsciously he took as his own personal, emotional defeat.

TELEPHONE LOG NIGHT OF MAY 8–9, 1970

9:22 P.M.	*Dr. Henry Kissinger*
10:35 P.M.	*Rose Mary Woods*
10:35 P.M.	*Tricia Nixon*
10:35 P.M.	*Secy. William Rogers*
10:37 P.M.	*Dr. Henry Kissinger*
10:37 P.M.	*H. R. Haldeman*
10:39 P.M.	*Mrs. Nixon*
10:50 P.M.	*Dr. Norman Vincent Peale*
10:56 P.M.	*Secy. John Volpe*
10:59 P.M.	*Cong. L. H. Fountain*
11:00 P.M.	*Hobart Lewis*
11:00 P.M.	*William Safire*
11:07 P.M.	*Secy. George Shultz*
11:11 P.M.	*Secy. Melvin Laird*
11:11 P.M.	*Dr. Henry Kissinger*
11:12 P.M.	*The Rev. Billy Graham*
11:21 P.M.	*John Ehrlichman*

11:26 P.M.	*H. R. Haldeman*
11:28 P.M.	*Secy. Walter Hickel*
11:31 P.M.	*Rose Mary Woods*
11:31 P.M.	*B. Rebozo*
11:38 P.M.	*Dr. Daniel P. Moynihan*
11:40 P.M.	*Cong. Jos. Monaghan*
11:47 P.M.	*H. R. Haldeman*
11:50 P.M.	*Cliff Miller*
12:03 A.M.	*Rose Mary Woods*
12:18 A.M.	*H. R. Haldeman*
12:20 A.M.	*H. R. Haldeman*
12:24 A.M.	*Dr. Henry Kissinger*
12:29 A.M.	*U. Secy. V. Alexis Johnson*
12:33 A.M.	*Dr. Henry Kissinger*
12:46 A.M.	*H. R. Haldeman*
12:47 A.M.	*Ron Ziegler*
12:48 A.M.	*Patrick Buchanan*
12:48 A.M.	*Dr. Henry Kissinger*
12:58 A.M.	*Gov. Nelson Rockefeller*
1:07 A.M.	*Herb Klein*
1:13 A.M.	*Nancy Dickerson*
1:15 A.M.	*Ron Ziegler*
1:22 A.M.	*Helen Thomas, UPI*
1:26 A.M.	*B. Rebozo*
1:29 A.M.	*Atty. Gen. John Mitchell*
1:31 A.M.	*Gov. Thomas Dewey*
1:41 A.M.	*H. R. Haldeman*
1:51 A.M.	*Rose Mary Woods*
1:55 A.M.	*Dr. Henry Kissinger*
3:24 A.M.	*Paul Keyes*
3:38 A.M.	*Dr. Henry Kissinger*
3:47 A.M.	*Ron Ziegler*
3:50 A.M.	*Helen Thomas*
4:22 A.M.	*Manolo Sanchez*

Defeat was like death—which was linked to his childhood fear of death. Being essentially passive and now depressed, he was unable to act out his aggression in a personal relationship. However, having a compelling need to express his anger, he had as President, and commander in chief of the armed forces, bombed and invaded Cambodia. His aggressive actions were impersonal.

While his actions in the war also were in part dictated by what he saw the military situation to be, they were reinforced by his innate hostile feelings. Nixon also identified with Presidents Lincoln, Wilson, Theodore Roosevelt, and to a lesser degree Franklin Roosevelt, all of whom had been involved in war. Yet it was Richard Nixon whose angry self was involved to the highest degree with his military and political decisions. This explains his erratic behavior as President.

We see many examples of Nixon's contradictory behavior. The President who opposed Communism for a quarter of a century opened up communications with the People's Republic of China. His enthusiasm for the visit to China was so great that his trip took place in February 1972 instead of May as first planned. It was the drama of the event which pleased the President. In view of his long years of bitter hatred toward Communism and his profound emotional fear of defeat, his decision to advance the date is not surprising.

Through his visit he made sure he would be remembered as being at the center of the world stage. It may well be that he went to China to work for peace. Knowing, however, his strong condemnation of Communism, we cannot accept this as the full story. We have no information on Kissinger's role, but we can say that Nixon was in the midst of a drama created by himself and with himself as the main actor.

Nixon's unusual behavior is also clearly evident in his handling of the case of First Lieutenant William C. Calley, Jr., who in 1971 had been convicted for his random shooting of twenty-five Vietnamese civilians, including nine children. Nixon interfered with the military court and ordered that Calley be released from stockade confinement and placed in quarters instead of prison during the appeal period.[19] President Nixon, and there are those who agreed with him, excused Calley for the killings when three times during a press conference he referred to Calley as though he were innocent. By denying the killer's guilt, he seemed to deny his own criminal acts in Vietnam.

Through his intervention in the Calley matter, Nixon also showed his intense need to be at the center of things and to control events. Being President had heightened his desire. The same impulse had led him more and more to know everything that was to be known.

Although other Presidents had a natural desire to be in the public eye, to control events, and to be secretive, Nixon outdid them all. And out of his intense need to be mysterious and secretive, he laid the foundation for his downfall. This emotional oscillation between secrecy and exhibitionism reached a dramatic and tragic extreme when, in the summer of 1970, according to Alexander P. Butterfield, deputy assistant to the President, he ordered the Secret Service to install a taping-system listening device in the Oval Office and in the Executive Office Building of the President.[20] A taping device was also installed in the Cabinet Room.

"He wanted," as one close observer of Nixon has said, "to know every detail about everything." He also wanted control, and so he was much disturbed about the publication of the Pentagon Papers, which Dr. Daniel Ellsberg was charged with stealing and releasing for publication. But Nixon's pursuit of Ellsberg took on a special character: in many ways it paralleled his pursuit of Hiss. If he could destroy Ellsberg—in the name of national security—Nixon could once again serve as the great protector, just as he had saved America from Hiss and the Communists. Unconsciously, he felt that his own security was threatened.

Nixon was also angry because Ellsberg had leaked the Papers to the press, an action that he considered a threat to "national security." Once again it was his own security which had to be defended at all costs. After first winning a temporary victory over the press, Nixon was determined to get Ellsberg. The Special Investigating Unit, the "plumbers" unit, set up by the White House, searched the office of Dr. Ellsberg's psychiatrist to find incriminating evidence.

The break-in of Dr. Lewis J. Fielding's office on Labor Day 1971 was a criminal fiasco. The burglars didn't find any incriminating evidence against Ellsberg. Dr. Fielding confirmed to me in February 1975 what he had stated to the court in the Los Angeles trial of the "plumbers"—that they had opened his file cabinet where he kept his papers about Ellsberg. To him it was evident that they had looked through the papers, but he knew they could not get any useful evidence out of them.*

One secretive, forbidden act usually leads to another.

---

* If the burglars had been familiar with psychoanalytic practice, they would have known that few practitioners make notes about their patients, and those that do, use, as I do, abbreviations or their own form of shorthand to make it impossible for anyone else to read their notes.

It came as a shock when the public learned that, in the case of Ellsberg, Nixon, through John Ehrlichman, had secretly offered the presiding judge the directorship of the FBI. While the reason for such an offer is transparent, more important is that Nixon pursued Ellsberg by every means he had available.

Nixon's vindictive act against Ellsberg was but one of many that led to the Watergate break-in.

During 1972 when Nixon was preparing for his re-election and created the Committee for the Re-Election of the President (CREEP), he gave the impression of being calm and collected. He gave this impression all during the campaign. And yet his emotional state and what was going on mostly behind the scenes was chaotic.

James W. McCord, Jr., was discharged as chief security officer for CREEP; on June 30 John Mitchell resigned as the President's campaign manager; Nixon in a news conference on August 29 said about Watergate: "No one in the White House Staff, no one in this administration presently employed was involved . . ."; Mitchell, testifying on September 2 in the Democratic National Committee's suit against CREEP, said he had no advance knowledge of the bugging incident, which Nixon and he knew was a lie; Maurice Stans had approved the transfer of $100,000 in campaign funds through Mexico to conceal the identity of the donors; a federal grand jury on September ·15 indicted the men arrested in the break-in (including G. Gordon Liddy and E. Howard Hunt, Jr., the latter a former White House consultant); on September 20 Robert C. Mardian and Frederick C. LaRue, two CREEP officials, had destroyed financial records after the break-in; on October 10 an illegal campaign of political sabotage directed by White House officials and CREEP had been organized; Donald H. Segretti, a former Treasury Department lawyer, had been hired by Dwight L. Chapin, President Nixon's appointments secretary, to direct the sabotage; Segretti was paid by the President's personal lawyer, Herbert W. Kalmbach; and the CREEP group—Maurice Stans, Jeb Magruder, G. Gordon Liddy, and Herbert L. Porter—controlled a special cash fund which in spite of denials had been used to sabotage George McGovern's campaign. The threat to Nixon's presidency, were the full facts revealed, would unnerve anyone. Far from being "cool," Nixon was tormented.

And yet in a *New York Times* interview Nixon after his election could say: "I find to handle crises the most important qualities one needs are balance, objectivity, and ability to act coolly. . . . The great decisions in this office require calm." [21]

People were attracted by the contradictions in Nixon's behavior; they were fascinated by his preoccupation with himself and his practice of total seclusion prior to the announcement of major decisions or nationwide addresses. This pattern of turning inward suggests how tense and cold he was. He took himself completely seriously, as if his words, coming from a mystical force, were infallible. Moreover, his sense of being "above" others—or at least different from them—discouraged any sense of personal fellowship. It impelled Nixon to become inaccessible, thereby heightening his isolation and mystique. While he claimed that there were times when he could relax and be carefree with some of his intimates, he was most often self-preoccupied and brooding.

These qualities were intimidating and aroused fear and anxiety in those around him. Strange as it may seem, he had a hypnotic effect on many of his subordinates. This explains, in part, the readiness and the submissiveness with which so many carried out his intentions and will.

Through a well-planned scenario, he was re-elected in 1972. In the role of President, he acted more like a hero in a dramatic play.

His life took on a Kafkaesque tone: still suffering from an obsession with the presidency, his mystique had become his alibi. However, the taping system in the White House was like a time bomb that would make it impossible for Nixon to survive his last crisis.

10

Throughout Nixon's personal and political life, he was unable to accept and absorb most emotional experiences. Any sadness or deep sorrow that he experienced touched him only superficially, so he could not contemplate his experiences and thereby increase his insight and maturity. Nixon brings to mind Ibsen's *Peer Gynt,* in which Peer, after a long and selfish life, tries to find out who he is.

[*Takes an onion and pulls off layer after layer.*]

There lies the outermost layer, all torn:
that's the shipwrecked man on the jolly-boat's keel.
Here's the passenger layer, scanty and thin;—
and yet in its taste there's a tang of Peer Gynt.
Next underneath is the gold-digger ego;
the juice is all gone—if it ever had any.
The coarse-grained layer with the hardened skin
is the peltry-hunter by Hudson's Bay.
The next one looks like a crown;—oh, thanks!
we'll throw it away without more ado.
Here's the archaeologist, short but sturdy;
and here is the Prophet, juicy and fresh.
He stinks, as the Scripture has it, of lies,
enough to bring the water to an honest man's eyes.
This layer that rolls itself softly together
is the gentleman, living in ease and good cheer.
The next one seems sick. There are black streaks upon it;—
black symbolises both parsons and niggers.

[*Peels off several layers at once.*]

What an enormous number of swathings!
Isn't the kernel soon coming to light?

166

[*Pulls the whole onion to pieces.*]

I'm blest if it is! To the innermost centre,
it's nothing but swathings—each smaller and smaller.—
Nature is witty!

[*Throws the fragments away.*][1]

Nixon too has layer upon layer around the supposed center
of his personality. But when we begin to peel away these
layers—defensiveness, secretiveness, passivity, happylessness,
compensating aggressiveness with viciousness—we may well
question the core of Nixon's character. The disquieting truth
is that in all probability there is no core, no integrity, no real
values.

In 1968 Nixon claimed, "There certainly is a new Nixon.
I realize, too, that as a man gets older he learns something.
If I haven't learned something I am not worth anything in
public office." [2] There was, however, no change in Nixon's
character. He remained immature, tied to his childhood,
fastened to his mother, from whom he never was weaned
emotionally. Because of his undeveloped feelings, he had difficulty in seeing his behavior as originating in himself. Therefore he felt little or no guilt in carrying out antisocial and
criminal acts.

Many years before, Nixon had said to a close associate (who
prefers to remain anonymous), "You don't know how to lie.
If you can't lie, you'll never go anywhere." His associate
added that Nixon sounded like a lawyer for the Mafia.

Nixon sold himself elaborately in the elections of 1968 and
1972. In doing so he was, again, like Peer Gynt, when Peer's
mother, exasperated by Peer's lies, cries out:

> Yes, a lie, turned topsy-turvy,
> can be prinked and tinselled out,
> decked in plumage new and fine,
> till none knows its lean old carcass.
>
> That is just what you've been doing,
> vamping up things, wild and grand . . .
> lying right and lying left . . .[3]

While many politicians use advertising and public relations

people to project their image, none has done so as well and as systematically as Richard Nixon, who used advertising techniques to create an image of himself and package his political policies. He was a questionable product polished up to look good. Every year it seemed that there was a new, improved Nixon.

While this kind of image making—selling, packaging—is perhaps representative of Madison Avenue, Nixon collected and used far more money than other candidates to corrupt the art. Although *all* the blame for using advertising techniques in an election campaign should not fall on Nixon, since our times demand it, he was certainly responsible for the degree of misrepresentation.

Nixon had no ideological core; in both his personal and political life he had no guiding principles, no genuine ideals. For this the United States can be grateful. For if he had, he would in all probability have been far more dangerous than he was.

Nixon's behavior, as he entered his second term, indicated more and more his lack of insight regarding himself. In a *New York Times* interview he stated, "I never watch TV commentators or the news shows when they are about me. That's because I don't want decisions influenced by personal emotional reactions." [4] Nixon wanted to separate himself from his feelings, as if this were possible.

In the same interview he said, "The major weakness of inexperienced people is that they take things personally, especially in politics, and that can destroy you."

Though passivity pervaded his makeup, in an interview in 1968 with the London *Observer*'s Kenneth Harris, Nixon stated that he "didn't have his parents' passivity" and that he "didn't believe in being passive under attack."

Saying that he didn't believe in being passive when attacked suggests that he was aware that in fact he was passive unless attacked. It also suggests that as a passive person he invited attack. People who like to take on those weaker than themselves often have an uncanny way of singling out their targets. They sense when a person is receptive or vulnerable to either verbal or physical attack, and seize the opportunity to exploit this weakness. When a person is afraid of being attacked, as Nixon was, it usually means that he unconsciously desires it. Fear and hostility work hand in hand.

Governed by his unconscious passivity, unable or afraid to

confront his own conflicting emotions, in particular his hostility, he required that his actions be carried out by his White House associates.

Behind the burglary of Dr. Fielding's office and his other subversive acts was the hostile mind of Richard Nixon. He showed this hostility openly when in July 1971 he announced to his staff:

> I want every son of a bitch in the State Department polygraphed until you find the guy [responsible for leaks at the State Department] . . . I don't give a good goddamn about [legalities]; it's more important to find the source of these leaks than worry about the civil rights of some bureaucrats.[5]

Nixon was so fearful and defensive and angry that he was capable of destroying anyone who threatened him. He was combative, a man who believed as he had written in *Six Crises,* "Instinctively I knew I had to counterattack. You cannot win a battle in any arena of life merely by defending yourself." [6] Offense was the best defense. This is how he tried to disassociate himself in order to deny any responsibility for the Watergate burglary, and attempted to prevent any objective investigation of his activities. When, for example, on February 25, 1974, the House Judiciary Committee requested that Nixon submit tape recordings of forty-two conversations between him and his staff members in order to obtain possible evidence for impeachment, Nixon interpreted this (and rightly so) as a personal threat. The tapes would prove whether or not he was guilty of "high treason and misdemeanors." Since the President did not yield to this request, the committee was forced to subpoena the crucial evidence.

Nixon, however, was an old warrior who believed he could fight off the subpoena with his combativeness. It was the same Nixon who had said, "When you hit a king, kill him." Instinctively, he was out for the kill. But he had to be sure of his target. An earlier target was Special Prosecutor Archibald Cox, whom he had appointed to investigate the Watergate break-in. When Cox, however, had to go further into the case than Nixon, for good reasons, wanted him to, he fired Cox in the now famous "Saturday Night Massacre" of October 20, 1973. Elliot Richardson, the Attorney General, refused to fire Cox and resigned, so that Nixon had to order Solicitor

General Robert Bork to do it. Bork was appointed Acting Attorney General. He in turn appointed Leon Jaworski as Special Prosecutor.

Nixon's second target became the House Judiciary Committee, which he symbolically wanted to kill and destroy. Yet even someone holding the power of the highest public office cannot "kill" anyone, even figuratively, without severe psychological repercussions. A man who has the "instinct to kill," figuratively or actually, unconsciously first wants to kill himself. Hateful aggression directed against someone else without any overt bodily harm is initially directed against the self.

Feeling that defeat would symbolize his own death, Nixon had refused to yield the complete transcripts. Instead, he had given the committee edited transcripts, a performance which he dramatized on nationwide television on April 29, 1974. But the transcripts Nixon provided lacked crucial material, as was quickly discovered, and were therefore less incriminating than the complete tapes would have been. These edited transcripts did, however, disclose Nixon's crude, vicious language and amoral judgments. They were shocking because they revealed that Nixon's lifelong façade of righteousness and virtue was hypocritical. When President Nixon released the edited transcripts, which comprised many volumes, he may have thought—and quite unrealistically—that they would not be widely read.

The transcripts showed how Nixon intended to "stonewall" the grand jury. He had said, "You can say, I don't remember. You can say, I can't recall. I can't give any answer to that. That I can't recall." The tapes revealed more than this clear intent to deceive. Nixon spoke of using the Federal Bureau of Investigation and the Internal Revenue Service to persecute his enemies. Most important, the tapes implicated Nixon and his entire staff in the cover-up.

Given Nixon's natural resistance to revealing his involvement in the Watergate scandal, it is ironic and almost unbelievable that he expected a favorable reaction to the publication of the transcripts. I suggest that one reason for his miscalculation was that he was isolated from and out of touch with public feeling. The cause, however, went deeper.

Nixon had always been preoccupied with himself. This self-absorption was due primarily to a conflict in Nixon, which must have occurred very early in his life. There was the "bad" Nixon, who thought and acted in ways of which his mother and father would never approve, and of which ultimately he himself could not approve. Then there was the "good" Nixon. The one he longed to be, the one he wished the world, particularly his mother, to see and approve of.

I have said that Nixon had always had a vivid imagination and a talent for acting. He would "eliminate" the bad Nixon. To do this he had to deny any feelings or actions that did not jibe with his picture of the good Nixon! Thus, he was alienated from his real feelings, his real self. In his imagination, he was "the good Nixon." Acting the role became second nature to him. If he could think no wrong, he could do no wrong.

I believe that the success of his Checkers speech in 1952, after he was charged with having a secret slush fund, also led him to believe he could repeat the performance. He would once more turn defeat into success. Fortunately for the country, his luck ran out.

Another aspect of Nixon's psychological makeup was his lifelong need for total control over those around him. To consolidate and strengthen his presidential power, he had appointed in 1969 an "inner cabinet," a group of men totally loyal to him. This inner cabinet was in part comprised of young, ambitious men unknown to the public, some of whom had come from advertising firms, such as J. Walter Thompson (H. R. Haldeman, Ronald Ziegler, Dwight Chapin). Then there were John Dean, John Ehrlichman, David Young, and Egil Krogh. A few joined the inner group after 1969. Others, belonging to an older generation, included John Mitchell, Henry Kissinger, Alexander Haig, Raymond Price, Leonard Garment, Charles Colson, and Spiro Agnew. They were all men of his own choice, "his people," whom he thought he could rely on or manipulate. In establishing his complete authority, Nixon was to make them and others his victims.

Everyone, consciously or unconsciously, has tendencies to victimize others. Stimulated by sadistic inclinations, many people hurt, use, and abuse others and thus derive conscious or unconscious pleasure. While this kind of behavior does not necessarily lead to physical harm, there is a *hidden* and insidious kind of victimization in which the one who inflicts pain sets out to destroy the spirit and well-being of the victim. It is a deadly form of psychological warfare.

The Nixon White House was a bloody battleground for just this kind of war.

Nixon's deep-seated sensitivity regarding his personal worth fostered a desperate need to control others—as well as events —in order to gain and maintain power. He was a classic victimizer.

Paradoxically, of course, the victimizer can change roles— and become the victim.[7] This occurred with Nixon.

It is clear that whatever the emotional cost to his colleagues, to himself, and to the nation, Nixon had to be the master. The fall of Nixon's inner circle during and after his second term testifies to his sadism. Some associates went to prison, some were disbarred, others left the Administration with broken families, as well as broken in mind and spirit. He betrayed his subordinates.

As Nixon was incapable of sustaining relationships based on mutual respect, those that he entered into were distorted and sick. With the exception of his association with Henry Kissinger, they fell into a master-slave pattern in which one was superior, the other inferior—a pattern we often see between husband and wife or between homosexuals.

H. R. Haldeman was the staff member closest to Nixon from the beginning of his first term until Haldeman's resignation in March 1973. Their relationship was symbiotic. Haldeman's knowledge of the existence of the tape recorders reveals the quality and importance of their mutual dependency.

As public concern about Watergate grew and began to focus on the Nixon White House, the question of what to do with the tapes became crucial. It is reasonable to assume that Haldeman knew what the tapes contained and that they incriminated him and Nixon as well as others. Why didn't Haldeman advise Nixon to destroy the tapes?

Mike Wallace interviewed Haldeman in two long television broadcasts aired in March 1975. His replies to Wallace are pertinent. When Nixon questioned whether the tapes should be destroyed, Haldeman told Wallace, "my strong recommendation [to him] . . . was that they should not be destroyed. But this was before anyone knew that the tapes existed, except the technicians and the President and me." He suggested to Wallace that the reason for his recommendation was: "I thought they would be valuable to the President in knowing what actually had been said at various meetings in his office."[8]

Asked what it meant from a moral point of view to undertake these recordings, Haldeman answered, "I would say that even with what we now know has happened it was a disastrous thing to have done. But what has happened is a total perversion of what was being done. What was being done was the production of the tapes for the President's own use, for confidential use."

At the Senate Watergate Hearings in July 1973, Haldeman had stated, "I had never really thought that the existence of the tapes would be known. I know that seems a little dense, I guess it did, but I really hadn't just—that wasn't within the range of alternatives of what might happen in my mind." But he *knew* how damaging they could be.

In the first interview with Wallace, we learn that while Haldeman agreed that as a practical matter the release of the tapes would be damaging, he admitted, "When it got to the point of having to release them, it should have been in my opinion, no—destroyed. . . . On a personal basis, on a non-business basis, I was not close to Richard Nixon. . . . I did not love Richard Nixon. I do not love Richard Nixon. I have an enormous respect for Richard Nixon.[9] . . . Nixon is weird in the sense of being inexplicable, strange, hard to understand." [10]

The interviews not only throw light on Haldeman's attitude toward the tapes, but also illuminate the relationship between the two men. Haldeman was tense in Nixon's presence and afraid of him; Nixon intimidated even his closest associates.

One reason for surreptitiously recording conversations was to be able to exploit what Nixon assumed to be his infinite power. He alone would know what people had said; they would not know what *he* had said. Nixon liked to victimize people; he was indirect, devious, secretive, and suspicious, and he enjoyed listening to secretly recorded conversations. In view of the fact that the Pentagon Papers had been stolen and published, Nixon may have thought that the secret White House recordings might also find their way into unfriendly hands. This may be one reason why he told Haldeman, although the time is not given, that perhaps the tapes should be destroyed. On the other hand, one reason for not wanting them destroyed might very well derive from Nixon's own self-destructive tendencies and his previous failures. When we realize, however, his own limited insight into himself, we should not be very surprised that he was unaware of these inclinations. John Osborne learned that when he was asked whether visitors should be informed that they were being taped by the

President of the United States, Nixon replied, "That would be terrible." According to Osborne's source, Nixon said:

> Jesus Christ, you know it would just never do for that to get out, that the President was taping conversations with people in the Oval Office, that would be terrible. Of course, if anything did happen, we would just have to say that, we only recorded, we only retained those things which had to do strictly with national security, for the record, business of state and that sort of thing, and that all the rest was destroyed.* [11]

Haldeman's role in preventing Nixon from destroying the tape recordings is important. Why was he so much against it? His comments on CBS-TV offer us some insight: " . . . nor did I think through the enormous damage that would be done to me and to Richard Nixon, and to all the other participants."

Significantly, he mentions himself first. Later in the Mike Wallace interview he says, "There isn't much him and I—him and me—to say about Watergate. He knows what I know and I know what he knows and . . . there isn't much to add or subtract from that." [12]

In other words, Nixon and Haldeman each knew exactly the extent of their illegal activities. Haldeman may well have been concerned about how Nixon might turn on him and make him a scapegoat. Nixon may have had the same concern. Nixon clearly knew that Haldeman as well as Ehrlichman was implicated in the Watergate break-in and cover-up, and yet on April 30, 1973, Nixon stated on television:

> Today, in one of the most difficult decisions of my Presidency, I accepted the resignations of two of my closest associates in the White House—Bob Haldeman, John Ehrlichman—two of the finest public servants it has been my privilege to know. [13]

---

* It is also reported by Osborne that at the time Nixon was in Bethesda Naval Hospital in July 1973 suffering from a viral pneumonia, he urged Haldeman to remove the taping system and have the accumulated tapes destroyed. Haldeman argued against it, and Nixon later regretted that he had given in to Haldeman's persuasiveness and had not ordered him to do what he then thought and by midsummer was convinced should have been done.

In the same speech, he also talked about the difficult time he had had and how the 1972 campaign developed as it did. He was asking for help, for sympathy, as if to lessen the implications of the resignations.

Nixon called for the resignation of Haldeman and Ehrlichman to take the heat off himself. He was afraid of them because they knew too much—because Haldeman, in particular, knew too much. Why did Haldeman resist the idea of having the tapes destroyed once he sensed the political danger both to himself and to the President?

I believe that Haldeman didn't want the tapes destroyed because as long as they existed he had a hold on Nixon. If he had been truly loyal to Nixon, he would have acted on the fact that the tapes were highly incriminating and potentially very damaging. The tapes could serve as a means of blackmail, which is possible only if the intended victim allows it to succeed. The idea of blackmail in this case is not farfetched.[14]

Blackmail among the Watergate conspirators was well known. The best-known example concerns convicted conspirator E. Howard Hunt, Jr., who threatened to tell the truth about Nixon's involvement in the Watergate cover-up unless "hush money" in the amount of $120,000 was paid.

Haldeman was austere and puritanical and drove his staff hard; he was jealous and punitive, which may be the basis for his advice to Nixon about the tapes. He had become to a high degree an extension of Nixon's character. Nixon may have thought of Haldeman and Ehrlichman as his symbiotic brothers. Haldeman and Nixon served each other's emotional needs.

Haldeman's hold over Nixon meant that their roles had shifted. Whereas Nixon had been the victimizer, he now became the potential victim. It may well be that such a shift also occurred with other of Nixon's associates, such as John Mitchell and John Ehrlichman. Nixon had become a participant in one type of behavior only recently recognized—victimology.

Another aspect of Nixon's complex character structure is illustrated by his choice of Spiro Agnew to be his Vice-President. He selected him not only once, but twice.

It has been said that all Presidents can use a "bad" guy, and Nixon realized that, in addition to Charles Colson, he could use his Vice-President to express his own hostile feelings, to take the "low road." That Agnew was a vicious person is easily documented. One story told by Evans and Novak will suffice:

> . . . Agnew's onslaught against [Senator Charles] Goodell produced one seemingly small incident that was to prove the beginning of Spiro Agnew's decline in the campaign of 1970. In the draft of one speech he was writing for Agnew, Safire referred to Goodell as "a political Christine Jorgensen"—a coarse analogy between Goodell's quick conversion from conservatism to liberalism and the sexual transformation of a young male nurse as a result of an operation in Denmark into the female Christine Jorgensen. Reading Safire's draft aboard the chartered jetliner, Agnew laughed his small, contained laugh and said he liked it. Bryce Harlow, however, thought it was in bad taste. Everybody agreed, and the remark was deleted.
>
> But it was lodged in Agnew's consciousness. In a free and easy conversation with editors of the *New Orleans Times Picayune* and *States Item*, Agnew blurted out that Goodell was "the Christine Jorgensen of the Republican Party." He later told aides he assumed the meeting was off the record, but, in fact, it had been made clear it was *on* the record. The remark received front-page treatment, and Agnew, in character, subsequently defended it with vigor.[15]

Nixon chose Agnew, who, like Nixon, was enigmatic, angry, revengeful, and arrogant. While they were not as close to each other as Nixon was to Haldeman or Kissinger, they served each other's purposes well.

Since Agnew's illegal activities forced him to resign the vice-presidency in order to avoid prison, and Nixon's illegal actions forced his own resignation to avoid impeachment, it is not surprising that Nixon deliberately and yet unconsciously singled out Agnew, an unknown, as his Vice-President in preference to more able and experienced public figures. These two emotionally compatible men had found each other. Agnew was a man whom Nixon could control and manipulate, who would do his dirty work for him. And it may well be that their compatibility accounts for Nixon's failure to publicly denounce Agnew's crimes. His choice and actions were motivated by emotions which restricted his ability to make objective decisions.

Charles Gregory (Bebe) Rebozo, an obscure man with little political background, was personally closer to Nixon than anyone else. Although reporters have unearthed a good many details about Rebozo's career, he still remains a shadowy figure.[16]

Rebozo, the youngest of nine children, was born in Tampa, Florida, on November 17, 1912. His father was a cigar maker in Tampa who with his wife had emigrated from Cuba. Subsequently they moved to Miami, where Rebozo went to high school.

It was at Miami High School that he started to develop friendships with youngsters who came from a more privileged environment. Among them was George Smathers, who later, when he became a senator, introduced Rebozo to people of power and influence. Rebozo did well in high school. He was also named the best-looking senior. Perhaps more important was the relationship he had with a girl which is reminiscent of Richard Nixon's with Ola-Florence and Pat and helps to explain their identification with each other.

In 1930, Rebozo met a vivacious, attractive high school senior named Clare M. Gunn. Bebe was very much taken with her, so much so that he desperately wanted to marry her at once. At first she resisted. Infatuated by her, he insisted that she marry him immediately. Unable to take "no" for an answer, he pursued her week after week, begging her, flattering her. Clare became unnerved. She fell so far behind in her school work that she was not allowed to graduate with her class. Finally, one evening, perhaps to appease her ardent suitor and bring some quiet into her life, she consented to marry Rebozo, on the condition that their marriage be kept secret and that they would not live together. He agreed to this arrangement.

In the Broward County courthouse there is a marriage license dated July 14, 1931, which shows that Rebozo, then only eighteen years old, married Clare Gunn. They both had sworn that they were twenty-one and did not need parental consent. Clay Blair, Jr., former editor of *The Saturday Evening Post,* discovered the long-kept secret.

Following their marriage by a judge in Fort Lauderdale, Rebozo went back to work in a gasoline station and Clare returned to her home. They remained secretly married for three years until she filed for an annulment in 1934. Only then did she tell her parents of the marriage which had never been consummated. A transcript of the court hearing shows that Clare said:

> He became quite attentive, and came down to the house every night and began asking me to marry him. . . . He was very domineering, kept insisting and insisting. . . . It made me absolutely ill with pain and cramps, and I had to just break away, and then I would be sick the next day.

Rebozo was deeply upset by Clare's rejection and the court action, but he continued to work hard to get ahead. He opened a gas station in Miami in 1935. He began to specialize in recapping tires, and when tires became scarce during World War II, his business boomed. He had been a steward with Pan American Airways in 1930, and later, well aware of Clare's interest in airplane pilots, he learned to fly. In 1941 he became a civilian navigator for the Air Transport Command and ferried empty planes from Miami to Africa.

When the war ended, Rebozo, who was living with his mother and married sister in Coral Gables, went into real estate and the personal-loan business. To people hard-pressed for cash, he loaned money, in 1949, at the usurious rate of 42 percent per year.[17]

In 1939, Clare had married a Pan American Airways pilot, who died five years later in a plane crash in the Pacific. Although Rebozo had been rejected by Clare, he was still bound to her. Apparently not wanting to get deeply involved with any other girl, he lived the life of a sophisticated bachelor and was often seen in the company of beautiful young women.

When Clare became a widow in 1944, Rebozo sought her out and began courting her again. In 1946 they remarried, lived together for two years, and then broke up. Clare sued for divorce, in February 1950, and in 1953 she married again. She developed cancer and died in 1960. Rebozo apparently knew about her illness, since he visited her in the hospital and brought her flowers. She had divorced him but he still felt strongly tied to her.

Rebozo's relation to Clare is similar to Nixon's relation to Ola-Florence: neither man showed an ability to develop a deep emotional tie with the woman he made the object of intense pursuit. Rebozo may have felt after his first marriage to Clare that he had won a victory and through the act of marrying an attractive woman had proved to himself that he was a man. Although their first marriage was not consummated, she was the conquered object whose subjection confirmed his sense of manhood.

Yet, like many other men preoccupied with machismo, he had to hide his concern.

Following his divorce in 1950, he once again began to lead a glamorous life. A neighbor of those days says, "His house was always full of fillies—and I don't mean the kind that run on a racetrack. Every time I saw him at a party, he had a different girl and no one ever knew where they came from."

When the limelight turned on Rebozo and Key Biscayne, he gave up his role as a man-about-town. As the friendship between Nixon and Rebozo deepened, he was increasingly involved with Nixon. Rebozo was at his side in 1960 when Nixon lost the presidential election. He was with him in the evening when he lost the California governorship race in 1962.

In the early 1960's, Rebozo had become interested in Jane Ann Lucke, a Key Biscayne divorcee and legal secretary to Thomas Wakefield, his attorney and business associate. Later, Rebozo and Jane became White House insiders. She and Rebozo were the only outside guests for Julie Nixon's birthday. There are no reports on whether he has married, but his closeness to Nixon and his complex relationship with Clare suggest that another marriage for him is doubtful.

Since Rebozo was very close to Nixon, his financial success and dealings have come under scrutiny. When he was in the fifth grade, Bebe had a job slaughtering and plucking chickens. He never forgot his "most distasteful" boyhood job. His road to riches began with his tire-recapping business and then buying and selling small pieces of land and lending money at exorbitant rates. Many of his former classmates had gone into real estate or banking, and Rebozo learned from them. He also, as we have seen, was close to George Smathers, who later became a senator by defeating Claude Pepper "in what is remembered as the most vitriolic Florida congressional campaign in recent history." Smathers identified Pepper with the "Commies . . . Radicals . . . and fellow travelers," the same tactic used by Nixon when he campaigned against Helen Gahagan Douglas. Rebozo was one of Smathers' campaign workers, a loyal member of his goon squad. Through the later years Rebozo's various partnerships with Smathers, financed by the Maroon banks, expanded his speculative real estate operation. He assembled valuable business properties in Miami, Coral Gables, and the Biscayne area. In 1960 he went into the coin-laundry business. Later he became president and chairman of the Key Biscayne Bank and Trust Company. In 1971 it was estimated that his worth was well over the $1 million mark.[18] In 1974 it is estimated that he was worth $4.5 million.[19]

As a freshman congressman, Nixon had come to know his fellow congressman George Smathers. Smathers introduced him to Richard Danner, his 1946 campaign manager. And it was Danner who introduced Rebozo to Nixon in 1950. Danner, who knew his way around Miami (the former FBI agent had been the city's manager), later worked as Howard Hughes's liaison with Nixon.

There must have been an immediate attraction between Nixon and Rebozo. Nixon was already a prominent public figure; he could help Rebozo. Rebozo could also help Nixon—and he did. Their personalities were similar. Rebozo could be entertaining and talkative, but, like Nixon, he was a secretive loner. Smathers recognized that Rebozo has a complex personality: "He's a very mercurial guy. Some days he loves the world, others he's suspicious of everybody." [20]

Rebozo prefers to act behind the scenes, and so through the years he proved to be the perfect partner for Nixon. He was flattered by Nixon's dependence on him and enjoyed the clandestine quality of their friendship; he remained the man in the shadows waiting to serve him.

Smathers once said, "I've seen him [Nixon] and Bebe sit in a room for three hours and neither ever say a word. Nixon's a little bit of a mystic." [21] A hidden bond between Nixon and Rebozo made their relationship secretive and exclusive. Rebozo had become Nixon's bosom friend.

While Nixon was Vice-President, he frequently went to Key Biscayne, stopping at the island hotel or at Bebe's home. Mrs. Nixon, however, did not seem to like Key Biscayne, so he went by himself or with William P. Rogers, who later was to become his Secretary of State. Following Nixon's defeat in California in 1962, Rebozo included him in one of his Miami real estate trust deals, which earned Nixon close to $200,000 profit.

In the years that followed, Rebozo guided Nixon's real estate investments, with the result that Nixon was able to buy a home in Key Biscayne. It was Robert Abplanalp (a director of Rebozo's bank) who at the time of his first inauguration loaned Nixon $625,000 with which to buy a 30-acre tract in San Clemente for $1.5 million. In August 1973 the White House reluctantly admitted that Rebozo was Abplanalp's partner in an investment company that later paid Nixon $1,249,000 and canceled the $625,000 loan on San Clemente, for which Nixon gave up only 5.9 acres of the 30 acres he had bought.

Rebozo's success in obtaining loans, particularly from the Small Business Administration, has been remarkable. When Rebozo opened the only bank on Key Biscayne, the bank charter of a rival group had been turned down by the Comptroller of the Currency, despite the federal bank examiner's conclusion that Rebozo's bank was "so conservative that it is almost not a bank."

Representative Wright Patman declared in 1969, "From 1962 through the present, Mr. Rebozo has been a 'preferred customer' of the Small Business Administration. . . . There can be no justification for SBA lending money to an individual under the guise of a small businessman, who then turns around and opens a bank."

In March 1973 the Federal Home Loan Bank Board turned down for the second time an application for federal deposit insurance from a savings and loan association on Key Biscayne. In June 1973, Daniel St. Albin Greene reported, "Nixon appointed two new members to the three-man board, leaving one seat vacant. In July they granted insurance to the twice-rejected company. Two of the owners are directors of Rebozo's bank, and it operates out of his bank building."

Given the tie between Rebozo and Nixon, it is not surprising that Rebozo was the intermediary in secret transactions involving cash contributions of $100,000 from Howard Hughes to Nixon's campaign.[22]

Richard Danner, manager of Hughes's Sands Hotel in Las Vegas, delivered two illegal donations of $50,000 from Hughes to Rebozo when Nixon had been elected President. Rebozo's lawyer, Thomas Wakefield, issued checks in the amount of $45,621.15 to various accounts to pay local firms for a variety of expenses including improvements on the

Nixon estate in Florida.[23] It is noteworthy that during this time Rebozo did not have sufficient cash available to be able to make these deposits from any known source other than the political campaign contributions which he acknowledged in his Senate testimony. From 1969 until April 1972 Rebozo received from representatives of Howard Hughes and A. D. Davis contributions totaling $150,000.

It was Rebozo's lawyer, Thomas Wakefield, who, through a complicated series of bank withdrawals and deposits, "laundered" the money (which originally belonged to the Florida for Nixon Committee) used to buy platinum-and-diamond earrings for Pat Nixon's sixtieth birthday.

Rebozo says of himself, "I'm not a fund-raiser and I don't even like to handle money," and declared that "my relationship has been truly a social one with various people in high office from time to time." [24]

Rebozo in an interview also stated, "Money means nothing to him [Nixon]" and "I don't know that he has ever signed a check himself." [25]

Although Nixon didn't write checks, he was not averse to receiving them. CREEP collected $60 million during the 1972 campaign. It has also been disclosed that Nixon "personally accepted at his New York City apartment" in 1968 an illegal $50,000 campaign contribution to his first successful presidential bid.[26]

Rebozo's personality structure was such that Nixon felt he could rely on him completely. He found in Rebozo (as he had in Haldeman) a substitute brother, a man who possessed qualities Nixon himself wished to emulate. He came to admire Rebozo because of his financial successes. Even though Nixon was politically successful, he yearned for wealth and power and admired Bebe's business acumen. Rebozo had the Midas touch.

What we know of their personality structure and background and experience leaves me with the impression that each has been committed to only one person—himself. Yet they were drawn together by the pattern of their lives and the unusual mix of personality traits. Rebozo and Nixon always viewed themselves as outsiders. Rebozo, the son of a Cuban cigar maker (Catholic), had been thrown into a well-to-do middle-class environment (predominantly Protestant). Nixon, a Quaker from the small town of Whittier, California, had felt out of the mainstream of the eastern establishment. Each was fiercely determined to overcome his humble beginnings. And each had a mother with an iron will and ambitious for her children.

Both Nixon and Rebozo were strongly power-oriented, lacked the ability to become emotionally involved, and were secretive in their undertakings. While Nixon had the advantage of a college and law school education, Bebe succeeded through shrewdness and natural business ability. Each sought out a beautiful woman to affirm his manhood. They shared the middle-class work ethic and the same pastimes: lounging on Bebe's boat, charcoaling steaks in Rebozo's back yard, watching football on television.

There were also similarities in their patterns of courtship. Both were unusually tenacious and self-demeaning.

Most important, both seemed interested in women only as objects to satisfy their need to affirm their manhood, not as life partners with whom they could share deep emotions and feelings. On the contrary, their relationships with these women were a way of impressing others. Nixon and Rebozo remain very private men.

Henry Kissinger, who played a major role in Nixon's administration, remained outside Nixon's inner circle. In spite of the dissimilarity in their backgrounds, education, and outlook, they were able to work well together. Kissinger, a Jew, was born in Germany. He had attended Harvard University and taught there. He was part of the eastern establishment through his association with Nelson Rockefeller. Nixon's background, of course, was totally different.

But there were similarities. Both were highly self-centered. Both were self-made men brought up outside the mainstream of society. And both were secretive. Perhaps most important, their political orientation was similar. Kissinger, like Nixon, was deeply interested in foreign policy. Each thought he could control the other. Both were committed to success on the international front as an expression of personal glory and achievement. *Both hungered for power.*

The remarks of Thomas L. Hughes of the Bureau of Intelligence and Research, State Department, put it well:

Both were incurably covert, but Kissinger was charming about it. Both abhorred bureaucracy, but Nixon was reclusive about it. . . . Both jealously guarded against diffusion of power, but Kissinger dispensed balm. Both were inveterate manipulators, but Nixon was more transparent. Both insisted on extremes of loyalty, but Kissinger endeared himself to his critics. Both had a penchant for secrecy, but neither uniformly practiced what he preached. Both were deeply suspicious, but Kissinger was irrepressibly gregarious. Neither was widely admired for truthfulness. . . . Neither worshipped the First Amendment. . . . Both were intoxicated with diplomacy. . . . Both were fixated on their role in history.[27]

When Kissinger posed before the Sphinx in November 1973, he joked, "Which of us is the real Sphinx?" As there always is a real intent behind every joke, his question is an affirmation.[28]

Kissinger, like Nixon, had a strong need to control others. "Power," Kissinger once said, was "the greatest aphrodisiac." [29] Although he may have been unaware of the real meaning of his remark, it certainly shows that his sexual feelings and desire for power were intertwined. Further, only a secretive, power-oriented, egocentric, suspicious man would win the trust of Nixon. These qualities struck a chord in the President. While Kissinger demanded complete allegiance, he was loyal only when it suited him.*

Interesting in this regard are J. B. Atkinson's comments:

> Reluctant as he might have been to behave as a client to Nixon, Kissinger was naturally predisposed to behave as an autocrat to his subordinates—men such as Alexander Haig, Alexis Johnson, and David Young. If his subordinates chose to treat him as a patron, he was disinclined to enlighten them.[31]

Kissinger, who has been likened to Bismarck, followed his dictum that "diplomacy is the art of the possible." Kissinger

---

* In a political film shown on August 23, 1972, at the Republican National Convention, he said that there was a "certain heroic quality about how he [Nixon] conducts his business . . ." In 1968, Kissinger, who supported Rockefeller, was quoted as saying, "Richard Nixon is the most dangerous, of all the men running, to have as President." [30]

said in an essay on Bismarck, "Facts cannot be changed; they can only be used." Since Kissinger, like Bismarck, responded primarily to opportunity, his ideological conviction became weakened. He is a man who believes solely in *Realpolitik*.

Nixon, too, was intent on playing on the global chessboard. Both *needed* power.

Nixon's view of the role of a Secretary of State could hardly have pleased Kissinger, although he had expressed that view before Kissinger was appointed to that post. Nixon said:

> I have always thought this country could run itself domestically without a President. All you need is a competent Cabinet to run the country at home. You need a President for foreign policy; no Secretary of State is really important. The President makes foreign policy.[32]

There were deep motivations for this preposterous reasoning. In one breath Nixon dismissed domestic affairs. Although he said that the Cabinet could run the home front, in fact his Cabinet was notoriously weak. Through wiretapping, "enemies lists," the White House "plumbers," the soliciting of illegal campaign funds, and many other illegal acts, he personally assumed more and more control of domestic affairs. The tighter his control of the country, the less he thought he had to fear. There were, perhaps, more personal loyalties involved in domestic affairs. And loyalty—or the lack of it—always posed a greater threat to his integrity. Because of Nixon's all-consuming desire for allegiance, he looked upon disagreement on domestic issues as an offense against his integrity.

More important to Kissinger was Nixon's arrogant dismissal of the importance of any Secretary of State. But Kissinger knew history and the intimate details of foreign affairs; he was a brilliant negotiator. He was gregarious, and could thus do what Nixon could not do. Nixon needed Kissinger, and this fact gave Kissinger great power.

The conviction grew in Nixon that he was omnipotent. He went beyond the constitutional powers vested in the President in foreign affairs (notably in Southeast Asia) because he desperately wanted to make his name in the world: Henry

Kissinger was of immeasurable help in achieving that goal, in making his daydreams about the world come to life.

Although modern Presidents since Franklin Roosevelt have, with some exceptions, tended to draw more and more power into their hands, Richard Nixon went further than any. He brought into play feelings of godlike power that made the presidency resemble a monarchy. A minor example of Nixon's attempts to surround himself with the trappings of royalty is readily seen in his pathetic desire to have the White House police dressed in tunics and helmets. A storm of ridicule brought an end to it.

Another characteristic—officiousness—gives evidence of Nixon's character disturbance. Feeling unsure of himself, unable to trust himself and others, he "wanted to have his finger in every detail." The need to compensate for his low self-esteem made him want to be concerned with and be the center of everything in the White House. Emotionally, however, he was an outsider.

During the Senate Watergate Hearings, Alexander Butterfield revealed that Nixon spent a great deal of time, for instance, on how curtains should be hung, where he or Cabinet members should stand at public functions. A President who is so concerned with detail shows his compulsive nature.

A person who displays anal traits is also a perfectionist, and Nixon fits that definition. When he appeared in public or on television, he never wore eyeglasses. He was, as Haldeman said, "very vain." [33] While many of us are vain and are eager to look and do our best, Nixon had an obsession to be perfect in the eyes of everyone. He needed to appear impeccable because he had such a low opinion of himself.

He desired desperately to be in control of any and all situations. Anal orientation leads to an overwhelming desire to control oneself and others, even the whole world, which harks back to Nixon's earlier childhood desire to see the world and finally to master the world of politics. For him it was much more than a professional interest in the political scene. Unconsciously and consciously he wanted to control it.

Self-control may lead to something salutary: true independence. But Nixon's form of control led to stubbornness and rigidity, a kind of *hyper*-control.

His hyper-control we observe in the unbending rigidity of

his body. Although his body movements are awkward, clumsy, giving him the appearance of being inept, like that of a graceless adolescent, he held tight control over his public posture. In pictures he seems stiff and doesn't know what to do with his arms, as though they are not really a part of him. In one picture taken at a football game, his left hand is stiff and with his right hand he rigidly holds on to his right thigh. In the picture of his twenty-year class reunion at Whittier College in 1954, he stands in front of all the others, alone and awkwardly braced.

Observing his body movements, we find that his unfree, uncertain, and hesitant arm movements mask his aggressive inclinations. Trying to repress these feelings, he gives the impression of freezing. His gestures become rigid and uncoordinated, all giving the illusion that in his whole appearance he is immobile.

He was terrified of being dominated. Murray Chotiner found him "the hardest candidate of all to manage." [34] The desperate need to control is invariably mobilized by fear. Self-discipline becomes so exaggerated that a person becomes a caricature. Yet to Nixon this self-discipline was a positive characteristic of which he was proud. When he told Mazo, "I have a fetish about disciplining myself," [35] Nixon didn't understand the implications of his statement.

By exerting self-control he could well have been led into the illusion that he could not do anything wrong. Such a mechanism was strengthened by his undue repressions of his hostile, antisocial, criminal feelings, which, as mentioned earlier, led to their being encapsulated within him. He was cut off from them because of his character disorder. And this disturbance became evident in his undeveloped feelings of guilt. This stunted ability runs like a thread through his behavior pattern. It became difficult for him to differentiate between right and wrong.

While we all have traces of both oral and anal traits, Nixon had unusual oral and anal *fixations*. We have seen his strong oral orientation. Among his many anal traits, we also must stress his "tightness" and acquisitive characteristics. He was not generous. He tried to reduce his taxes through illegal means, and his tax-deductible gifts while he was President were small indeed. Nixon's income and charitable contributions for the four years from 1969 to 1972 were:

	Income [36]	Contributions [37]
1969	$328,161.52	$3,150.00
1970	262,942.56	7,512.00
1971	262,384.75	2,524.00
1972	268,777.54	295.00

Of the $7,512 Nixon contributed in 1970, $4,500 was given to the Billy Graham Evangelistic Association; $1,000 was given to the Baptist Community Hospital; $1,000 went to the UCLA Alumni Association. His charitable donations, contrary to common practice, went to an almost completely different list of organizations each year. Although he and his wife filed a joint return, her name did not appear as a donor to any charity.

Nixon also had deducted $576,000[38] in 1969 for his vice-presidential and presidential papers which he donated to the federal government. The deductions were disallowed, however, because the deed had been illegally backdated.

Through his acquisitive nature, which had been reinforced by his childhood anal characteristics, he was during his presidency prompted to acquire wealth as well as two mansions, one on the east coast in Key Biscayne and one on the west coast in San Clemente. In addition, of course, he lived in the White House and used Camp David in Maryland. Symbolically he had acquired all America.

Nixon wanted to be everywhere and yet was nowhere. He was a man without a home.

It is said that he was generous to those who worked for him or those who came to visit him for public causes. While at times he could be kind, it does not seem that kindness was an outstanding attribute.

His kindness was of a peculiar type. One person on his staff pointed out, "I could talk for a long time with him about what was on his mind. But then suddenly he stopped and the conversation was over." He was so self-preoccupied that even when he could be kind he could not maintain this sense of friendliness.

We also know his tenderness as a child when he remembered how his little brother Arthur called his mother into his room two days before his death:

He put his arms around her and said that he wanted to

pray before he went to sleep. Then, with closed eyes, he repeated that age-old child's prayer which ends with these simple yet beautiful words:

"If I should die before I awake, I pray Thee, Lord, my soul to take."

There is a grave out now in the hills, but, like the picture, it contains only the bodily image of my brother.

And so when I am tired and worried, and am almost ready to quit trying to live as I should, I look up and see the picture of a little boy with sparkling eyes, and curly hair; I remember the childlike prayer; I pray it may prove true for me as it did for my brother Arthur.[39]

We know about the compassionate letters Nixon sent to widows whose husbands had been killed in the Vietnam War. These deaths may have reminded Nixon of his two dead brothers.

Yet this aspect of Nixon's character is in sharp contrast to reports from former colleagues. Kissinger, for example, publicly declared that "Nixon was unpleasant."[40]

Philip Mayher, a senior lieutenant in the Navy who had been with Nixon at the Ottumwa, Iowa, Navy camp in 1943 and 1944, told me that Nixon, who was a junior lieutenant, hardly spoke with anyone below him in rank. He didn't even express friendliness to those who were his immediate superiors. He only sought the friendship of the lieutenant commander of the post and those of similar rank. Nixon was known to be a "bootlicker," or, as my source characterized him, a "brown-nose" par excellence. "Already at that time he was playing politics."

His lack of trust in others is clearly shown in the White House transcripts, in which there is little or no expression of Nixon's trust in our national institutions or in government on any level.

The tapes showed Nixon's indecisiveness and fear. He said, "It is better to fight it out. . . . It is better to fight it out and not let people testify. . . . And now, on the other hand, we realize that we have these weaknesses—that we have these weaknesses—in terms of blackmail." "This is a war. We take few shots and it will be over."

"What is the situation anyway with regard to the situation of the sentencing of the seven? When in the hell is that going to occur? . . .

"Another way to do it . . . is to continue to try to cut our losses. Now we have to take a look at that course of action. First it is going to require approximately a million dollars to take care of the jackasses who are in jail. That can be arranged."

". . . . You know when they talk about a 35-year sentence, here is something to think about. . . . ." "What the hell do they expect though? Do they expect clemency in a reasonable time? . . . You couldn't do it, say, in six months."

"It's about $120,000. . . . That would be easy. It is not easy to deliver, but it is easy to get. Now."

"That's why for your immediate things you have no choice but to come up with the $120,000, or whatever it is. . . . Would you agree that that's the prime thing that you damn well better get that done? . . ."

"It's a hell of a lot different than John Dean. I know that as far as you're concerned [Haldeman and Ehrlichman] you'll go out and throw yourself on a damned sword. . . . I'm trying to think the thing through with that in mind because, damn it, you're the two most valuable members on the staff. . . . It's not bull—it's the truth. . . . I'm not ruling out kicking him [Dean] out. But I think you got to figure what to hell does Dean know. What kind of blackmail does he have?"

"The point is, if you break it off with him [Dean], then he could go out and say, 'Screw the . . .'"

"Frankly, the Dean thing troubles the hell out of me—I would like, in one sense I would like to see the poor bastard, you know, out of it and in another sense I think the immunity thing scares me to death."

In connection with raising the money, Nixon said, "No, it is wrong, that's for sure." [41] Thus referring to a criminal act, he stated the obvious; it is what a child would say. However, it is also an expression of Nixon's disturbed character. Further, the violent language, the gutter language displayed may indicate that he almost was trying to rub people's noses in the dirt. The tapes confirm a strong disdain for others and the anger and contempt that filled his mind. An angry, hostile man is seldom kind.

On the tapes, Nixon expressed the thoughts he really had about people. These tapes provided the outlet he needed to get back at his enemies, since he was unable to deal with them directly. To a high degree, the ideas he expressed on the tapes follow an unconscious pattern of retaliation and revenge. Nixon started this taping for unconscious reasons, which may be why he continued with the taping long after the Watergate investigation had begun. It may have been why he would not destroy them, because the tapes were really part of him, *part of his unconscious mind*. For once he wanted to get out what was really on his mind. He was convinced that the President, his imperial presidency, was beyond sanction. However, psychologically he had an overwhelming need to vent his anger against those whom he thought were against him.

We receive the impression that Nixon was entirely consumed by his emotions. ("Eaten up with himself" might be a better expression.) He couldn't forget the snubs, the injuries he had received throughout his life, and he was now giving it back, word for word. Revenge was at the core of his feelings. Not once did he talk about a wrongdoing he had committed. His behavior here followed his early pattern: fighting belligerently while proclaiming innocence. It is therefore not surprising that, after he returned to San Clemente, in a lengthy deposition made to regain custody and disposition of White House documents and tapes, he claimed a right to decide the future of these papers and tapes. He evaded the problem that this material contained evidence of the illegal acts that compelled him to resign in order to avoid impeachment.[42] As usual, his rhetoric was strong but the substance was weak.

In his deposition, as in all his speeches, he was bent upon showing that he was right, and that he was not insignificant. He wanted to be manly. Consciously and unconsciously, he was attempting to show his mother that he was important. He had once made a comment about America not being a "pitiful, helpless giant." This is a remarkable and revealing statement. Unconsciously, it clearly refers to feelings he had about himself. He was far from unimportant, but inwardly he felt so, and he wanted desperately to reassure himself.

Nixon's personal and political behavior originated in his passive-aggressive personality structure. My formulation is different from that of James David Barber, who describes Nixon's character as being "active-negative."[43] By this description, Barber means that Nixon is fundamentally aggressive, but that he controls himself, so that his frustrations and anger are kept within him. In speeches, Nixon moves "from defense to attack, larding his rhetoric with aggressiveness."[44]

Barber has underestimated the underlying element in

Nixon's behavior; his passivity. In my view it is only by recognizing this passivity that we can understand, psychodynamically, the inner working of his mind—his indirectness, deviousness, ambivalence, secretiveness, and hysterical exhibitionism, his shattered superego, his destructiveness. Nixon suffers from a character disorder. He can, in fact, be described as a *psychopathic personality*. Such individuals are frequently aggressive and passive—either alternately or simultaneously. They may be alcoholics, drug addicts, or sexual deviants—they may be bisexual or homosexual. They may be antisocial. They are generally impulsive, unreliable, prone to lie and to commit criminal acts. They are highly narcissistic. Since their character formation has been distorted, they act out their conscious and unconscious fantasies almost immediately. They are unable to tolerate frustration, and require immediate gratification.

Predominant in Nixon's character were his egocentric and paranoid feelings, which brought to the fore his secretive, manipulative, and omnipotent attitudes.

Character is the sum total of the thoughts and feelings (conscious and unconscious) and the views and aspirations that come through in an individual's behavior. Character is revealed in the way a person expresses every thought and every feeling, the way he or she carries out or avoids action. A person may have a passive, receptive character, such as Nixon's fundamentally passive one, which he tries to deny by becoming overly aggressive. On the other hand, a person with an aggressive character will typically solve emotional problems by carrying out actions directly in an aggressive way. If a person is passive, he will respond to problems by conforming to the situation. Character, then, presents the dominant set of the person's feelings, the emotional attitudes which determine how he or she will function. Character means the *personality structure* which determines and decides the pattern of behavior. It is the power of motivation, the force around which the person moves and from which he receives his incentive.

Character is the core of any person's psychology. Character and psychology are related as anatomy relates to physiology. While a person's outward behavior may change, his character remains unchanged.

The formation of character begins at birth and develops in a definite direction in accordance with the child's instinctual forces and his responses to family environment. As a youngster's feelings, which dictate his evaluation of this environment, are subject to constant variation, evaluations change accordingly. This kind of alternating emotional pattern may upset character formation, leading to permanent instability. Yet, despite this variance in behavior, the child retains certain fundamental traits which form the basis of his attitudes and actions, which in turn shape his behavior pattern. In fact, when the child becomes an adult, his basic style of behavior and feelings remains the same since his character already has been defined. Not all characters are strong or positive. Although character as such does not change, its nature may be vague and indefinite, indicating a weak or almost nonexistent character.

That Nixon held back his feelings implied that he was frightened, protective of himself, defensive and vulnerable. His self was splintered, broken, but many pieces of his personality still hung together. He was not a whole person. A person who holds back his feelings is fundamentally cold, heartless, isolated. He is a person who rejects. He is alone.

Unable to trust anyone, Nixon created an imperial presidency that corrupted the power of the Chief Executive far beyond that of any earlier President. While previous Presidents used and misused power, Nixon went further than any of his predecessors. He came to rule as if his power were a "divine right."

11

Was Nixon as President capable of rationally discharging his responsibilities? While on the surface it would seem that many of his White House decisions were based on national interests, he reacted mostly to public issues under the influence of his personality needs. It is impossible to differentiate between when he was acting dispassionately and when he was acting out of his deeply ingrained instinctual drives. Often it was a simultaneous process.

In determining the extent of the disturbance of a person's character, we should not be misled by what we perceive as his intelligence. Many people who suffer from a character disorder are highly intelligent and talented. But this intelligence is frequently blocked; people often become involved in situations in which their unconscious desires to destroy or punish themselves predominate over rational judgment. They become their own victims.

Although Nixon is not an intellectual, his intelligence is far above average. According to some of his White House associates, he was able to analyze a political problem with great insight—"down to the bone." However, Nixon feared being considered wrong or less than perfect, which caused him to be overcautious in approaching any problem. Intelligence presupposes spontaneity. Nixon, who was never spontaneous, could not use his intelligence to the fullest. It was constricted, and thus his judgment was often faulty.

Nixon's intelligence was limited by interference from his fears. It was these fears which, to a large extent, propelled him in a constant search for power. And having gained power, he was unsure of how to use it for the well-being of others. Even after he was in the White House he was so obsessed with being re-elected that he substituted CREEP for the leadership of the Republican Party. And the methods he used were illegal. He would use any means to achieve his end. Being the President meant that he already had power over the running of domestic affairs. He also wanted to extend his power to encompass the world.

Therefore, he had to develop a strategy for acquiring even more power, and this fascinated him. Apparently he used the same strategy here as he used when campaigning or playing poker. He was out to win. Power became an end in itself. It was a personal strategy geared to his own advantage. Since his power-gathering increased his narcissism, it restricted his ability to deal with substantive issues on a rational basis.

Unconsciously Nixon must have realized this—and the knowledge only added to his feelings of being overwhelmed, put upon. He reacted as he always did when threatened: with defensive paranoid feelings. It was not *his* fault. He couldn't be expected to do *everything*. In his mind he justified his desire for more power—as stemming from his deep need to serve the country. He was the leader. He had to have power to lead properly. His problem was that he didn't know how to lead, how to *act*, because of his essential passivity.

One particular influence in shaping Nixon's behavior was the pattern of rejection and failure that he experienced repeatedly at different turns in his career. This pattern had become an important part of his personality and reflected passivity. Unconsciously Nixon sought failure. He had become attracted to it. Failure had become a compulsion one might compare to a sexual compulsion wherein a person is driven by desire and a need to masturbate. The need to fail stemmed from his guilt feelings—feelings which he could never acknowledge, even to himself. Although these guilt feelings were rooted in his early sexual yearning for his mother, it does not necessarily mean that he actually desired sexual intercourse with her. The yearning reflects, as it does with most people, only a need for closeness to his mother.

However, the mind of a child cannot make this distinction. He knows only that his wishes are somehow forbidden. To want what is forbidden calls for punishment. Thus the circle begins. To a man such as Nixon, failure is the worst possible punishment he can conceive. So he becomes in effect his own executioner. He punishes himself by arranging his own failures.

But once his need for punishment was fulfilled, Nixon, mobilized by his hysterical traits, had to show that he could come back dramatically with spectacular success and remain in the limelight. Each comeback was an emotional return from death to life. Having been brought back to life, he created another situation which again would lead to failure, to defeat. He thus established a pattern of self-destruction, which, I feel, because it was associated with the death of his two brothers, became an unconscious re-enactment of his own death. His apparent recovery from each defeat (I say "apparent" advisedly, because it was only temporary until another failure beckoned) showed that after all he was not a "loser," as people had thought. And he would also proclaim that he was not a "quitter."

Nixon's behavior pattern was one of projective defense against attacks, both real and imagined. When people imagine they are being attacked, they may unconsciously wish for it. They may feel they deserve it, or they feel others are "against" them. They are projecting their own feelings onto others. Nixon exhibited all the signs of a *paranoid personality*. Such a person may be psychotic but not always so. People with a paranoid personality are often highly talented and educated. But they are self-centered, rigid, morbidly sensitive, easily angered, secretive, and calculating. Often they impugn the motives of others about even minor and irrelevant matters.

This description, as we have seen, applies to Nixon.

During the last years of his presidency, the impairment of his mind grew and could be seen in his overt behavior. He had established the "Enemies List" against "those who had done us in"—an extension of his paranoid feelings—and he also showed his virulent anger against the press. As William Safire has recounted:

> "The Press is the *enemy*" to be hated and beaten, and in that vein of vengeance that ran through his relationship with another power center, in his indulgence of his most combative and abrasive instincts against what he saw to be an unelected and unrepresentative elite, lay Nixon's greatest personal and political weakness and the cause of his downfall.[1]

Nixon had become suspicious to an inordinate degree. Roy M. Cohn told me:

> I think he was one of the *most* suspicious men I have ever met in my life. I think he was suspicious of every-

body and everything. I think he was like a fellow who always thought of himself as being in a corner, and trying to see who is trying to trap him. I think he looked at everybody with suspicion and had complete second thoughts and saying, what's his game and how is it going to affect me? No question about that. I would say that without a moment's hesitancy. He was tough and suspicious.

In March 1973 Nixon commented to John Dean, "Nobody is a friend of ours. Let's face it." This feeling pervaded the White House. Thomas Charles Huston remarked, "No one who had been in the White House could help but feel he was in a state of siege."[2] Herbert Porter, after he had been at the White House a couple of days, said, "Dwight Chapin said to me, 'One thing you should realize early on, we are practically an island here.' "[3]

Campaign movies and tapes made during the presidential primary in New Hampshire in March 1968 show an apparently confident Nixon who appeared strong and definite. This sense of confidence and well-being is in sharp contrast to his manner in 1974, when, in spite of his attempts at self-control, he was severely tense, ill at ease, distracted, brooding. His worries over Watergate were etched in the lines of his face. Emotional tension, and paranoid suspicion, had taken their toll.

The case of Nixon raises the question of determining a President's physical and mental fitness. It is a matter of great public importance when a President or any high government official suffers from a psychiatric disorder which influences his decision-making capacity.[4] People who are intrinsically unhappy, hostile, and therefore depressed, are a threat, to themselves and others—and of course can prove most dangerous when they occupy a powerful public position. Nixon belongs in this category.

While psychiatry has made great strides in delineating the nature of mental health, a person's emotional stability under stress is difficult to predict. The emotional health of a person depends upon a variety of factors—the constitutional strength of his instincts, how well the ego can modify his behavior, early childhood traumatic experiences and the way he reacted to them.

Generally, good mental health means that a person understands and accepts his emotional strengths and weaknesses

197

and can function satisfactorily within the limits they impose. Good mental health means that a person is able to feel and show enthusiasm and be spontaneous. It means he is able to establish adult emotional relationships with men and women and able to give and receive love without fear. It means an ability to express anger when necessary, an ability to make independent decisions and follow through on them. Above all, it signifies a capacity to grow emotionally, intellectually, and spiritually. It means being able to set realistic goals, to face adversity and to continue to grow, and develop a profound sense of self. A person who is mentally healthy is able to give freely and still have the emotional energy to deal with those deep inner needs that make for well-being.

On the basis of these principles, it is obvious that Nixon deviated from the norm. Nixon was neither enthusiastic nor spontaneous. He was indirect, hesitant, secretive, uncertain, and cautious. Conversely, he could be highly impulsive in reacting to people or situations which threatened him. Because he felt people were against him, he was incapable of judging people or events objectively. This lack of realistic appraisal made it impossible for him to feel at peace with himself.

That Nixon was intense may falsely lead us to believe that his feelings, his libido,* his psychic energy were strong and powerful. His intense feelings, however, had little to do with the strength of his libido—the stream of his emotions behind his sexual drive. Rather, his intensity came from strong unresolved conflicts between his hostile aggressive and passive feelings. These conflicts, centering basically on his relationship with his parents, meant that his Oedipal situation was unresolved. In effect, these unresolved feelings were repressed and beyond his personal control.

What is interesting is that many, like Nixon, who seem to have a strong libido are able to find other outlets which can give expression to their inner aggression. When we psychoanalyze people, we frequently find that where the libido is weak there is little flow of emotions, since they are blocked. A large part of them has dried up. Instead of a flow of the libido there is only a trickle.

Nixon does not seem to have an emotionally rich life. He identified with his mother, who approached the role of a "sub-

---

* Libido is not identical with any kind of desire. Only the power behind the sexual drive can be termed libido.

stitute wife," and since he had to repress this identification, it is clear that his inner life was impoverished very early.

Richard Nixon's great love object, if any, during his growing years and through the rest of his life, was his mother. She meant more to him emotionally than anyone, except himself. She was in his eyes an ideal, a saint. Much more of his emotional energy, his libido, found an outlet through his relationship with her than with his father. But reconciling his conflicting attitudes toward her was difficult. Actually, he was never able to solve his conflicts with either parent.

As he was frustrated in part in relationship with his mother, however, his great love objects became his narcissistic self and his ambition. In politics he gratified both. All other pursuits had to give way for the one to which his libido was anchored —politics. Politics provided the outlet for his infantile oral and anal drives—talking and controlling.

The fact that Nixon's emotional life was impoverished meant that he had little personal regard for himself. Though he was obsessed with self-importance, he spoke like a man who felt a deep inner sense of alienation. Actually he isolated himself. What is ironic is that, in becoming President, Nixon remained the little boy, the rejected youngster from Yorba Linda—a small town that nobody in Washington had ever heard of.

A man must mean something to himself before he can mean something to others and to the world. Nixon always suffered from a sense of dejection and was always emotionally unstable. Most of his emotions were directed to the difficult task of controlling himself. The last days of his presidency were a climax of despair, thwarted anger, and bitterness. He was innocent, he maintained. "What wrongdoing?" he asked.

Jeb Magruder's comments about the cover-up are illuminating:

> . . . there was no question that the cover-up began that Saturday when we realized there was a break-in. I do not think there was ever any discussion that there would not be a cover-up.[5]

Nixon's inability to acknowledge his involvement with the Watergate break-in, the cover-up, and the obstruction of justice, leads one to question whether, even within the most private recesses of his mind, he believed he was involved. Nixon repressed his criminal acts by blocking out memories of them. They became nonexistent. These acts which Nixon repressed had a life of their own with little conscious connection between them and himself. They were then beyond his conscious control.

Such a process is not unusual. We often find it in people who have an inflexible, narcissistic ego, whose fear of being hurt reaches the point where all hurt, all pain, has to be repressed. When Nixon said he "hadn't done anything wrong," he was in one sense right because the wrongs had been pushed out of his conscious mind so that he indeed consciously felt innocent.

A friend, Clinton Harris, who had known Nixon since their school years, told me that he talked with Nixon in April 1975. At no time did Nixon admit that he had made a mistake or done anything wrong. Robert Finch told me that when he talked with Nixon in April 1975, Nixon simply said, "We made some mistakes." What surprised Finch, who had known Nixon for many years, was that "he never said, 'I made a mistake.'"

Because of his deformed superego and ego-ideal formation, Nixon had difficulty in making the connection between morality and his behavior. Despite his denial, we detect, from our knowledge of Nixon's personality structure, his motivation and capability for instigating, promoting, and carrying out the high crimes and misdemeanors with which he was charged in July 1974.

As a result of his contradictory personality traits, he acted at times like his mother, at others like his father. This conflict in him made Nixon prefer to play a role, to be an actor, and caused a dissociative reaction in him—creating emotional stress which he had to repress, separate, encapsulate.

Because his repressed hostile aggressive emotions were incompatible with the rest of his personality, they often broke into his consciousness and became almost a secondary subpersonality. What we see is a double image. Friendly and at the same time abrupt, argumentative, self-absorbed, he was of two minds.

These two Nixon postures are often found in introverted (schizoid), preoccupied, and secretive persons. This disunity has given the impression that Nixon had a double personality, a person who simultaneously seems to display entirely different thoughts, feelings, attitudes, and character.

This duality has been the fundamental cause of Nixon's undoing, and at the same time accounts for his impulsive or "manufactured" charisma. The fact that his double personality enables persons of completely opposite viewpoints to identify with him may help to explain Nixon's ability to remain politically prominent from 1946 until 1974.

Nixon's behavior, most appropriately described as a character disturbance, and possibly of no small order, has lasted since early childhood. This conduct, reflecting an unusual range of acting-out activities, may collectively be considered not normal behavior. It was *abnormal*.

What is remarkable is that more people, aware of Nixon's moral dishonesty, his combative instinct of "going for the jugular," did not raise their voices against him when the lurid details of Watergate became more and more linked to the Nixon White House.

While it has been said politics is the art of the possible, in Nixon's case it was the art of the impossible. Politics is a game of seduction. Many people unconsciously like to be deceived, or duped. They are suggestible, easily seduced, and they follow readily, particularly when they are in a crowd, where individuality is reduced to a minimum and suggestibility raised to a maximum.[6]

Nixon was a master in being able to turn almost any situation to his advantage, regardless of the principles involved.

Politics was Nixon's specialty, the only life he knew. His existence was a pattern of acquired behavior developed to seduce others. He was the consummate politician.

Despite his awkwardness, Nixon had an uncanny hold on people because they discovered in him traits that lifted him "out of the ordinary." Even when he was young, he knew how to exploit a situation, and for this people admired him; he could fool people, and for this they admired him. He could crush a political antagonist into pulp. He could be blunt, even brutal, and for this people admired him. People *secretly* admired Nixon for daring to do what they were unable to do. He had a hidden fascination as a dramatic actor, a relentless debater, an ardent aggressor. The public empathized with him —and, what is more important, they voted for him. And for Nixon it was not morality or justice that counted. It was the final victory, the end justifying the means.

In discussing politics, he admitted as much: "There is no mileage in doing the right thing here, there's only mileage for demagogues."[7]

We know that he harbored a grudge against fate, which he believed had been unkind to him in denying him what other people had. His reasoning, which enabled him to place himself above the law, may have originated in his conviction that he should be compensated for the hardships of his early years, that he was entitled to get his "due reward." This may in part explain why Nixon has reacted to Ford's pardon as if he felt he had it coming to him.

Again, Nixon has been able to get by. He has fooled the American public and he has fooled himself. Worse, his pardon has prevented him from having any incentive for rehabilitation. Usually a criminal is pardoned when he has shown remorse and has openly admitted his crime. But such an admission has been far from Nixon's mind. He argued vehemently in defense of his innocence*—in the same way he had debated and argued to prove his point ever since the fifth grade. This same combative pattern had defined his behavior since childhood—to argue and argue and never give in. The President under attack still had the little boy Richard within him.

It is true that the pardon, according to Attorney General Edward H. Levi, "saved the country the trauma òf watching a former President dragged through the criminal legal process." But the country, which already had paid too high a price for its President, also had to pay the price of being deprived of the evidence that would be brought out in a trial.

President Ford did not simplify Nixon's role in the illegal Watergate activities. He complicated it. Whereas most of us would agree that we should temper justice with compassion, it can also be said that compassion could only be rendered when the full scope of Nixon's misdeeds had been brought to light. He had, however, and I repeat, felt entitled to get his "due reward."

---

* The situation turned out to be quite different for Haldeman and Ehrlichman. During the last days of Nixon's regime, they frantically called to ask him to pardon them. The telephone calls, however, never reached him, and perhaps this was not accidental. "The President is not available" was the official response. At that time, we suspect, Nixon was too caught up in his own desperate situation to be concerned about others. His own narcissistic hurt was too overwhelming to permit concern for others to enter his mind.

It was this sense of restitution that allowed him to feel he had the right to be an exception to the rule, to breach custom, regulations, and laws. Feeling highly competitive with those who had been blessed with the "good" life, he became an injustice collector; he had always been given less than he deserved.

Why hadn't he been born into the eastern establishment? His whole demeanor, his brooding, his loneliness, his ungainly body made him an easy target for ridicule. This anger at himself may have made him as defiant as Macbeth, who says, "I am reckless. I do to spite the world."

Nixon fits Shakespeare's description of Richard III, whose crimes were a way of avenging his physical deformity:

> But I, that am not shaped for sportive tricks,
> Nor made to court an amorous looking-glass;
>
> . . . .
>
> Cheated of feature by dissembling nature,
> Deform'd, unfinish'd, sent before my time
> Into this breathing world, scarce half made up,
> And that so lamely and unfashionable
> That dogs bark at me as I halt by them;
>
> . . . .
>
> I am determined to prove a villain,
> And hate the idle pleasures of these days.
> Plots have I laid, inductions dangerous . . .[8]

Nixon's emotional illness influenced his actions as much as if he had been physically defective. Such emotional deformity may, depending on its extent, make itself felt in one's behavior. He had been defiant and spiteful. He had manipulated and intrigued. Because of his emotionally crippled state, he found it difficult or was unable to act in a social and legal way. He, like Richard III, consciously or unconsciously chose to play the villain.[9] I say "chose" deliberately, for we know that although Nixon was "impulse-ridden" in the sense that many of his acts were instinctive and unconscious, he also had, as we have so often seen, conscious impulses emerging from his ego. Both conscious and unconscious motivations brought about his singular need for power. While his indirectness and deviousness were rooted in his instincts, they were also mobilized, instigated, and nurtured by his ego.

Nixon's sense of self-importance was so great that he believed he was indispensable to the country. When he was threatened with impeachment, he may have considered it inevitable that everything would go down with him, including the United States. In his mind, he may have thought, "If I go down, everyone goes down." In his fantasies, his downfall was to be his *Götterdämmerung,* the "twilight of the gods."

We know that Nixon had an active fantasy life. In thinking about and planning transgressions, he undoubtedly first fantasized about them. Because of these fantasies, crippled as his superego may have been, some remorse may have been present. We should allow him the benefit of the doubt. Maybe there was some zigzagging and seesawing in his antisocial activities: two steps forward, one step back. Hesitant, perhaps doubtful, he may also have believed that his wrongdoings would never come to light.

Some may ask whether Nixon's emotional problems indicated that he was merely a neurotic person or whether he suffered from a more deep-seated disturbance. We have shown that his personality development was arrested. His childhood feelings of anger and bitterness remained static, fixed, repressed. The fact that he described his *Six Crises* as political rather than emotional in nature is important. His lack of principles and convictions on one side and his character disturbance on the other were intricately intertwined. We know that crises do occur in the maturing process, but in Nixon's case these crucial events did not seem to change him. He gained no insight; his consciousness was not expanded. He viewed these events as external to himself.

If his emotional development, up to the point of the Judiciary Committee's decision in favor of impeachment, had been in the direction of emotional maturity, we could say that he may have had only a neurotic condition. His behavior, however, particularly on the night and morning of May 8-9, 1970, at the Lincoln Memorial, indicates that his disturbance went deeper. In my professional view, his behavior was abnormal. In the final analysis, Nixon was a deeply disturbed person whose prevailing symptoms intensified under the overwhelming pressure of his last two years in office.

Nixon's antisocial or illegal activities had become an intrinsic part of his being. While they may not have been fixed formally in his mind, one may say he was unable to stop himself.

This is perfectly illustrated by Henrik Ibsen in *Rosmers-*

holm. With keen insight he has shown the conflicting feelings in Rebecca, who, through her subtle behavior toward Beate, Rosmersholm's wife, became instrumental in her death. In despair Beate threw himself into a waterfall and drowned. As the play moves forward, Rebecca admits:

> I wanted to get rid of Beate, one way or another. But I never really imagined it would ever happen. Every little step I risked, every faltering advance, I seemed to hear something call out within me: "No further. Not a step further!" . . . And yet I could not stop. I *had* to venture a little bit further. Just one little bit further. And then a little more . . . always just a little bit more. And then it happened. That's the way things like that do happen.[10]

To say that in Rebecca's case "things do happen," or in Nixon's case that criminal activities "just took place," is not true. If Nixon's transgressions occurred without his really wanting them to happen, he still must have had some association with them, but here again his repression played a fatal role.

Clearly, at the height of his power, he fell by his own hand. In psychoanalysis we often see successful people who manage to destroy their success. Since they feel undeserving—guilty —they do everything in their power to demolish themselves.

Nixon, who had achieved world recognition, rejected his position of power. He couldn't have saved himself. He couldn't have admitted that he had done wrong and that he regretted it. The American people would have accepted his apology and his admission of guilt. But he couldn't apologize. The arrogance of power made Nixon feel it was beneath him to admit any wrongdoing. As President he felt that he should be respected by every American. How could he be respected if he were to admit to serious wrongdoing? To save himself this way never entered his mind. Only later and indirectly, by acquiescing in Ford's pardon, has he indirectly implied admission of guilt.

Did Nixon *wish* to save himself? The answer simply is no. He couldn't and didn't. Despite his low self-esteem, he felt he was *destined* to be important. In his imagination he was someone so far beyond others that he did not see the *necessity* to save himself. He was omnipotent.

Like Peer Gynt, he undoubtedly was guided by a single compelling conviction:

> . . . thou art come of great things,
> and great things shall come of thee.[11]

Possessed by this thought, he felt he was one with destiny. He went beyond the presidency. As the chief of the most powerful state, he wanted to be the supreme architect of global politics. He gave the presidency an imperial dimension. He may very well have felt that his presidency was the nation's benevolent destiny as well as his own.

In 1976, Julie Eisenhower wrote:

> In 1968, I asked my mother why she, an intensely private person, supported the decision to seek the Presidency. She answered: "He's a great man, a man of destiny." She was to repeat those words in 1974 when friends asked what sustained her.[12]

Apparently he wanted to return to where he once had been. His own destruction had to do with this desire, which separated him from happiness, from personal tranquillity and inner peace. He was incapable of innocence, a state of mind relatively free of brooding, guilt, or doubt. Even though he held the highest office in the United States, it had little meaning for him in terms of his feelings. What he lacked was the sense of innocence, that vital source which enables people to strive to be worthy.

As the Watergate scandal unfolded, Nixon's self-preoccupation and instability grew. A close associate told me that in the last few months, from May to August 1974, "Nixon did slide down. It was as if a sense of doom had come over him."

Despite fervent denials, there is little doubt that the former President was unnerved. A high official in one federal agency, which previously had received guidelines from the White House, told me that during the last half year of Nixon's regime, despite much prodding, no guidance was forthcoming. Finally the agency was compelled to act on its own.

A year after Watergate, Kissinger declared that Nixon "barely governed during the eighteen months of the unfolding

Watergate scandal which eventually forced him to resign. His hostile and destructive feelings against himself and against others played havoc with him."[13]

The United States survived Nixon because of his lack of principles and the enduring strengths of our Constitution. Being without principles and trying to play different roles to different people, he had no sense of being a real person, alive with feelings, ideas, opinions, and passion. In effect, he had become an abstraction of the hard-working President rather than an alive, human Chief Executive.

Even as the curtain for the last act of his presidency was coming down, his family and his White House associates were deceived by his declarations of innocence. Why didn't his family or anyone in the White House know about the extent of Nixon's transgressions?

The answer is twofold: they wanted to see Nixon as President of the United States; they did not want to see or believe in his crimes. Nixon, on the other hand, never gave anyone a full account of the true Watergate situation. Nobody knew the full story, except possibly Haldeman.

Not telling anyone the full story enabled Nixon to remain *in control* of his secrets.

He remained adamant. He was innocent. Even when two of his aides, J. Fred Buzhardt, Special White House Counsel for Watergate, and Leonard Garment, Counsel to the President, went to Florida at the beginning of November 1973 to suggest that he resign, Nixon refused to meet with them.[14] Whether it was Alexander Haig, White House Chief of Staff, or Ronald Ziegler, Nixon's Press Secretary, or Nixon himself who ordered the refusal to meet with Buzhardt and Garment, is not clear. It stands to reason, however, that it was Nixon who made the decision. He desperately wanted to remain President.

Nixon had become more and more isolated. We have seen that, in his last year and a half in office, he was unable to carry out his duties as President. He had lost interest in leading his country. Being self-preoccupied, he had become more and more introverted and hardly listened to his aides. Often he became impatient, a trait we have noted since his childhood, and he would interrupt an ongoing discussion. At times he would become almost incoherent; he was unable to listen to what others said. Instead he would sink back into his own world of memories.

As accusations began to mount, more and more attention became focused on the President himself. For the first time since Andrew Johnson, the American public and the House of Representatives began seriously to consider impeaching the President.

Faced with this threat, Nixon tried to appear unconcerned. He showed no feelings of guilt or moral scruples. The show had to go on. Yet what appeared on the outside was not necessarily what he experienced internally. The only concern he displayed regarding possible impeachment was narcissistic. "You know," he said to Colson, "that if I am impeached, I'll be wiped out financially—no pension . . ." [15] He was incapable of acknowledging faults or personal failings. But inwardly he felt uncertain and afraid, which is one reason why he could say, "You know, Chuck, I get down on my knees every night and just pray to God." [16]

In the final analysis he wanted to be his own counsel. Not even his lawyer, James St. Clair, knew much about Nixon's predicament. The President seemed unable to evaluate his situation objectively, for in June 1974 he maintained that he was not legally and constitutionally bound to hand over the complete tape recordings of the White House conversations, which Leon Jaworski, the Watergate Special Prosecutor, and Judge John J. Sirica had demanded. Publicly, Nixon continued to deny the seriousness of his position and dismissed the possibility of impeachment. Privately, he must have been angry and frightened. He ordered an all-out White House campaign, called Operation Candor, to clear himself of any guilt. Operation Candor was led by Dean Burch, the President's Political Counselor, and Raymond K. Price, one of Nixon's best speech writers.

Nixon isolated himself from most people and was ill at ease in conversation unless he was with someone who was not threatening and who would not intrude on his thoughts, such as Bebe Rebozo. Ironically, it was, we may suspect, during these times of seclusion that his thoughts intruded more deeply upon him, frightening, troublesome thoughts which made him even more aloof and depressed. Whether or not he was aware that he refused to be emotionally involved in issues or with people, there is reason to believe that he was incapable of any involvement except with himself. Self-absorption had become essential to his own existence. In his own world he was still safe and secure. The outside world was important to him only if it could afford him the respect he felt he deserved.

One of Nixon's assistants told me that, after the resignation, he called the former President to say goodbye. "This was a private conversation," he said, "and Nixon was, as always, very polite. At the end, Nixon said to me, 'You are going out of the White House clean.' Nixon said it with a very strange laugh. It sounded to me as if Nixon's strange laugh came from his unconscious, a voice from the grave." His laughter may have meant that somehow his former assistant had been fooled, that Nixon felt outside what was going on in his own province—the White House.

This deep sense of detachment may have been caused by Nixon's need to believe that he was not involved in Watergate. In the words of another White House assistant, Nixon played a "complicated game"; he relied on "executive privilege" to put himself above the law. And this strong belief had strong repercussions. The President, in effect, created a fourth, isolated branch of the government, in which he felt above the government.

Many of his foreign and domestic activities he carried out in secret, under the cloak of "national security." And the illegal actions were carried out without accounting to anyone except himself. He compartmentalized his presidency—as he had compartmentalized his personal life.

It has been reported by Woodward and Bernstein, among others, that Nixon had begun to drink. Naturally, a man frightened by the threat of losing his high office might well seek ways to lessen his anxiety and fear. The choice would be alcohol or drugs or suicide. As a psychoanalyst, it does not surprise me that Nixon chose drinking as a way of escape. From his earliest years, from infancy on, Nixon had a compelling oral drive. Unable to face his Watergate opponents openly in debate, he still had to satisfy his oral drive. What was left for him? He was disinterested in eating. He was distant from his wife, unable to communicate affection to her even by kissing.* It is not surprising, then, that Nixon chose drink as the pressures increased. Haldeman has recounted that Ehrlichman "expressed concerns about Nixon's lifestyle, specifically in the area of drinking."[18] Nixon, however, thought

---

* When Marine Lieutenant Colonel Jack Brennan, the President's military aide, joked that his duties included "briefing Nixon on how to kiss his wife,"[17] this was no joke.

he had to be perfect, just as his mother, Hannah, had taught him to be. In his final White House days it is apparent that he often drank alone, afraid to risk embarrassment.

It was feared by some that Nixon would commit suicide rather than face total loss of power and respect. I personally thought he never would because he was too much in love with himself. He felt at times that he was the center of the universe.

While it must also be stated that Nixon had strong self-destructive tendencies, they would, however, not move him to act directly. Nixon's death wish surfaced in a different form. In *The Final Days*, Woodward and Bernstein tell of Nixon's trip to Egypt in June 1974. In Salzburg, Austria, he developed phlebitis. Very possibly it was psychosomatic in origin. His left leg became swollen and inflamed. Whether or not he unconsciously chose it, to his ego, to his perception, it was an honorable illness. Only his body had failed him. His doctor, Walter Tkach, felt this was a very dangerous condition because of the possible formation of blood clots, which could be fatal. He urged Nixon not to continue the trip to Egypt and strongly recommended that he return to Washington. Nixon refused to take his physician's advice and continued his trip despite severe pain and great danger to himself. He risked destroying himself indirectly.

One of Nixon's few strong relationships has been with his younger daughter, Julie. During the 1972 political campaign and the hectic Watergate period, Julie was an ardent spokesman for her father. She believed until the last minute, and may still believe, that he was innocent. However, one person who knew the family well (he prefers to remain anonymous) told me: "At a historical meeting on March 16, 1975, in Montebello, California, Julie Eisenhower was invited to speak. She was very frank at times about the relations at home between her mother and father. She said indirectly that she felt her father had done something wrong." What we may conclude is that to this day Nixon has never told the truth to anyone, including his daughters. When Nixon finally decided to resign, on August 7, 1974, and told his family about it, White House photographer Ollie Atkins was called in to take pictures. As Atkins describes the scene:

It was obvious that some shocking news had happened.

He had told his family about his resignation. In taking the pictures everyone tried to be brave. The only one who showed tears on her face was Julie Eisenhower and after the picture-taking was over, she broke down. Nixon embraced Julie but he didn't cry.[19]

The photograph of Nixon and his daughter illustrates how close they are. It is my feeling that there is a great deal of emotional similiarity in their makeup. Yet, whatever their identification, the loyalty she and other family members have shown must be one of the few constructive, emotionally gratifying elements in Nixon's adult life.

On the evening of August 8, 1974, about an hour before Nixon was to deliver his resignation speech to the nation, he met in the Cabinet Room with twenty senators and twenty-six members of the House.

"They all," my source told me, "cried and wept, and so did Nixon, and finally he had to be carried to a chair. One congressman was so angry and upset that he banged the wall."

Nixon was under great strain. Until the day before, Wednesday, he wasn't absolutely sure he was going to resign, although the previous Monday and Tuesday he had more or less agreed to do so. Possessive of his presidency, he couldn't let go of it. The presidency belonged to him. Nobody else.

According to a close associate:

> Of course, he was under tremendous strain. I don't know how he lasted through those last meetings. Of course, when he came out and saw the people the night just before he resigned, I think that meeting was instinctive, the breakdown. He cried so that he could get it out of his system so that he could go on television and be under control.
>
> [I interrupted and said that this was the thing for him to do, to cry.]
>
> Yes, so that he wouldn't cry on television.
>
> [I reminded him that Nixon was a great actor.]
>
> Yes, I can understand that, but here I think he had to cry. This was not an act. He had to cry. Either he could cry then or while he was on television. He preferred to cry with his friends in the privacy of the Cabinet Room.

Another associate described that meeting as "the breakdown at the end":

> He was overcome by tremendous depression at seeing everything lost in defeat. I believe his behavior at that meeting can be characterized as a mental breakdown. He couldn't hold himself together; he had to be helped to a chair.

My source added:

> With all his friends . . . I mean this gathering of his whole life, we might say. These were the men he campaigned with, schemed with, talked with, and now he was saying goodbye to them. It was a kind of death tableau.

The loss of the presidency, a loss which to him represented death, may unconsciously have been associated with the fear of losing his life he had when young; the loss reinforced his depression as he surrendered his high office. A White House official told me that twenty-five minutes after the meeting with his congressional friends, when Nixon was giving his resignation speech to the country on television, "he had almost regained his composure and talked almost as if nothing had happened. But Nixon was a doomed man and felt so too."

Nixon's apparent belief in his innocence was rooted in a lack of identification with reality, which helps to explain his recalcitrant, stubborn stand in the face of overwhelming facts.

The morning after the announcement of his resignation, Nixon addressed the White House staff to say his farewells. He extolled his mother, "the saint." She meant more to him emotionally than anyone. He was filled with self-pity. Later, with outstretched arms, he bade America goodbye from the helicopter and smiled as if to say, "The show must go on." Again, it was a seemingly noble gesture but filled with self-pity.

As the helicopter lifted from the White House lawn and disappeared over the treetops, President Ford walked slowly into the White House holding his wife's hand. Nixon certainly felt grieved as he left behind all the power he had come to crave. We may never know the tears shed on that trip.

We do know, however, from Atkins, that on the plane flight "it was quiet. Everyone was meditating. President Nixon was in his own compartment. Pat Nixon in her own compartment on Air Force One."[20]

He chose not to sit with his wife. He was—as always—alone.

Unpredictable and oscillating as Nixon's past has been, with a spectacular career, crushing defeats, and immeasurable humiliation, his fundamental character traits are still present. In 1976, when he went to China acting like a former rather than a deposed President, he showed his disdain for the American people and President Ford. Revisiting Peking was a calculated attempt to play the role of world leader and to erase the disgrace he had brought on himself and the office of the presidency. It was also as if he were trying to spite the American public—the public which had rejected him. David S. Broder wrote in the *Washington Post:* "That his trip is an enormous political embarrassment to the President who pardoned him is inconsequential to Nixon. . . . Nothing shames him; nothing deters him."[21]

Unaware of his emotional shortcomings, he will, one may predict, continue to live preoccupied, bitter, and brooding, as he did as a child, adolescent, and adult—all the time desperately trying to return to the political arena. But even a modest comeback would *not* gratify his wounded ego.

Nixon's inner conflict, his fight against himself, was the wellspring of his success as a politician as well as the pain and depression he felt when he left the presidency. Unaware of the enemies in his own mind, he projected them onto others. He withdrew into himself to live there with his loneliness, his hypersensitivity, his narcissism, his suspicion, his secrecy. His childhood fears and anger never left him, even when he became the most powerful figure in the United States. Whatever rudiments of character one has, no one, and this includes Nixon, can go beyond the limitations of his character. This is the tragedy: the never-ending battle of Nixon vs. Nixon.

Notes

A Note on Interviews and Correspondence

Much of the material in the book derives from interviews and correspondence between the author and persons familiar with particular aspects of Richard Nixon's life. It would be tediously repetitive, for author and reader alike, to cite in a formal note each and every contribution these people have kindly made to my account of Richard Nixon. Unless otherwise indicated, then, the reader may assume that the sources of my "personal communications"—except for the many anonymous ones—are the following:

Frederick Albrink, interview, April 1976

Roy M. Cohn, interviews, November–December 1974

Robert H. Finch, interview, May 1975

Clinton Harris, interview, May 1975

Edwin P. Hoyt, interviews and correspondence, January, February 1975

Donald Jackson, interviews and correspondence, March 1975–September 1976

Rose Olive Marshburn, interviews and correspondence, March, May, November 1975 and March 1976

Philip Mayher, interviews, January, March, April 1976

Bradley Morrah, interview, March 1976

William Perdue, interview, April 1976

Irving Wallace, interviews and correspondence, October 1975–June 1976

Jessamyn West, interviews and correspondence, December 1974–April 1975

Merle West, interview, May 1975

Lois Elliott Williams, interviews and correspondence, August, September 1976

Preface
1. *The New York Times,* July 19, 1974.
2. "Behavior: Second-Hand Shrinking," *Time,* August 12, 1974, p. 47.
3. Victor Zorza, *Washington Post,* January 12, 1975.

1.

1. *Richard M. Nixon: A Self Portrait* (script of a film prepared for the 1968 presidential election campaign), p. 3.
2. Richard M. Nixon, *Six Crises* (Garden City, N.Y.: Doubleday & Company, 1962), p. 296.
3. Bela Kornitzer, *The Real Nixon: An Intimate Biography* (Chicago: Rand McNally & Company, 1960), p. 71; Edwin P. Hoyt, *The Nixons: An American Family* (New York: Random House, 1972), p. 101.
4. "Richard M. Nixon," Associated Press Bio. Sketch 3953 (1955), sheet 2.
5. Hoyt, *op. cit.,* p. 102.
6. Raymond Martin Bell, *The Ancestry of Richard Milhous Nixon* (Washington, Pa., 1972) (typescript), p. 46.
7. *Ibid.,* p. 21; Frieda Fateley Crawford, *An Indiana Sojourn: The Milhous Family,* 1854–1904 (privately printed, 1974), p. 28.
8. Hoyt, *op. cit.,* p. 163.
9. *Columbus* (Indiana) *Republic,* October 2, 1967.
10. *Los Angeles Times,* October 1, 1967.

2.

1. Bell, *op. cit.,* p. 16; Hoyt, *op. cit.,* pp. 171–72.
2. Jessamyn West, *Hide and Seek: A Continuing Journey* (New York: Harcourt Brace Jovanovich, 1973), p. 238.
3. Crawford, *op. cit.,* p. 42.
4. West, *op. cit.,* p. 239.
5. *Ibid.,* pp. 238–40.
6. Stewart Alsop, *Nixon and Rockefeller: A Double Portrait* (Garden City, N.Y.: Doubleday & Company, 1960), p. 126.
7. "The New President: Richard M. Nixon," *U.S. News & World Report* (article prepared but not printed, July 4, 1958).
8. Hoyt, *op. cit.,* p. 184.
9. "The New President: Richard M. Nixon," p. 2.
10. Hoyt, *op. cit.,* p. 180.

11. Earl Mazo, *Richard Nixon: A Political and Personal Portrait* (New York: Harper & Brothers, 1959), p. 13.

12. *Ibid.*, p. 12.

13. Hoyt, *op. cit.*, p. 178.

14. *The Daily News* (Whittier, California), January 18, 1969, and *East Whittier Review*, January 19, 1969, p. 13.

15. Alsop, *op. cit.*, p. 219.

16. Hoyt, *op. cit.*, p. 180.

17. *Time*, September 12, 1974, p. 20.

18. West, *op. cit.*, p. 239.

3.

1. "The New President: Richard M. Nixon," p. 2.

2. *News Tribune* (Fullerton, California), November 7, 1968.

3. *Ibid.*

4. Kornitzer, *op. cit.*, p. 35.

5. Mazo, *op. cit.*, p. 16.

6. *Nixon: A Self Portrait*, pp. 5–6.

7. *Ibid.*, p. 8.

8. Ralph de Toledano, *One Man Alone: Richard Nixon* (New York: Funk & Wagnalls, 1969), p. 19.

9. *Nixon: A Self Portrait*, p. 4.

10. *Ibid.*, p. 7.

11. *Ibid.*

12. *Ibid.*, pp. 7–8.

13. Alsop, *op. cit.*, pp. 185–86.

14. Bela Kornitzer, "My Son: Interviews with Rose Kennedy and Hannah M. Nixon," *This Week Magazine*, September 18, 1960.

15. *Ibid.*

4.

1. *Los Angeles Times*, October 1, 1967.

2. *Time*, August 25, 1952, p. 13.

3. "The New President: Richard M. Nixon," p. 2.

4. Mazo, *op. cit.*, p. 16.

5. James David Barber, *The Presidential Character: Predicting Performance in the White House* (Englewood Cliffs, N.J.: Prentice-Hall, 1972), p. 400.

6. *Ibid.*, p. 402.

7. Kornitzer, *The Real Nixon*, p. 50.

NOTES

8. Barber, *op. cit.*, p. 401; originally cited by Kornitzer, *The Real Nixon*, p. 57.

9. *Nixon: A Self Portrait*, p. 6.

10. Mazo, *op. cit.*, p. 20.

11. Donald Jackson, "The Young Nixon," *Life*, November 6, 1970, p. 54B.

12. Kornitzer, *The Real Nixon*, p. 79.

13. *News Tribune* (Fullerton, California), November 7, 1968.

14. West, *op. cit.*, p. 240.

15. Kornitzer, *The Real Nixon*, p. 19.

16. Alsop, *op. cit.*, pp. 184–85.

17. *The Daily News* (Whittier, California), January 18, 1969, and *East Whittier Review*, January 19, 1969, p. 9.

18. Kornitzer, "My Son: Interviews with Rose Kennedy and Hannah M. Nixon."

19. Arthur Woodstone, *Nixon's Head* (New York: St. Martin's Press, 1972), p. 102.

20. Jackson, "The Young Nixon," p. 54B.

21. *The Reporter*, April 19, 1956, p. 11.

22. *The Daily News* (Whittier, California), March 23, 1929.

23. *The Daily News* (Whittier, California), January 18, 1969, and *East Whittier Review*, January 19, 1969, p. 17.

24. *Ibid.*, p. 19.

25. *Ibid.*, p. 34.

26. Barber, *op. cit.*, p. 366.

5.

1. Quotations from Nixon's composition are from Kornitzer, *The Real Nixon*, pp. 61–65.

2. See also Kornitzer, *The Real Nixon*, p. 46; Barber, *op. cit.*, p. 404; Mazo, *op. cit.*, p. 5.

3. *Nixon: A Self Portrait*, pp. 3–4.

4. Nixon, *Six Crises*, p. 295.

5. *Nixon: A Self Portrait*, p. 4.

6. *Ibid.*, p. 12.

7. *Ibid.*, pp. 12–13.

8. *Ibid.*, pp. 13–14.

9. *Los Angeles Times*, October 1, 1967.

10. Mazo, *op. cit.*, p. 23.

11. Jules Witcover, *The Resurrection of Richard Nixon* (New York: G. P. Putnam's Sons, 1970), p. 22.

12. *The White House Transcripts: Submission of Recorded Presidential Conversations to the Committee on the Judiciary of the House of Representatives by President Richard Nixon* (New York: Bantam Books, 1974), pp. 644, 782.

13. *Nixon: A Self Portrait,* pp. 6–7.

14. Mazo, *op. cit.,* p. 20.

15. Communication, March 21, 1976.

6.

1. Jackson, "The Young Nixon," p. 58.

2. *Nixon: A Self Portrait,* p. 9.

3. Lael Morgan, "Whittier '34 Most Likely to Succeed," *West Magazine, Los Angeles Times,* May 10, 1970, p. 35.

4. Donald Jackson, "Coming of Age in America: The Youth of Richard Nixon" (typescript, 1970), p. 9.

5. *Ibid.*

6. Morgan, *op. cit.,* p. 34.

7. Jackson, "Coming of Age in America," p. 6.

8. *Ibid.,* pp. 9–10.

9. Kornitzer, *The Real Nixon,* p. 56.

10. Morgan, *op. cit.,* pp. 34–35.

11. Jackson, "Coming of Age in America," p. 10.

12. Morgan, *op. cit.,* p. 34.

13. Interview, September 1976.

14. Jackson, "The Young Nixon," p. 60.

15. Jackson, "Coming of Age in America," p. 10.

16. Kornitzer, *The Real Nixon,* p. 54.

17. Morgan, *op. cit.,* p. 35.

18. *Ibid.*

19. *Ibid.*

20. Jackson, "Coming of Age in America," p. 11.

21. Interview, September 1976.

22. Morgan, *op. cit.,* p. 35.

23. *Ibid.*

24. Interview, September 1976.

25. Myra MacPherson, "Whittier College '34," *Washington Post,* July 13, 1970.

26. Alsop, *op. cit.,* p. 47.

27. Jackson, "The Young Nixon," p. 60.

28. Interview, August 1976.

29. Morgan, *op. cit.,* p. 35.

7.

1. Jackson, "Coming of Age in America," p. 12.
2. *Ibid.*
3. *Ibid.*, pp. 12–13.
4. *Ibid.*, p. 13.
5. Kornitzer, *The Real Nixon*, p. 120.
6. Alsop, *op. cit.*, p. 132.
7. Jackson, "Coming of Age in America," p. 14.
8. *Ibid.*
9. Communication from Irving Wallace, October 22, 1973.
10. *The Daily News* (Whittier, California), January 18, 1969, and *East Whittier Review*, January 19, 1969, p. 52.
11. Alsop, *op. cit.*, p. 195.
12. Statements also printed in the District Court of Appeals, Second Appellate District, State of California, Division One, 2nd Civil no. 13774, pp. 19, 20, 23. Appellant's Reply Brief, Daniel A. Knapp, pp. 5, 16. See also Respondent's Brief, David Schwartz, p. 3, 4, 27.
13. Jessamyn West, "Pat Nixon—As She Is," *The Reader's Digest*, April 1971; condensed from *Good Housekeeping*, February 1971.
14. Jackson, "Coming of Age in America," p. 16.
15. Kornitzer, *The Real Nixon*, p. 136.
16. Jackson, "Coming of Age in America," p. 16.
17. Trude E. Feldman, "The Quiet Courage of Pat Nixon," *McCall's*, May 1975, p. 116.
18. *Ibid.*, p. 75.
19. *The New York Times*, March 14, 1971.
20. *Writer's Digest*, February 1974, p. 12.
21. *Ibid.*, p. 17. Steinem's interview strongly indicates that she was protective of Pat and had no intention of upsetting her.

8.

1. Toledano, *op. cit.*, p. 37.
2. *Nixon: A Self Portrait*, pp. 10–11.
3. *The Daily News* (Whittier, California), January 18, 1969, and *East Whittier Review*, January 19, 1969, p. 24. Information reprinted from *The Daily News*, November 2, 1945.
4. *Ibid.*, p. 53.
5. My source for this and the following information pre-

fers to remain anonymous. Interviews took place in October 1975 and January and April 1976.

6. E. B. Potter and Chester W. Nimitz (eds.), *The Great Sea War: The Story of Naval Action in World War II* (Englewood Cliffs, N.J.: Prentice-Hall, 1960), p. 292.

7. E. B. Potter and Chester W. Nimitz (eds), *Triumph in the Pacific: The Navy's Struggle Against Japan* (Englewood Cliffs, N.J.: Prentice-Hall, 1963), p. 36.

8. Samuel Eliot Morison, *Breaking the Bismarcks Barrier: 22 July 1942–1 May 1944,* Vol. IV of *History of United States Naval Operations in World War II* (Boston: Houghton Mifflin Company, 1950), pp. 412, 414, 417.

9. Kornitzer, *The Real Nixon,* p. 146.

10. *Nixon: A Self Portrait,* p. 1.

11. *Ibid.,* p. 11.

12. *Washington Post,* October 16, 1975.

13. William A. Reuben, *The Honorable Mr. Nixon* (new ed.; New York: Action Books, 1960), p. iii.

14. *The Daily News* (Whittier, California), January 18, 1969, and *East Whittier Review,* January 19, 1969, p. 25. Information reprinted from *The Daily News,* November 3, 1945.

15. Reuben, *op. cit.,* p. iv.

16. *Nixon: A Self Portrait,* p. 12.

17. Nixon, *Six Crises,* pp. 3–4.

18. Courtesy Peter H. Irons, Boston State College Library, Cambridge, Massachusetts.

19. "The Hiss Case: A Lesson for the American People," Speech of the Honorable Richard M. Nixon of California in the House of Representatives, Thursday, January 26, 1950, p. 16.

20. Speech given in Wheeling, West Virginia, February 9, 1950.

21. *News Tribune* (Fullerton, California), November 7, 1968.

22. "Letters from Readers," *Commentary,* December 1975, pp. 12–16.

23. Reuben, *op. cit.,* p. 133.

24. Ralph de Toledano and Victor Lasky, *Seeds of Treason: The True Story of the Hiss-Chambers Tragedy* (New York: Funk & Wagnalls, 1950), p. 250.

25. Kornitzer, *The Real Nixon,* pp. 180–82.

26. "Douglas-Marcantonio Voting Record" (leaflet).

Courtesy the Boston State College Library, Cambridge, Massachusetts.

27. Nixon, *Six Crises*, p. 22.

28. *Ibid.*, p. 30.

29. Arthur Edward Rowse, *Slanted News: A Case Study of the Nixon and Stevenson Fund Stories* (Boston: Beacon Press, 1957), pp. 8–9.

30. "The Hiss Case: A Lesson for the American People," p. 14.

31. Nixon, *Six Crises*, pp. 73–74.

32. *Ibid.*, p. 73.

33. *Ibid.*, p. 74.

34. *Ibid.*, p. 104.

35. *Ibid.*, pp. 110–11.

36. Morgan, *op. cit.*, p. 36.

37. Mazo, *op. cit.*, p. 23.

38. *Ibid.*, p. 22.

39. Garry Wills, *Nixon Agonistes* (Boston: Houghton Mifflin Company, 1969), pp. 95–96.

40. Woodstone, *op. cit.*, p. 30.

41. *Ibid.*, p. 31.

42. Nixon, *Six Crises*, p. 164.

43. *Ibid.*, pp. 164–65.

44. *Ibid.*, p. 165.

45. Earl Mazo and Stephen Hess, *Nixon: A Political Portrait* (New York: Harper & Row, 1968), p. 15.

46. Witcover, *op. cit.*, p. 23.

47. Woodstone, *op. cit.*, p. 33.

48. *Ibid.*

49. Nixon, *Six Crises*, p. 161.

9.

1. Merle Miller, *Plain Speaking: An Oral Biography of Harry S. Truman* (New York: Berkley Publishing Corporation, 1973–74), pp. 178, 135.

2. Alsop, *op. cit.*, pp. 195, 200–01.

3. Nixon, *Six Crises*, p. 408.

4. Woodstone, *op. cit.*, p. 8.

5. A few days after Nixon's California defeat, Howard K. Smith on ABC-TV gave a commentary entitled "The Political Obituary of Richard Nixon."

6. Kornitzer, "My Son: Interviews with Rose Kennedy and Hannah M. Nixon."

7. According to a reliable source who prefers to remain anonymous.

8. Joe McGinniss, *The Selling of the President 1968* (New York: Trident Press, 1969), p. 103.

9. The story of the filming has been provided by an anonymous source.

10. "Lucky Dick," *Newsweek,* March 27, 1972.

11. *Newsweek,* January 25, 1971.

12. See Martin Wangh's book review of Walter C. Langer, *The Mind of Adolf Hitler: The Secret Wartime Report* (New York: Basic Books, 1972), in *Psychoanalytic Quarterly,* XLIII, No. 1 (1974), 131.

13. Robert B. Semple, Jr., "Nixon's Presidency Is a Very Private Affair," *The New York Times Magazine,* November 3, 1969.

14. William Safire, *Before the Fall: An Inside View of the Pre-Watergate White House* (Garden City, N.Y.: Doubleday & Company, 1975), p. 184.

15. *Ibid.,* p. 203.

16. *Ibid.,* p. 204.

17. *Ibid.,* p. 205.

18. *Ibid.,* p. 210.

19. David Abrahamsen, "Is There a Bit of Calley in Us?" *Look,* June 1, 1971, pp. 76–77.

20. *The Watergate Hearings: Break-in and Cover-up. Proceedings of the Senate Select Committee on Presidential Campaign Activities* (New York: Bantam Books, 1973), pp. 435–36.

21. *The New York Times,* January 14, 1973.

10.

1. Henrik Ibsen, *Peer Gynt,* Act V; translated by William and Charles Archer (New York: The Heritage Press, 1957), pp. 264–66.

2. McGinniss, *op. cit.,* p. 70.

3. Ibsen, *op. cit.,* Act I, p. 13.

4. *The New York Times,* January 14, 1973.

5. J. B. Atkinson, "President Nixon's Advisory System as a Variant of the Patron-Client Model of Association: A Case Study," Master of Philosophy Examination Paper, Yale University, April 1974 (unpublished), p. 33.

6. Nixon, *Six Crises,* p. 83.

7. David Abrahamsen, *The Murdering Mind* (New York: Harper & Row, 1973), p. 83.

8. This quotation and several immediately following are from the *Washington Post*, March 23, 1975.

9. *The New York Times*, March 23, 1975.

10. *Washington Post*, March 23, 1975.

11. John Osborne, *The Last Nixon Watch* (Washington, D.C.: The New Republic Book Company, 1975), pp. 26–27.

12. *Washington Post*, March 23, 1975.

13. *The White House Transcripts*, p. 799.

14. This opinion is shared by a person (who prefers to remain anonymous) who worked with Nixon in the White House.

15. Rowland Evans, Jr., and Robert D. Novak, *Nixon in the White House: The Frustration of Power* (New York: Random House, 1971), pp. 333–34.

16. Part of the material in this section on the career of Bebe Rebozo is derived from two sources. Unless otherwise cited, facts and quotations are from Clay Blair, Jr., "Bebe Rebozo's Search for *Machismo*," *Boston Sunday Globe*, October 4, 1970, or Daniel St. Albin Greene, "He's Nixon's Best Pal: Rebozo's Friendship Profits Both Men—in Many Ways," *National Observer*, February 2, 1974.

17. *Newsday*, special report on Bebe Rebozo, October 6, 1971, p. 6R.

18. *Ibid*.

19. J. Anthony Lukas, *Nightmare: The Underside of the Nixon Years* (New York: The Viking Press, 1976), p. 362.

20. Myra MacPherson, "Bebe Rebozo: The President's Publicity-Shy Friend," *Washington Post*, March 23, 1969.

21. Witcover, *op. cit.*, p. 38.

22. *The New York Times*, August 4, 1974.

23. *Ibid.*, July 11, 1974.

24. *Philadelphia Inquirer*, November 1, 1973.

25. *Ibid*.

26. *The New York Times*, February 19, 1976. The money was turned over by William W. Weekler, according to the court papers.

27. Thomas L. Hughes, "The Bismarck Connection: Why Kissinger Must Choose Between Nixon and the Country," *The New York Times Magazine*, December 30, 1973.

28. Marvin Kalb and Bernard Kalb, *Kissinger* (Boston:

Little, Brown and Company, 1974), caption below photograph following p. 360 (November 8, 1973).

29. Josiah Lee Auspitz and Clifford W. Brown, Jr., "What's Wrong with Politics?" *Harper's Magazine*, May 1974.

30. Kalb and Kalb, *op. cit.*, caption below photograph following p. 360 (August 23, 1972).

31. Atkinson, *op. cit.*, p. 21.

32. Anthony Lewis, *The New York Times*, July 17, 1971.

33. Interview with Mike Wallace on CBS-TV, March 16, 1975.

34. Barber, *op. cit.*, p. 374.

35. Mazo, *op. cit.*, p. 5.

36. *Examination of President Nixon's Tax Returns for 1969 through 1972*. Prepared for the Joint Committee on Internal Revenue Taxation by Its Staff (Washington, D.C.: U.S. Government Printing Office, 1974), pp. A-690, A-718, A-735, A-752.

37. *Ibid.*, pp. A-699, A-730, A-750, A-758.

38. *Ibid.*, p. 13.

39. Kornitzer, *The Real Nixon*, pp. 65–66.

40. *Washington Post*, October 16, 1975.

41. *The White House Transcripts*, pp. 157, 63, 85, 166, 85, 87, 165, 172, 623–24, 645, 686, 33.

42. *The New York Times*, August 23, 1975.

43. Barber, *op. cit.*, p. 363.

44. *Ibid.*, p. 364.

11

1. Safire, *op. cit.*, p. 343.

2. Lou Cannon, "The Siége Psychology and How It Grew," *Washington Post*, July 28, 1973.

3. *The New York Times*, August 5, 1973.

4. Alexander L. George, "Assessing Presidential Character," review article on Barber, *op. cit.*, in *World Politics*, Vol. XXVI, No. 2 (January 1974).

5. *The Watergate Hearings*, p. 259.

6. See David Abrahamsen, "Mass Psychosis and Its Effects," *Journal of Nervous and Mental Disease*, XCIII, No. 1 (January 1941), 63–72.

7. Safire, *op. cit.*, p. 238.

8. *Richard III*, Act I, Scene I.

9. Freud pointed out: "Richard seems to say nothing more than 'I find this idle way of life tedious, and I want to enjoy myself. As I cannot play the lover on account of my defor-

mity, I will play the villain; I will intrigue, murder, do anything I please.' " Sigmund Freud, "Character Types in Psycho-Analytic Work," *Collected Papers*, Vol. IV (3rd ed.; London: Hogarth Press, 1946), p. 322.

10. Henrik Ibsen, *Rosmersholm*, Act III, translated by James Walter McFarlane, in McFarlane (ed.), *Ibsen*, Vol. VI (London: Oxford University Press, 1960), p. 363.

11. Ibsen, *Peer Gynt*, Act II, p. 73.

12. Julie Nixon Eisenhower, "My Mother," *Newsweek*, May 24, 1976, p. 13.

13. Mike Garvey, *Washington Post*, October 16, 1975.

14. Bob Woodward and Carl Bernstein, *The Final Days* (New York: Simon and Schuster, 1976), pp. 21–30.

15. Charles W. Colson, *Born Again* (New York: Chosen Books, 1976), p. 179.

16. *Ibid.*

17. Woodward and Bernstein, *op. cit.*, p. 165.

18. H. R. Haldeman, as told to Joseph Scott, "Inside the Nixon White House," New York *Daily News*, June 23, 1976, p. 43.

19. Interview with Dan Rather, *60 Minutes*, CBS-TV, May 16, 1976.

20. *Ibid.*

21. *Washington Post*, February 25, 1976.

Bibliography

Abrahamsen, David. "Mass-Psychosis and Its Effects," *The Journal of Nervous & Mental Disease*, Vol. 93, No. 1 (January 1941).
———. *The Mind and Death of a Genius*. New York: Columbia University Press, 1946.
———. *The Road to Emotional Maturity*. Englewood Cliffs, N.J.: Prentice-Hall, 1958.
———. *The Psychology of Crime*. New York: Columbia University Press, 2nd printing, 1967.
———. *Our Violent Society*. New York: Funk & Wagnalls, 1971.
———. *The Murdering Mind*. New York: Harper & Row, 1973.
Alsop, Stewart. *Nixon and Rockefeller: A Double Portrait*. New York: Doubleday & Company, 1960.
Arena, Richard. "Whittier College Richard Nixon Oral History Project," *Oral History Association Newsletter*, Vol. VIII, No. 2, Summer 1974.
Atkinson, J. J. "President Nixon's Advisory System as a Variant of the Patron-Client Model of Association, a Case Study," Yale University, April 1974 (Philosophy Examination Paper, unpublished; Supervisor, Professor R. E. Crane).
Auspitz, Josiah Lee, and Clifford W. Brown, Jr. "What's Wrong with Politics?", *Harper's Magazine*, May 1974.
Barber, James David. *The Presidential Character: Predicting Performance in the White House*. Englewood Cliffs, N.J.: Prentice-Hall, Inc., 1970.
Bell, Raymond M., with special assistance from Frank R. Baird (Westchester, Pennsylvania, and Stuart P. Lloyd (Summit, N.J.). *The Ancestry of Richard Milhous Nixon*. Washington, Pennsylvania Edition, 1972.
Bernstein, Carl, and Bob Woodward. *All The President's Men*. New York: Simon and Schuster, 1974.
Blair, Clay, Jr. "Bebe Rebozo's Search for Machismo," *Boston Sunday Globe*, October 4, 1970.
Colson, Charles W. *Born Again*. New York: Chosen Books, published by William R. Barbour, 1976.
Crawford, Frieda Fately. *An Indiana Sojourn: The Milhous Family 1854–1904*. Privately printed, 1974.
Dean, John. *Blind Ambition: The White House Years*. New York: Simon and Schuster, 1976.

BIBLIOGRAPHY

Erikson, Erik. *Young Man Luther. A Study in Psychoanalysis and History.* New York: The Norton Library, W. W. Norton & Company, Inc., 1962.

Feldman, Trude B. "The Quiet Courage of Pat Nixon," *McCall's,* May 1975.

Fenichel, Otto. *The Psychoanalytic Theory of Neurosis.* New York: W. W. Norton & Company, 1945.

Freud, Sigmund. "Character in Psycho-Analytic Work," *Collected Papers,* Vol. IV, edited by Ernest Jones. The International Psycho-Analytical Library, Third Edition, Hogarth Press and the Institute of Psychoanalysis, 1946.

———. *Leonardo da Vinci: A Study in Psychosexuality.* Introduction by A. A. Brill. New York: Random House, 4th printing, 1947.

———. *On Psychotherapy* (1904) *Collected Papers,* Vol. I, Third Edition. New York–London–Vienna: The International Psychoanalytical Press, 1946.

George, Alexander L. and Juliette. *Woodrow Wilson and Colonel House.* New York: John Day, 1956.

George, Alexander L. "Assessing Presidential Character," Review Article, *The Presidential Character: Predicting Performance in the White House* by James David Barber. Englewood Cliffs, N.J.: Prentice-Hall, World Politics, Vol. XXVI, No. 2, January 1974.

Hoyt, Edwin P. *The Nixons: An American Family.* New York: Random House, 1972.

Hughes, Thomas L. "The Bismarck Connection: Why Kissinger Must Choose Between Nixon and Country," *The New York Times Magazine,* December 30, 1973.

Ibsen, Henrik. *Peer Gynt.* Translated with an introduction by William and Charles Archer. Illustrated by Per Krohg. New York: The Heritage Press, 1957.

———. *Rosmersholm.* In *Collected Works* (Samlede Dikterverker), Vol. V. Oslo: Gyldendal Norwegian Publishing, 1930.

Jackson, Donald. "Coming of Age in America: The Youth of Richard Nixon." In manuscript, 8/28/70.

———. "The Young Nixon," *Life Magazine,* November 6, 1970.

Kalb, Marvin and Bernard. *Kissinger.* Boston: Little, Brown & Company, 1974.

Kornitzer, Bela. *The Real Nixon: An Intimate Biography.* Chicago: Rand McNally & Company, 1960.

———. "My Son," interviews with Rose Kennedy and Hannah M. Nixon, *This Week Magazine,* September 18, 1960.

Langer, Walter. *The Mind of Adolf Hitler: The Secret Wartime Report.* New York: Basic Books, Inc., 1972.

Lucas, J. Anthony. *Nightmare: The Underside of the Nixon Years.* New York: Viking Press, 1976.

MacPherson, Myra. "Bebe Rebozo: The President's Publicity-Shy Friend," *The Washington Post,* March 23, 1969.

BIBLIOGRAPHY

Mazo, Earl. *Richard Nixon, A Political and Personal Portrait*. New York: Harper Bros., 1959.

McGinnis, Joe. *The Selling of the President, 1968*. New York: The Trident Press, 1969.

Newsday, "Special Report on Bebe Rebozo," October 6 & 7, 1971.

Nixon, Richard M. "The Changing Rules of Liability in Automobile Accident Litigation," *Duke University Bar Journal of Law and Contemporary Problems*, Vol. 3, No. 4 (Fall 1936).

———. "The Hiss Case, A Lesson for the American People," Speech in the House of Representatives, January 26, 1950.

———. *Six Crises*. New York: Doubleday & Co., Inc., 1962.

———. *A Self-Portrait*. Script Xerox copy, United States Information Agency, November 15, 1968.

———. "Nixon's Views of His Wife: A Strong and Sensitive First Lady," *The New York Times*. March 14, 1971.

Reuben, William A. *The Honorable Mr. Nixon*. New York: Action Books, Sixth Printing, 1960.

Richardson, Elliot. "The Saturday Night Massacre," *The Atlantic*, March 1976.

Rogin, A. M., and T. Lattier. "The Inner History of Richard Nixon," *Transaction*, Rutgers University, 1971.

Rowse, Arthur Edward. *Slanted News: A Case Study of the Nixon and Stevenson Fund Stories*. Boston: Beacon Press, 1957.

Safire, William. *Before the Fall: An Inside View of the Pre-Watergate White House*. New York: Doubleday & Company, 1975.

Schlesinger, Arthur M., Jr. *The Imperial Presidency*. Boston: Houghton Mifflin Company, 1973.

Smith, John Chabot. *Alger Hiss: The True Story*. New York: Holt, Rinehart and Winston, 1976.

Steinem, Gloria. Interview in *Writer's Digest*, February 1974.

"The Examination of President Nixon's Tax Returns for 1969 through 1972." Prepared for the Joint Committee On Internal Revenue Service by its Staff, U.S. Printing Office, Washington, D.C., April 3, 1974.

Wangh, Martin. Book Review of *The Mind of Adolf Hitler, The Secret Wartime Report*, by Walter C. Langer, Basic Books, Inc., New York, 1972, *The Psychoanalytic Quarterly*, Vol. XLIII, No. 1, 1974.

The Watergate Hearings. Break-In and Cover-Up Proceedings, The New York Times. New York: Bantam Books, October 1973.

West, Jessamyn. *Hide and Seek: A Continuing Journey*. New York: Harcourt Brace Jovanovich, Inc., 1973.

The White House Transcripts. The full text of the Submission of Recorded Presidential Conversations to the Committee on the Judiciary of the House of Representatives by President Richard Nixon. Introduction by R. W. Apple, Jr., *The New York Times*. New York: Bantam Books, 1974.

BIBLIOGRAPHY

Wills, Garry. *Nixon Agonistes.* New York: New American Library, 1969–1970.

Witcover, Jules. *The Resurrection of Richard Nixon.* New York: G. P. Putnam's Sons, 1970.

Younger, Irving. "Was Alger Hiss Guilty?", *Commentary Magazine,* Vol. 60, No. 2, August 1975.

Zorza, Victor. After Brezhnev . . . ? *The Washington Post,* January 12, 1975.

Index